D0936942

NOV

N
Ci

FE

FEB

THE
PRESIDENT
AND
FUND RAISING

THE
PRESIDENT
AND
FUND RAISING

James L. Fisher

Gary H. Quehl

AMERICAN COUNCIL ON EDUCATION
Macmillan Publishing Company
NEW YORK

Collier Macmillan Publishers
LONDON

824125

Mitchell Memorial Library
Mississippi State University

Copyright © 1989 by American Council on Education
and
Macmillan Publishing Company,
A Division of Macmillan, Inc.

All rights reserved. No part of this book may be repro-
duced or transmitted in any form or by any means, elec-
tronic or mechanical, including photocopying, recording,
or by any information storage and retrieval system, without permission in writing from the Publisher.

Macmillan Publishing Company
866 Third Avenue, New York, N.Y. 10022

Collier Macmillan Canada, Inc.

Library of Congress Catalog Card Number: 88–27264

Printed in the United States of America

printing number
1   2   3   4   5   6   7   8   9   10

Library of Congress Cataloging-in-Publication Data

The President and fund raising.

(The American Council on Education/Macmillan series
on higher education)
    Includes index.
    1. Educational fund raising—United States. 2. Univer-
sities and colleges—United States—Finance. 3. College
presidents—United States. I. Fisher, James L. II. Quehl,
Gary H. III. Series: American Council on Education/
Macmillan series on higher education.
LB2336.P74 1989   379.1'3   88–27264
ISBN 0-02-897151-5

CONTENTS

III
CONDUCTING THE FUND-RAISING PROGRAM

IV
REACHING THE APEX IN FUND RAISING

PREFACE

It is no secret that formal leadership is under siege throughout American society. Whether in business, government, or education, executives are under enormous pressure to respond to a range of difficult problems. Most require creative approaches. All demand new insights and skills.

For the most part, our colleges and universities are well served by the men and women who lead them. These are unusually gifted individuals who possess boundless energy and are deeply committed to the welfare of their institutions. The demands of their office arise from the needs of various quarters: to improve educational quality and verify performance, expand educational opportunity and ensure educational success, retain the national workforce, foster economic development.

The one demand that supersedes all others, however, is the unrelenting pressure for college and university presidents to raise money. Lots of it. Some presidents shrink from this responsibility; those who ignore fund raising ultimately lose their jobs. Most presidents, however, embrace the advancement role enthusiastically, and their efforts often are rewarded with remarkable results.

Presidents of independent colleges and universities have long understood the centrality of fund raising from private sources. In most public institutions, where past government support provided adequate funding, the president's energies were directed to the legislative process, often to the exclusion of private fund raising. Today, however, needs have outdistanced government appropriations at most public institutions. This means that every college and university—whether public or independent—must look to private giving as a principal source of funding. It also means that the college or university president must lead the entire fund-raising effort as *the* chief advancement officer for the institution.

The President and Fund Raising is, therefore, an important book as well as a timely one. It is the first of its kind to provide the chief executive officer with vital insights on fund raising and its relationship to the institution. Regardless of institutional type or size, this book offers fundamental concepts in which every president must be well grounded—from the case statement to the role of governing boards, from the annual fund to planned giving. Further, it provides perspectives and principles for refining existing fund-raising activities and implementing new programs, focusing on the major elements found in any successful development program. Each chapter, by one or more of the nation's leading thinkers and practitioners, offers presidents a working knowledge of basic methodology as well as benchmarks to measure the effectiveness of the advancement program.

Not all presidents find themselves enthusiastic about fund raising, but all honor their real need to possess a working knowledge of the field and of the fundamentals of development. The annual fund, for example, provides an institution with current support *and* serves as a "living endowment." Presidents must be conversant with proven methods for encouraging both first-time gifts and renewals from past donors. Larger annual gifts that require personal solicitation by the president will be increasingly important in providing program support and budgetary relief.

Whereas the annual fund provides a broad base of institutional support, planned giving is at the apex of the development process. Wills, trusts, and pooled income funds preserve institutional quality by establishing endowed scholarships, chairs, and professorships. Presidents, in coordination with staff or key volunteers, are crucial to soliciting these gifts and providing careful stewardship and attention to this group of donors. Planned gifts provide examples for others to follow, and the president must be at the forefront in this fund-raising activity.

Obviously the significant involvement of major constituencies is crucial to the success of any institution's development program. Students, parents, faculty, alumni, business and government leaders—all have important roles to play. Key among the leadership groups is the institution's board of trustees. For example, the feasibility study, which determines the direction and potential for an institution's development activities, must involve board members as well as other major supporters. Although not all board members are outstanding solicitors, most possess other assets in fulfilling their board responsibilities. They can introduce, host, open doors, and endorse the development activities, thus lending the president critical support in solicitation strategy and implementation.

Presidents also need to know the role and value of external consultants to the fund-raising program. Whether advocates of existing programs or implementers of new activities, consultants must understand and be able to articulate the institution's mission, work closely and well with various constituent groups, and maintain the highest ethical and professional standards.

In sum, *The President and Fund Raising* provides a fresh, all-encompassing look at fund-raising practices, interpreting for today's market-driven environment a full range of long-established principles. Without question, this book will help presidents become more knowledgeable in a field that demands nothing short of their dedicated involvement and expertise.

Finally, in the full spirit of this book, we wish to thank the Xerox Foundation, most notably Mr. Glegg Watson, without whose encouragement and support this book would not have been possible.

Gary H. Quehl   James L. Fisher
President   *President-emeritus*
CASE   CASE

THE
PRESIDENT
AND
FUND RAISING

I

AN OVERVIEW OF
PHILANTHROPY

ESTABLISHING
A SUCCESSFUL
FUND-RAISING
PROGRAM
James L. Fisher

You are a newly appointed college president. You are pleased, even excited, but also a bit confused and uncertain—and so it is only natural that, to some extent, you are bound to do a little posturing. Since you are an educated and practicing academic, this situation makes you more than a little uncomfortable. After all, at least *some* things that you are presumed to know are all but completely foreign to you. Yet no one asks whether you might need a little time to learn *anything*. Rather, from the first day, you are expected to be off and running—a combination of Abraham Lincoln, Mother Theresa, Nicholas Biddle, and Father Hesburgh.

You make some phone calls to a few presidential friends, take a few trips, and even attend a three-day seminar for new presidents; but somehow you are still unsettled. You know that the first steps you take probably will eventuate in some mistakes, but you intend from the start to keep errors to a bare minimum. You also know that those first steps can ultimately spell the difference between presidential success and failure; whether your administration is a plus or a minus, bland or piquant. What if you appoint the wrong vice president, create the wrong office (or fail to create the right one), or postpone confronting the reality of a difficult decision that, when put off, only festers? So many "what ifs"! Nonetheless, you remain pleased and excited about your presidency, because in your entire life you have never had such an opportunity to play a major role in realizing your dream. And that is worth all the anxiety.

This chapter is designed to help obviate at least some of your anxiety, to give you a higher degree of confidence as you address one of the most important areas of your administration: development, or fund raising. That is one area where, quite simply, you just cannot afford to make serious mistakes.

Institutional advancement, the area of college and university administration that usually includes development, public relations, and alumni activities (and sometimes also mistakenly includes government relations, athletics, admissions, and even placement), is perhaps most frequently the area with which newly appointed college and university presidents are least familiar. Yet it is this area, more than any other, that will determine the extent to which your administration is deemed worthy or unworthy.

The idea of asking for money makes you feel uncomfortable. You know little about the history of philanthropy and its important role in human institutions. There are few courses taught, and books written, on the subject and you aren't sure where to start—or whether you should start at all. Of course, if you survive the first three years in office, your attitude will change. But is there time?

The contention of this book is that, if handled thoughtfully and seriously, your institutional advancement area can be not only extraordinarily successful but one of the most rewarding and most intellectually stimulating of your presidential responsibilities. The key is to approach fund raising head-on, with both eyes open, and utilizing all the mental faculties at your command, *at the beginning of your term.*

Colleges and universities in the United States and Canada employ nearly 9,000 full-time development officers. There are over 7,500 public relations and publications professionals, and about 4,500 professional alumni administrators. Assuming that, like you, other presidents are the chief advancement officers of their institutions, then another 3,000-plus can be added to the list. And so we are considering more than 24,000 persons engaged in institutional advancement activities for colleges and universities in North America. Although a number of other countries (England, Scotland, Ireland, Germany, Mexico, Brazil, Australia, Hong Kong, Indonesia, India, and others) are beginning to fashion development programs on the American model, most are only at the instructional and translational levels. Papers, meetings, special conferences, and (recently) Fulbright grants promise that within a few years many American-type fund-raising programs should be in full operation around the world.

What follows is a simple, concise, research- and experience-tested formula for college presidents to follow in establishing and maintaining a successful fund-raising program. Although there are a number of variations on this approach (some of which are discussed elsewhere in this book), you should test any significantly contrary ideas on at least one experienced, trusted, and candid friend before seriously considering them.

1. *Start a Personal Fund-Raising Library*

In addition to Frances Pray's *Handbook on Educational Fund Raising* and Wesley Rowland's *Handbook of Institutional Advancement,* read everything you and your assistant can find on philanthropy. Robert Payton, at the end of Chapter 3 in this book, lists some excellent suggestions, and all college presidents should have his book *Philanthropy* on their bookshelves. You should also become familiar with the seminars and programs offered by CASE (Council for Advancement and Support of Education) and by AGB (Association of Governing Boards of Colleges and Universities). You will then be ready to use what you've learned.

2. *Keep or Replace an Incumbent Vice President*

You will probably have in place a vice president or director for development, college and university relations, or institutional advancement. You must intelligently but quickly determine whether that person should go or stay. The imperative here is that you examine the accomplishments before you get to know the incumbent so well that you cannot comfortably and objectively make a change. Many new presidents assume that because the incumbent vice presidents are experienced, they also are qualified. Because of uncertainty you may want to wait before making any dramatic move. However, by the time you confirm what you knew instinctively, you might already be hostage to the sticky tenure of politics and friendship.

Because faculty members, students, and even board members are generally as unsophisticated as college presidents about fund raising, that is often the area where presidents appoint instead friends, political compromises, or music men or women who make grand promises. Some have speculated that as many as half of the fund-raising vice presidents in place today are mistakes. While this is undoubtedly an overstatement, it dramatizes the point that if you aren't exceedingly careful in choosing your chief fund raiser, you could rue your decision.

The track record of the development division (I prefer calling the area "development" rather than "advancement" because the former more nearly suggests bottom-line evaluation) of your institution is the most documentable of any of the conventional line divisions. Either the institution has raised money of it hasn't. And if it hasn't, regardless of whether yours is a public or private institution, look very critically at the incumbent vice president and all of the reporting offices. Don't easily accept statements like "People won't give to our college; we don't have the potential" or "We're not ready for a capital campaign" or "Your predecessor wouldn't allocate sufficient resources for us to do much" or "President So-and-So didn't expect us to raise much money." Whatever the case, if your institution hasn't raised much money, you have a presidential problem. And if your incumbent vice president doesn't enthusiastically endorse your assessment, then immediate change is in order. Yes, there also are indices of effective community and public relations activities, as there are of alumni activities, but for the new and relatively inexperienced president the best index is "How much money has been raised?" *Every friend-making activity should be translated into these terms—cash or kind.* You'll receive advice that contradicts this statement. Ignore that advice.

3. *Appoint a Fund-Raising Consultant*

Shortly after you assume office, appoint a consultant (and do this before appointing a new vice president). After discussing your plans with your board chair, call CASE in Washington, D.C. at (202) 328-5000 for advice about consultants. Get the names of four or five. Approach fund-raising consultants as you do the entire advancement area: based on track record. Find out for whom the candidate firm has worked, and then phone fellow presidents. Unless other presidents view you as a direct competitor, they will almost always be candid.

If you are completely (or even a little) befuddled about your advancement area, ask CASE to put together a team that will come to your campus and audit your present advancement functions. This will give you a better idea of what you need and the kind of vice president you should have. But even with a CASE evaluation, you still will need to appoint a consultant. Whether you should appoint the consultant before or after an evaluation is debatable, but my advice is to do it either before or at the same time.

Your consultants should come to the campus one or two days every month, and always be as near as the phone. Rates vary, but they usually go from $1,500 to $3,000 per day. Some will charge a flat $10,000 or so per year, with a prearranged contract calling for a specific number of visits and accomplishments within the contract period. Most consultants are full-time, and you should select a tested professional from among this group. However, a number of able and highly qualified persons who hold campus positions do consulting. If they are experienced, they will advise you about both their time and interest limitations. Often, particularly in short-duration assignments, they can be both exceedingly helpful and less costly. Many newly retired persons fall into this category. They have expertise and time, and are not highly driven by financial needs. *Whatever the price—within reason, of course— a good consultant is worth the money. And it is a naive president who tries to raise money without one.*

If you do have a satisfactory vice president in place, you should bear in mind that since you will hold that person accountable for accomplishing your fund-raising goals, you must grant authority and involvement consistent with your delegation. *But stay involved yourself.*

4. *Conduct a Feasibility Study*

Assuming you have a written fund-raising plan, your consultant will usually suggest a feasibility study and develop a case statement. Today, some respected authorities suggest alternatives to the classic feasibility study, but by-and-large these "alternatives" are simply more equivocal ways of achieving the same purpose. The study will determine the extent to which your various institutional publics have the capacity and willingness to give (cash or kind) to your institution. Either your consultant, or yet another firm, may conduct it. Be sure of sufficient experience, because you must place great confidence in the results.

If you are at a more sophisticated institution that already has such a study, ask to see it. (Most institutions should update a feasibility study every five or six years.) Your vice president will be surprised and impressed that you know about these studies. At the very least, update the study consistent with the time of your appointment and your own particular dream or mission for your institution. Be sure the study is conducted according to your terms, not the consultant's or the vice president's. Always remember that, regardless of what came before, this is *your* administration!

A feasibility study usually will cost between $10,000 and $50,000. Don't blanch at the amount; it's worth it. If yours is a new development program your consultant, after reviewing the results of your evaluation/ audit, may advise you to announce your new direction through a modest fund campaign (usually $1–5 million). This can get you up and going within 15–20 months, and a thorough feasibility study can follow your campaign. But whatever the advice, *listen to your consultant.*

5. *Develop a Case Statement*

The best research indicates that a formal, written, concise case statement characterizes an "overproductive" fund-raising program. It provides evidence of a clear sense of mission: where you were, where you are, and where you want to be. It also provides tangible evidence of a well-managed institution that seeks to control, rather than be controlled by, its environment. Here again, *appoint a consultant.* The best course is usually to talk with a good writer on your staff about your ideas for a case statement, and ask for a draft. You should edit the draft and present it to your consultants (who may recommend dramatic changes.) You can get it done for from $2,000 to $8,000.

6. *Appoint an Extraordinary Vice President for Development*

The state of things on campus will probably demand that you use a search committee to appoint a new vice president (should you need one). But, at all costs, do not allow the participatory system on your campus to intimidate you. Remember, if the vice president doesn't work out, it's your fault; but if he or she turns out to be brilliant, be sure to give your advisors all of the credit.

The search committee (don't call it "selection") should probably include representatives of the faculty, the student body, the alumni association, and perhaps even trustees. But be careful: It's better not to have lower-ranking advancement professionals on the committee; they will only inhibit candidates from speaking candidly about a modestly successful program. If you must have *any* administrators on the committee, appoint *one* from another line division of the institution (preferably business affairs).

Although your college councils (faculty, student, alumni) will want to play a role in your search committee appointments, it is important that you personally have at least one appointee or agent on the committee (if one can't do the job for you, then you've got the wrong agent). Your appointee should ordinarily be your presidential assistant, or someone else in whom you have complete confidence. The committee should recommend to you three to five qualified candidates, not in rank order (although somehow you will know the rank). This leaves you free both to *make* the selection and to be *perceived as* making the selection (both are important). Here again, most experienced presidents will employ a search consultant to work with themselves and the committee. CASE can give you the names of several top firms or individuals. These consultants usually charge from 20–33⅓ percent of the first year's salary.

The twin criteria for a vice president for development are (1) track record (once again) and (2) chemistry. Note the word "twin"; one is not more important than the other. I have known presidents who feel so foreign in the company of fund-raising activities and people that they appoint to their top position a person with an impressive resume but who makes them uncomfortable. Almost invariably they later regret their choice when they engage in the even more uncomfortable task of getting rid of the person. My advice is this: If you don't find a qualified person who makes you feel comfortable, then go with chemistry over experience. I once appointed a professor of English whom I had grown to admire and enjoy. Today he is the vice president for development at one of our most impressive institutions, and has won over a dozen national awards for his advancement achievements.

Should you decide to go the limited- or no-experience route, be sure the person is bright, educated, enthusiastic, and has a past record demonstrating extraordinary motivation. Also be certain that, *during the first few months* in office, your inexperienced vice president attends a CASE Summer Institute in Fund Raising and two or three conferences on especially pertinent subjects (annual fund, capital campaigns, planned giving, and so on). The vice president will both learn about the field, and meet key professionals who will become part of a valuable information directory.

You should pay the vice president what you must to get the one you want. And if you decide to appoint an experienced professional (which is usually your best bet), you may have to pay this person more than you do the other vice presidents. Or you might even need to make a special trip to the head of your board. Go ahead. Be bold. You're the president.

7. *Give the Vice President an Impressive Office Near Yours*

Why do I mention something so apparently pedestrian? Because so many presidents make the mistake of putting vice presidents in the wrong place. The position and look of an office make a difference. Quite simply, the vice president's office should look attractive, prestigious but reserved. Preferably, it should be adjacent to your own suite. It should be tastefully decorated, without a lot of school rah-rah (save that for the alumni office). Quiet understatement is in order. For instance, quality pieces of art that have been given to the institution convey a number of messages.

Ideally, the other offices in the development/advancement area (with the possible exception of the alumni office) should be near the vice president's. But if this is not possible, put the vice president alone in an office near yours. Obviously this office placement speaks to lots of inquirers—faculty and staff members who are skeptical; potential contributors who always seem to know that the most important people are located near the president; and visitors who are prompted to ask "What is development?"

8. *Make the Vice President an Important Member of Your Top Advisory Council*

Like the vice president's office, the key to making your fund-raising program a success is to recognize its tenant as an integral part of your chief advisory group. Too often this vice president either is not in-cluded—especially in "kitchen councils". If these vice presidents are invited, their opinions may be discounted (and this is even worse) during mainstream discussions about the institution. This not only makes a person feel less important, but it is a sure way to create a disenchanted, superficially knowledgeable, and less productive advance-ment area. A good officer, when treated this way, will begin quietly to lay plans to move on, and you will have committed a basic presidential mistake.

Advancement professionals are first and foremost educators, be they in development, public relations, alumni administration, or publications. And even if some of them don't initially believe it themselves, you must make them educators. Only then will they be able to approach their maximum self-esteem and professional achievement. And so, start-ing at the top, you must *sincerely* include your fund-raising vice president in all substantive discussions about the institution and its affairs. If you can't do this, then you have appointed the wrong vice president, and either you're already in trouble or you're headed that way. Your message will filter down. You will see it in your publications, hear it at alumni meetings and over coffee and cocktails, and in presentations to potential benefactors. In time, your obvious respect and appreciation for your advancement staff will energize the entire division. And don't think that you can "respect" them by simply appreciating the number of dollars they bring in or the number of people they affect. We feel this way about good carpenters. Advancement officers aren't trades-persons; they are professionals. And in higher education, the *only* sure way they can be truly committed to the mission is to be considered full-fledged members of the team.

Off-campus and with your board of trustees and the alumni board, this vice president should be perceived as your surrogate. These groups should view your vice president as so important that they feel, in speaking with the vice president, that they virtually are speaking with you. Obviously you can delegate this much responsibility only to an exceptional person, and so you must invest a great measure of presi-dential trust and confidence therein. This is perhaps the main reason you must have an extraordinary relationship with your vice president. Perhaps more than any other of your top associates, he or she can hurt your career. This person must have such a well integrated and healthy personality that there is little or no discomfort in identifying with you. (Identifying with the institution is not identifying with you.) This is especially true when you are not present.

Watch for the tendency of your vice president to use the first person singular. It's a bad practice that you should nip in the bud. If you don't, you will soon lose the reins. On the other hand, if you choose not to grant surrogate status to your vice president, you won't have this potential problem (at least not to this degree). But neither will you be free to exercise yourself as freely in the conduct of your presidency, nor will the vice president be as effective as you would like. It's a trade-off, and I encourage you to take the chance. Talk about it now and then with your vice president. Never assume anything that has to do with your leadership, regardless of what people say to you. In the long run, your closest advisors will be your greatest test.

9. *Approve a Budgetary Allocation That Is More than You Are Initially Inclined to Grant*

Because a president should adopt a general style designed to get more for less, it is important to emphasize that in institutional advancement, particularly development, your thinking should take a different course. You'll get more with more, at least initially. Numerous studies indicate that the most "overproductive" programs invest more money in development. Be aware that you'll have great difficulty in carrying out this philosophy if you have a new, unsophisticated program—one that doesn't raise much money, regardless of what "they" say. As a rule of thumb, you can expect to take three years before you break even, which means that you may have a real selling job to do on all your potential critics (the board of trustees, the faculty, and other staff, most notably your business officer). In time, your average fund-raising cost per dollar raised should be approximately eight cents in a private institution and approximately twelve cents in a public.

I vividly recall saying year after year to my development officer, "Next year, Paul" when he pressed me to allocate additional funds for a planned-giving officer. If I had listened to Paul's strong plea, we would have raised several million dollars in unrestricted funds. Since that time, he has been responsible for raising more than $300 million for other institutions. I asked him recently why he hadn't raised that kind of money for me. He responded, "Jim, it was because you wouldn't let me."

Don't let this happen to you. If you take these words seriously, it needn't. Now, although this statement could be stretched to a fault, I make it nonetheless: *Every college or university, regardless of size, should have a full-time planned-giving officer.* The only exception is a new institution with mostly younger alumni.

Of course, in making what appears to be a generous allocation of resources to your development area, you will need to both defend and evaluate zealously. Other vice presidents may carp, and some may resort to questionable behavior. Stop this sort of thing quickly or, in time, the criticism will erode popular confidence in your development program. This is not to suggest that you automatically question or consider devious your other top-level associates. They cannot be expected to be as farseeing as their president, and it is your job to buoy their spirits and stay their tongues when resources are scarce. Only you, the president, can do it.

In a similar vein, don't tolerate even casual informal asides that belittle your development efforts. If you do, the criticism will surely grow, and you will regret your tacit support. It is so easy to become disenchanted in the first and last stages of a fund-raising program (campaign). No matter how you feel in the heat of the particular fiscal moment, be as enthusiastic as you are bottom-line oriented. Be tough and specific in tracking the fund-raising program, even during the three-year grace period. A really good vice president will anticipate this action yet be persistent. Find out what you are getting for the money spent. And don't accept generalizations, clichés, or vagaries as answers. In the end, this style will make your advancement staff feel better. In the beginning, however, be prepared for anxious defensiveness; most presidents aren't so demanding.

In retrospect, were I to serve my decade as a college president again, I would evaluate more rigorously every advancement activity (alumni, public relations, and publications) using development as a model. Money raised may be a rather gross index to some, but even the most sophisticated programs use this measure. That's the reason I would put a development officer in charge of the advancement division (as the vice president). For obvious reasons, these officers are by nature more inclined to accept and expect performance indices relating to the amount of money raised.

All of this notwithstanding, an extraordinary public relations or alumni officer can also do a good job as your vice president. But you must be careful to stress from the start the importance of written measurable objectives for which that person will be accountable. Be mindful that in addition to financial objectives, you can also establish measurable objectives in alumni and public relations areas. Anything that you can count, weigh, or otherwise measure should be included in the annual mission goals.

10. *Be Lean in Organizing and Administering Your Advancement Area*

After my suggesting that you be generous in the budgetary allocation to your development area, you may be nonplussed by the suggestion that you be lean. Here's why. After you start making impressive strides (and you will) in your development efforts, you may tend to (1) accept any proposal for additional positions or programs, and (2) become more amenable to solving personality conflicts and other problems by adding staff or building around them. These things happen most in wealthier and larger institutions where predecessors have already incorporated the fat and the inefficiencies. And because of your lack of experience, you could find yourself in danger of simply accepting such arrangements, or situations.

If an established development program costs more than 15 percent of the total dollars raised, you probably have a problem, and you certainly should ask for an explanation. But rarely do people ask questions— so the institution continues, year after year, practices that shouldn't have been accepted in the first place. (Remember, revamped programs, like start-up costs, cost more.) This wasteful and less effective condition also occurs in liberal arts colleges and similar public institutions. Often they are smitten by the "big time," and quickly adopt some version of the Harvard, Stanford, Michigan, or Berkeley models, all of which are more inefficient than you can probably afford.

The most obvious costly practice is to create separate vice presidencies in both development and public affairs (or public relations). Some even create alumni vice presidencies. This practice is most evident in major private and public universities. Despite this trend, there has never been evidence that such organization makes things better, more successful, or more efficient. I am convinced that these operations would raise more money than they do (and they raise staggering sums) if they had more efficient organizations. Unfortunately, even some consultants support the practice, usually to mollify president and staff. If you are inclined this way, go ahead; but be aware of the price. At the very least, you'll spend money that could have been allocated to your academic program (or perhaps better spent on a management seminar). Even more fundamentally, such an arrangement makes it more difficult to conduct and evaluate your advancement activities with the bottom line in mind.

Here especially, beware of the advisor who counsels you that "public relations is valuable for the sake of public relations." This position is sheer nonsense. Your public relations program exists to enhance the ability to generate resources for your most precious activity, your academic program. The idea of not attempting to cash in on your cultivation activities is as naively and mistakenly academic as it is rarely done. Conduct your development (advancement) program to raise money; the cause is more than worth such a candid assessment. Do this, and you will find all of the critics of your program converted to enthusiastic supporters. This same style should apply to every social event, every president's party, every news release, and all publications. If *you* don't insist on such accounting efforts, chances are that no one will. And you will have generated less support for your fine institution.

Some presidents have created separate vice presidencies in public relations, development, and alumni affairs because of personality conflicts or because of perceived or real limitations of the incumbent officers. Every situation like this that I have known occurs because the sitting president doesn't want to make a tough decision about which officer should be subordinate to the other, or which should go. And once the arrangement is in place, it usually remains. Not long ago, I spoke at a prestige campus that had gone this route. After my speech, I spent some time talking with staff, all of whom dislike *their* arrangement. Why did they feel that way? Well (to cite an unusually pertinent example), the next day, Bob Hope was coming to be involved in the institution's public relations and fund-raising activities. And despite the fact that the institution had vice presidents, each highly respected, there was no way, short of involving the president as referee, to effectively coordinate Bob Hope's activities for the advancement, public relations, and alumni offices. Everyone was relieved when Hope left two days later.

Understandably, important activities in development, and particularly in public and alumni relations, will not be readily measurable. Results of many valuable public relations activities often are difficult to gauge, and all of your advancement offices participate in them. These activities include such apparent disparities as sending out news releases, producing publications, media relations efforts, parties, alumni meetings, and tours and trips. On your part, they include appearances on TV and radio, speeches, newspaper and magazine articles, political fund raisers (both sides of the aisle), and countless parties with the landed and the shakers and movers. All of these goings-on influence your fund-raising program.

Another of the less financially measurable activities is the work that advancement offices do with the academic and administrative departments. These efforts will seldom bear immediate results, but they are valuable and should be carried out under the direction of your advancement division. Include everything from departmental brochures and college catalogs to faculty participation in development, public relations, and alumni activities.

Sooner or later, your public relations and alumni officers will have to work more closely with the admissions office to enhance efforts to match the institution with prospective students. While the prime authority and accountability for "marketing" activities should remain in the admissions office, it is wise to bring the expertise and involvement of these advancement functions to bear on the ever-important area of admissions.

A special word about alumni associations. Although the early alumni associations served their alma maters, alumni fellowship and continuing institutional service and education are considered legitimate alumni activities. These areas are quite difficult to reduce to fund-raising specifics. Recognize them as important and legitimate activities but, at the same time, press for closer (regardless of the present condition) relationships between the alumni and development offices. Some presidents have found it worthwhile to assign the annual fund to the alumni office. Often this arrangement can set a better tone for all alumni activities.

There is another special condition about organized alumni activity that most newly appointed (and some experienced) presidents don't understand—the differences between dependent and independent alumni associations. Most alumni associations are dependent—that is, largely funded by the institution. While the dependent association may charge dues and engage in other revenue-generating activities, this office clearly is an institutional activity, and staff are expected to conduct themselves within the same professional and management context as other advancement professionals. They must recognize that they are primarily accountable to the incumbent officers of the institution rather than to some vague college or university tradition and a vested alumni board.

Not so for the independent alumni associations! Their roles are not as clean-cut or easily explained. The independent association usually is significantly, if not completely, funded by its own activities. Its board of directors appoints and evaluates the staff. Its publications and other activities and programs are more autonomous than those of dependent associations. While the chief alumni officer works closely with other advancement professionals in development and public relations (*and* with you), his prime allegiance is to the alumni board. Because of this relative autonomy, many newly appointed presidents are wary of independent associations. Some quickly plan to bring them into the "comfort circle" by making them dependent despite the fact that it costs the institution more.

If you inherit an independent association, don't jump too soon. Although the arrangement is suspect from a presidential perspective, many, if not most, of the top alumni associations are independent. Their programs are impressive. Their suggestions to the institution usually are as helpful as they are uninhibited, and they contribute generously to your development program. I am not suggesting that you go one way or the other. Just wait until you know the territory before you leap. Some presidents have moved hastily and regretted it leisurely.

Yes, these indirect activities will cost, and the amount will be difficult to determine. But you must never cease trying, and pressing your associates to quantify these costs. This is the reason that bottom-line dollars and cents raised serve as such a good starting and ending point. And when the bottom line becomes vague, you should know why and how it will ultimately tie in with the amount of money raised for the institution.

There is another trend in institutional advancement that needs airing: the move to assign admissions, placement, athletics, and other externally related activities to the division. Except for rare instances (so rare that I can't think of any), you should avoid this situation. The rationale may appear logical, for each of the areas engages the external public, but the problem is one of efficiency, costs, and philosophy. These areas take too much management time from your vice president, who is (or should be) primarily responsible for raising private support for the institution. While it makes sense to tie your public relations (and publications are a part of your PR program) and alumni programs to your fund-raising effort, you reach a point of diminishing returns when you add other areas—that is, when you become less, rather than more, efficient. And finally, if yours is a larger institution with schools and colleges, *do not* establish autonomous development offices in each of them; and if you've inherited an autonomous arrangement, quickly appoint an outside consultant to make enlightened recommendations. All advancement activities, however remote, should report to your vice president or to his or her delegate.

11. *Establish an Efficient Development/Advancement Area*

Although the size and nature of your institution may necessitate modifications there from, the following figure shows the most efficient and effective general design for your fund-raising program. Be skeptical about anything that calls for additional staff, even though in time, with success, you will need to add them.

You cannot do without a vice president and director of development, a public relations officer, an alumni officer, a professional initially to do research and cultivation and begin your annual fund, and a planned-giving officer. This is a barebones total of five well-paid professionals. As your operation grows, you will want to consider recommendations from your vice president calling for additional development, public relations, and alumni staff. If you discriminate, do so on the side of the development staff. In time, you will need to approve an additional position for the capital campaign that your unprecedented success will

Figure 1.1. THE MOST EFFICIENT AND EFFECTIVE DESIGN FOR A FUND-RAISING PROGRAM.

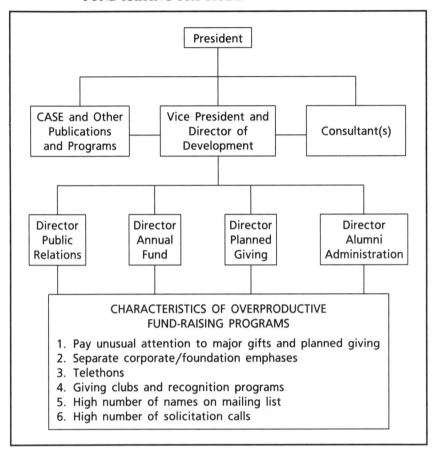

demand and merit. After such success, most institutions err on the side of too many staff, especially in public relations. Many public institutions have a number of public relations professional and absolutely no fund-raising staff. This practice should be unacceptable to you.

The following chapters will elaborate on the points made here. After reading them, keeping your enthusiasm high, you will be ready to involve deeply your full board of trustees and other good friends of the institution who will be your principal fund raisers. You will be able to create confidently a trustee development committee that will carry this message to the full board: "Give, get, or get off." The committees and the board will view you, your vice president, and staff as sufficiently sophisticated to merit their being gently orchestrated. And you will be on your way to a distinguished presidency.

2

A HISTORY
OF PHILANTHROPY

James L. Fisher

Philanthropy, or love of mankind, includes voluntary giving, voluntary service, and voluntary association, primarily for the benefit of others. What a wonderful term philanthropy is, and how in consonance it is with what a university is supposed to be! A university by whatever name (college, school, institute, and so on) exists for mankind, and its primary functions are to pursue truth, to interpret that truth gently with tentativeness and humility, and to create and appreciate beauty. There are no other fundamental purposes of a college or university.

Fund raising is a crucial dimension of philanthropy, and educational fund-raisers are completely engaged in the spirit and business and joy of philanthropy. Yet, few presidents think of philanthropy and fund raising together. Because of ignorance or inexperience, many presidents view fund raising as being distant from philanthropy, rather than as a part of the philanthropic process. Yet the worthy fund raiser is as much a part of philanthropy as the giver. They are both exhibiting a love of mankind and helping to reach a higher human condition. And the president, more than any other, is the one who must illuminate the institution, its programs, and its people so that others who care may find their way to it (Simic 1984).

My purpose in this chapter is to provide sufficient information about the history and nature of philanthropy to whet your appetite for pursuing the subject still further. I also hope to convince you that fund raising *is* philanthropy, and therefore is among the highest callings of your presidency. And as suggested in Chapter 1, you simply must get a copy of Robert Payton's book *Philanthropy* (ACE/Macmillan) for your personal library.

Philanthropy, The Unexamined American Tradition

It is uncomfortable for an academician to investigate the subject of philanthropy. Of all our important American traditions, it is least known, understood, and examined by scholars. Although generosity is perhaps our most unique national characteristic, until two years ago not a single college or university offered a course, or even a unit in a course, on philanthropy. The card catalog in the Library of Congress contains only three headings under the subject. And nowhere in all 2,918 pages of the 1983 edition of the *Random House Encyclopedia* does a listing for philanthropy appear.

Not one university has a division of philanthropy! In fact, this review unearthed only one institution with anything of that nature: The International Headquarters of the Seventh-Day Adventist Church has a Department of Philanthropic Services.

Most colleges and universities call the areas that deal with philanthropy "development," "institutional advancement," or sometimes "public affairs" or "external relations." All of these titles are acceptable, but they are cold terms for the important work of these offices. After all, the university president and the fund raisers, public relations officers, and alumni administrators who work under development are, in their highest and best form, engaged in philanthropy. Is the reason we avoid the term "philanthropy" because we are ashamed to announce what we are, or are frightened of being what we should be, or afraid we don't measure up? Is it because we don't want to seem pretentious? Or is it because we've never stopped to consider the beautiful occupations that fund raising and its related activities really are—loving mankind and the search for truth?

Charity and Philanthropy: An Important Difference

Although there is considerable historical debate about this, in Western society, philanthropy was born out of charity. The two terms have continued intertwined, although philanthropy is the more embracing term today (despite "charitable"-giving tax laws).

Charity is generally considered to be an act of goodness designed to reduce or eliminate human suffering, pain, or any other unfortunate condition immediately. Philanthropy is more general and long-term: It is an action directed at elevating humankind and preventing, rather than allaying, calamity.

Philanthropy is an activity that, if taken to its ultimate, eliminates the need for charity. Philanthropy is closely associated with the idea that the keys to self-sufficiency and freedom lie within the individual: Once the individual is independent, there will be no need for charity.

A vivid and amusing illustration shows the difference between charity and philanthropy:

A people lived in a village at the base of a great cliff. At the top of this cliff ran a much-used highway, and so many hapless travelers fell over the cliff that the kindly villagers were always busy picking them up and caring for their wounds. Finally, at great expense, the villagers bought an ambulance, which they kept ready at the base of the cliff to provide better care for the unfortunate wayfarers. One day, a thoughtful old man said, "Why do you not build a fence at the top?" But the screams of the suffering were loud in the villagers' ears, and helping the injured kept them so busy that they could not take time to climb the cliff and build the fence. And besides, they all knew, there is little charity in fence building. [Andrews 1950, 43—original source not certain.]

Charity, then, is generally for the short run, and philanthropy for the long run. We will probably always need both, but we can hope not. In universities, our most profound commitment should be to a society wherein philanthropy is so widespread that only the most unfortunate need charity.

Some Caveats on Philanthropic Motivation

Any discussion of the history of philanthropy requires us to acknowledge abuses in the practice of philanthropy. But then, there have also been abuses—in religion, politics, medicine, and most other professions. Even Robert Bremner, who has written the most candid (some say ruthless) historical assessment of philanthropy, proposes that ". . . philanthropy has been one of the principal methods of social advance." He continues: "The aim of philanthropy, in its broader sense, is improvement in the quality of human life. Whatever motives have animated individuals to become involved in philanthropy, the purpose of philanthropy itself is to promote the welfare, happiness, and culture of mankind."

Some of my colleagues in psychology insist that selfishness motivates giving. In the broadest sense, this may be true. In *The Art of Loving,* Erich Fromm wrote about altruism as the highest form of selfishness. That is, the more you think of others, the more others will think of you and the better you will think of yourself. There is nothing petty about this definition of selfishness. However, it is true that some, if not much, of modern philanthropy springs from the giver's desire for personal advancement, for special tax advantages, or to have a name put on a building for personal gain in the here or hereafter. I don't decry all such gifts, but suggest that a much higher order of giving should be the ultimate goal of the college president. After all, even the selfish are influenced for the better as they come in contact with those who give out of compassion and hope for their fellow beings. So long as the gift is not "tainted" (an old argument in philanthropy), the funds are used to advance the human condition and everyone is the better for the process, both giver and recipient.

Religion Gives Rise to Charity

Egyptian civilization yields perhaps the first Western evidence of charity. In the *Book of the Dead,* which dates back to around 4000 B.C., you can find passages praising those who give bread for the hungry and water for the thirsty (Budge 1967, 351). From the tombs of Harkhuf and Pepi-Nakht of the Sixth Dynasty (about 2500 B.C.) comes this record of giving and doing good because of a desire to improve the afterlife: "I desired that it might be well with me in the great gods' presence" (Breasted 1962, 151–52).

Clearly, the needs of the destitute held a high priority in ancient Egypt. Charity was an end in itself, and religion, rather than the bonds of family or clan, was the motivator. These same conditions mark charitable activities in most societies that follow, including twentieth-century America, although we see less religious motivation now.

Greco–Roman Origins of Philanthropy

As the cultures of Israel and Egypt gave us charity, classical civilizations gave us philanthropy (Payton 1982, 5). It was in ancient Greece and Rome that the first clear extension of charity resolved into what we call philanthropy. Those societies behaved more or less kindly "toward people or society in general," rather than exclusively toward the poor. It is important to note that this kind of behavior was not relegated to alms giving, for it had little or no connection with poverty. And it was seldom motivated by pity. Homer wrote:

And greatly was he loved, for courteously
He welcomed to his home beside the way
All comers. [*The Iliad*]

And about religion, he obliquely declared:

Happy the man and happy he alone
Who can call today his own;
He who, secure within, can say
"Tomorrow do thy worst, for I have lived today."

More to the point, perhaps, was Seneca, who penned this:

Religion for the intellectual is foolish; for the politician, useful; and for the masses, necessary.

Certainly, then, the motivation does not appear to be the promise of some special consideration after death. In the case of the Greek or Roman giver, the prime index of self-interest was measured in mundane terms rather than celestial benefits (Payton). The Athenian philanthropist Cimon, who built the Academy of Socrates and Plato, kept his house open for his fellow citizens, fed travelers, and shared his worldly goods (Plutarch 1932, 585). Classical philanthropy also reached out to the arts, festivals, education, and recreation.

Pre–Christian Romans followed the example of the Greeks. They gave for the benefit of any worthy citizen or for the state, rather than out of pity for the needy. Cicero wrote that all men were brothers, and "the whole world is to be considered as the common city of gods and men." Following this reasoning, the best example of morality would be a conscientious sense of obligation to this whole. In Roman terms, people owed it to themselves and to society to establish a sound economic base for their lives and subsequently to fulfill their duties as citizens (Cicero 1967, 54–62). These Roman thoughts remind me of the philosophy of Rockefeller and Carnegie, without the religious fervor of Rockefeller. But charity itself found little scope in Rome. As Polybius reported, "In Rome no one ever gives away anything to anyone if he can help it" (Durant 1944).

The Jewish Charitable Tradition

The Hebrews have a history of religiously motivated charity that dates back at least to the Egyptians. For them this sort of charity is called "tzedakah" and means "sharing what we have with the poor and doing good deeds" (Epstein 1970). Indeed, their charitable practices were similar to the Egyptians' and suggest a strong degree of mutual influence that, to my knowledge, scholars have never closely examined. In the Old Testament, Jacob saw a vision and promised to give a tenth "of all that Thou shalt give me" to God. The Mosaic Code required that all land be left fallow every seventh year (Shemitah); the crops that grew of themselves were for the poor, as were the "gleanings of the vineyards" every year. To give was a religious duty, and those who did not were "cursed." Today, in addition to being deeply involved in the broader charitable and philanthropic activities, tzedakah continues through efforts designed principally to serve Jewish interests.

The Christian Charitable Tradition

The teachings of Jesus set up a high ethic for givers, a standard that has yet to be achieved by most who give or recognize givers (certainly including colleges and universities). Jesus taught that the spirit of the giver is more important than the size of the gift:

> Woe unto you, scribes, Pharisees, hypocrites! for ye pay tithe of mint and anise and cummin, and have omitted the weightier matters of the law, judgment, mercy, and faith: these ought ye to have done, and not to leave the other undone. [Matthew 23:23]

The value of the gift is determined by the sacrifice of the giver; for the rich to merely tithe is not enough. Too, in the Book of Matthew Jesus advised the rich young ruler to "sell all that thou hast, and distribute unto the poor, and thou shalt have treasure in heaven."

Jesus taught that gifts should be given in secret, and not for public acknowledgment: "Take heed that ye do not your alms before men, to be seen of them, otherwise ye have no reward of your Father which is in heaven." Note that Jesus promises the heavenly reward only for the secret gift. It is more blessed to give than to receive, He says—but only if we keep quiet about it and ask those who receive, if they must know, to hold it private.

The Church, the Rise of Charity, and the Decline of Philanthropy

With the advent of Christianity as an organized religion under Emperor Theodosius I in the fourth century A.D., Roman philanthropy ground to a halt. The more restrictive form of giving, charity, replaced it—continuing virtually throughout the Middle Ages. The Catholic church depended for its support on charitable programs, which often were motivated more by secular and political factors than by religious ones. True, charity helped the poor, the widowed, the aged and infirm, orphans, and others. But not adequately. Like the Romans, the church tried to provide cultural elevation. But there were few meaningful attempts. And so the situation reversed itself: A period of little concern for the poor, and great attention to cultural elevation, changed to a period of almost exclusive concern for the poor, and little concern for the general betterment of the individual and society. One could only look to heaven for surcease.

This was a period of all but unbounded religious authority. The Catholic church, together with an acquiescing state, tried to enforce payment of tithes, grant indulgences, and sell the use of other religious devices to fund their charitable programs. Perhaps the earliest such action was around 800 A.D., when the capitularies of Charlemagne commanded tithes to maintain the bishop, the clergy, the poor, and the general purposes of the church (Andrews 1950, 36). All of these techniques assumed the idea that you could buy salvation.

Enter the State and the New Middle Classes

Religious motivation was considerably tempered by the reentry of a measure of philanthropy in the later Middle Ages. The first impetus was the rise of the secular state; the second, the rise of the new middle class. As the power and wealth of the state grew stronger, the church became less influential. In 1225, Louis VIII gave 100 sous each to the 2,000 leper houses in his realm. Similarly, nobles and other wealthy individuals began to make gifts to charitable causes. Importantly, although religion continued to be a prime motive for giving, the church was no longer the exclusive conduit.

The coming of the Mercantile Age brought both preindustrial cities and a higher level of general sophistication. With these came a new prosperity that left in its wake social alienation and a growing number of people who had neither a job nor the institutions of family and church for support. The traditional charities lacked the resources and the vision to attend to new problems, and so the rising middle classes stepped in.

Endowments for schools, scholars, sermons, and orphanages began to spring up, particularly in England. Because such gifts were so widespread, legislation was enacted. In 1601, during the reign of Queen Elizabeth I, the Statute of Charitable Uses was made a law of the land (Bremner 1960). Its purpose was to create, control, and protect such funds. This statute stands to this day as the cornerstone of our laws concerning giving, and as the legitimator of present-day American charitable foundations.

During this same period in England came the poor laws, which mark the real beginning of government's assuming responsibility for charitable activities. Indeed, Payton has concluded that the English poor laws marked the watershed between medieval and modern philanthropy (Payton 1982, 14). Under Elizabeth I, wrote Payton, poor laws "would suggest that the state had moved in to fill the vacuum [between church and nobility]." Early poor laws called for public collection of funds for the relief of the poor. These laws grew more specific through the years. They even came to include sanctions (mostly religious) for noncompliance. Eventually the Poor Rate in the Act of 1601 established outright taxation (Andrews 1950, 40).

Philanthropy in the United States

Most would agree that organized philanthropy supported by systematic fund raising developed in twentieth-century America (Cutlip 1965, 5). However, the fact is that the first systematic attempt to raise funds in America occurred in 1641, when the Massachusetts Bay Colony sent three clergymen to England to raise money for Harvard University. Until the twentieth century, however, philanthropy in America occurred on a small scale, largely financed by a wealthy few in response to personal "begging" appeals. The early years of the twentieth century finally provided the seedbed for today's philanthropic structure and success. It was during this period that institutions conducted the first major organized fund-raising campaigns, and universities hired the first fund-raising consultants and appointed the first development officers.

Harvard's Extraordinary Role in American Philanthropy

From the initial bequest of John Harvard in 1638, and for almost 100 years thereafter, Harvard University commanded the major share of philanthropic attention (Curti and Nash 1965, 4). Although the College of William and Mary was founded in 1693, and the Collegiate School of Connecticut (later renamed for its first major benefactor, Elihu Yale) opened in 1701, the experience of Harvard set the pattern for philanthropic practices and problems that exist today.

A number of America's first colleges (such as Dartmouth College and King's College) received some public support, but the primary source was private, and the moral force religious. (The religious motives were little different from those of the ancient Egyptians.) In 1633 Reverend John Eliot (one of the first masters of the philanthropic appeal) wrote to Simonds D'Ewes, seeking funds for Harvard:

> God has bestowed upon you a bounty full blessing; now if you should please, to employ but one mite, of that great walth which God hath given, to erect a schoole of larning, a college among us, you should doe a most glorious work, acceptable to God and man; & the commemoration of the

first founder of the means of larning, would be perpetuating of your name
and honour among us. . . . [Curti and Nash 1965, 5]

Harvard Slips

Although love of God was almost invariably the reason for a gift,
even this lofty impetus was insufficient to stay selfish motives. The
earliest example of questionable ethics in fund raising at American
colleges came when Harvard tottered on the brink of collapse in 1641.
Reverends Thomas Weld, Hugh Peters, and William Hibben went to
England to raise what funds they could without engaging in dishonorable
begging. Among the givers was the wealthy Lady Anne Mowlson,
visited by Rev. Weld (Curti, 1965, 6). Her gift called for the establishment of an endowment for the support of "poore schollar[s]," and
Weld, apparently looking out for his own interests, stated that the first
scholarship should go to one John Weld, his son. Young Weld never
received the scholarship because he was arrested for burglary, and ex-
pelled from Harvard. Despite this flaunting of moral laxity, however,
the university was saved. (The gift money totaled 500 pounds sterling.)

Names to Remember: Whitefield and Franklin

Perhaps the most dynamic, and certainly the most successful, early
college fund raiser in America was the evangelist George Whitefield
(1714–1770). In seven visits to the colonies, the young Rev. Whitefield
preached philanthropy. Although he sought gifts for his other, more
strictly charitable, causes, he also secured books and financial assistance
for hard-pressed colonial colleges. Harvard, Dartmouth, Princeton, and
the University of Pennsylvania all benefited from his assistance (Cutlip
1965, 6). Bremner (1960, 21–23) writes that if no single institution
can be regarded as Whitefield's monument, it is because he helped so
many.

Benjamin Franklin also figures in fund-raising lore. College presidents and trustees may find substance, or at least a source of wry
amusement, in this statement from Franklin about his fund-raising
activities: "I do not remember any of my . . . manoeuvres . . .
whenever, after thinking of it, I more easily excused myself for having
made some use of cunning" (Cutlip 1965, 7). Franklin was a successful
fund raiser because he never accepted a cause in which he did not
profoundly believe. He also shrewdly planned his appeal, and carefully
catalogued his prospective donors. He would always prepare a list

of special prospects, and then personally call on each one (Cutlip 1965, 6).

Experienced fund raisers will smile, reassured, at this letter about fund raising from Franklin to a friend:

> In the first place, I advise you to apply to all whom you know will give something; next to those whom you are uncertain whether they will give anything or not and show them the list of those who have given; and lastly, do not neglect those whom you are sure will give nothing, for in some of them you may be mistaken. [Cutlip 1965, 6]

Promoter Presidents and the Beginning of Systematic Fund Raising

From the early days of the Republic through the Jacksonian period, there were several attempts at systematic fund raising. Most failed, but there were successes. In 1829 a British chemist, James Smithson, left an estate of a half-million dollars "to the United States of America to found at Washington, under the name of the Smithsonian Institution, an establishment for the increase and diffusion of knowledge among men" (Cutlip 1965, 9). And in 1834 the indefatigable Miss Mary Lyon launched a fund drive to found Mount Holyoke College. She solicited subscriptions house to house for this women's seminary. Astonishingly successful, she almost singlehandedly raised $30,000 in less than two months.

Up to World War I, college fund-raising methods were much like Mary Lyon's campaign—"simple and homemade," dreams made real by extraordinary people (Marts 1961, 20–22). Western and Southern colleges used "financial agents"—frequently the college presidents—and sent them to Eastern cities to gather funds. Following the pattern of the original Harvard trip to England, Presbyterian financial agents went to New York City and Pittsburgh, Congregationalists to New England, and Methodists to New York State and Pennsylvania.

Throughout the nineteenth century, countless colleges stayed alive thanks to the personal fund-raising efforts of promoter–presidents. Even then a primary task of the president was to secure the resources to maintain and improve the institution. Cutlip (1965, 19) describes E. P. Tenney of Colorado College as typical of this group of effective presidents. When money was short, Tenney would board the next train for the effete East, to return with both money and students. As far as anyone knew, he never returned empty-handed.

In 1871, Smith College became perhaps the earliest example of how a matching gift could stimulate public giving when the citizens of

Northampton, Massachusetts, raised over $25,000 to meet the conditions of Sophia Smith's will.

Because of the role it was to play in later fund campaigns, we should also cite the founding of the American Red Cross. In 1881, a small group met in Clara Barton's house in Washington, D.C., to organize the "greatest venture of voluntary service in the world." This venture was destined to play an influential role in American philanthropy (Bremner 1960, 160).

Carnegie, Rockefeller, and Large-Scale Philanthropy

Large-scale philanthropy emerged when Andrew Carnegie and John D. Rockefeller created benevolent foundations. In a historic essay called "Wealth," published in 1889, Carnegie stated that millionaires should, instead of leaving their fortunes to their families, administer their wealth as a public trust during life. In that same year, Rockefeller, a student of the old-fashioned school of religious motivation, gave $600,000 to help found the University of Chicago. This was the first of millions that he was to give to that university (Bremner 1960, 6–117). Out of this came both good and bad: Great amounts of money were intelligently administered, but the "tainted money" controversy grew out of accusations that the rich robber barons were trying to buy both public favor and heavenly rewards. Reverend Washington Gladdon's article "Tainted Money" and Ida Tarbell's book *The History of the Standard Oil Company* played major roles in inspiring strong public criticism of the new big givers.

Ward, Pierce, and the First Fund-Raising Campaigns

During the early 1900s colleges and other institutions seriously began to use the campaign as a means to raise funds. This method, developed by YMCA secretaries Lyman L. Pierce and Charles S. Ward, marked the beginning of philanthropy as a broad public enterprise rather than a hobby of the very rich. Arnaud Marts, president of Bucknell University and cofounder of the fund-raising firm Marts & Lundy Inc., documented this shift. He reported (1961, 23) that it was not unusual in the early 1920s to see, at any given time, a half-dozen or more college presidents at New York City's Prince George Hotel. Each president was there seeking funds to meet campaign goals.

The essence of the Ward–Pierce Plan was to launch an intensive campaign to raise large sums of money in a short time. They did this by saturating the target public with appeals and by recruiting scores of volunteers to solicit many times their number. The first college to use the Ward–Pierce Plan was probably the University of Pittsburgh, in 1914, where the method succeeded in raising capital funds. It was after that, in 1916–17, that Ward and Pierce directed their famous $100 million campaign for the American Red Cross. This success prompted literally hundreds of colleges to use campaign techniques. Arnaud Marts' *Man's Concern for His Fellow Man* is a fascinating first-hand account of much of the work of Ward and Pierce.

Harvard Brings Refinement to Fund Raising

At the time Ward and Pierce were demonstrating their whirlwind campaign techniques, Bishop William Lawrence of Boston pioneered another effective, yet entirely different, approach. This son of a prominent New England family was repelled by the high-powered drives of Pierce, Ward, and their followers (Cutlip 1965, 51). In 1894 he became an overseer of Harvard, and in 1904 was elected president of the alumni association. In his presidential address that June, he called on Harvard alumni to give $2.5 million to increase the salaries of the faculty in liberal arts. Not surprisingly, Harvard president Eliot drafted Lawrence to organize the campaign to raise this great sum. Thus began the large-scale but less flamboyant alumni fund drive, which today constitutes a major financial activity in support of America's colleges, universities, and preparatory schools (Cutlip 1965, 52).

The First Fund-Raising Consultants

The next major development in college fund raising was the rise of professional consultants. Interestingly, while professional consultants predated the first full-time college development offices, they gave life to them. But today, unfortunately, many college and university presidents appoint people with virtually no fund-raising experience to the chief development position, and then compound their problems by refusing to consider a consultant. And these presidents wonder why they don't raise money.

In 1919, Charles Ward gave up his $8,000 annual salary with the YMCA to found the first fund-raising firm, Ward and Hill Associated. A few months later, the firm became Ward, Hill, Pierce (of YMCA fame), and Wells. The junior partners were Christian H. Dreshman, Olaf Gates, and Arnaud C. Marts (Marts 1961, 34) And the first staff member of the new firm was George E. Lundy of Canton, Ohio, who had also been a YMCA secretary. Other staff members were George Tamblyn, Bayard Hedrick, and Howard Beaver. And after World War I, two young former army officers, Carlton and George Ketchum, opened Ketchum Publicity. From Ward and Hill Associated came at least five of today's largest fund-raising firms—firms that have brought fundamental changes to American philanthropy (Cutlip 1965, 157–201).

John Price Jones Succeeds with Style

It was John Price Jones who, apparently without a plan, brought together the best of the schools of Bishop Lawrence and Ward–Pierce by codifying fund-raising principles and practice. His work included techniques of research and planning that were to elevate the field to a new level. A journalist by profession, he entered fund raising as a publicist in 1917 to work on the Liberty Loan Campaigns. The style of Bishop Lawrence at Harvard strongly influenced these campaigns. Jones, also a Harvard alumnus, blended his penchant for system, detail, and planning with the Lawrence technique. We have no direct report of it, but at this time he must have been aware of Ward–Pierce's extraordinary success.

In 1918 Robert F. Duncan, the Harvard Endowment Fund's first full-time secretary, appointed Jones to the Funds staff. Jones's appointment was to have far-reaching effects not only on Harvard, but also on the entire fund-raising profession. The university's $10 million campaign in 1919 made fund-raising history, and in fact changed the course of American higher education. Jones brought dignity and new techniques, as well as success, to fund campaigns. Cutlip says that Jones "sought to develop enthusiasm for giving to Harvard by dignified means without rough-and-tumble methods" (Cutlip 1965, 174). The university raised $14.2 million in less than ten months—a dramatic departure from the campaign of Weld, Peters, and Hibben.

The College President and Fund Raising Today

Today, $500 million campaigns are not uncommon. There are even billion-dollar campaigns. The patterns of philanthropy in American higher education seem set. The fund-raising drive is carefully organized—be it on behalf of capital, annual fund, or alumni (and even planned giving) campaigns. Prestigious leaders, including college presidents, spearhead the campaign and professional and institutional development officers and consultants stand behind (but not too far). These development experts carefully pinpoint prospects, organize solicitation and large numbers of volunteers, and help to build a climate for giving. Such activities are the only *proven* ways to generate significant private support for a college or university. Individuals who interest *other* individuals in investing in an institution raise the funds. And the primary initiative for this essential activity is the president.

Assuming that a thoughtful appreciation of the purposes of your institution and of the history of philanthropy undergird your program, you should have no uneasy feelings about fund raising. It is, after all, the grandest of presidential responsibilities.

Bibliography

Andrews, F. Emerson. *Philanthropic Giving.* New York: Russell Sage Foundation, 1950.

Boas, Franz. *Kwakiutl Ethnography.* Chicago: University of Chicago Press, 1966.

Breasted, J.H. *Ancient Records of Egypt,* vol 1. New York: Russell and Russell, 1962.

Bremner, Robert H. *American Philanthropy.* Chicago: University of Chicago Press, 1960.

Budge, E. A. Wallis. *The Book of the Dead.* New York: Dover Publications, 1967.

Cicero. *On Moral Obligation,* trans. John Higginbotham. Los Angeles: University of California Press, 1967.

Curti, Merle, and Roderick Nash. *Philanthropy in the Shaping of Higher Education.* New Brunswick, NJ: Rutgers University Press, 1965.

Cutlip, Scott M. *Fund Raising in the United States.* New Brunswick, NJ: Rutgers University Press, 1965.

Durant, Will. *Caesar and Christ, The Story of Civilization: Part II.* New York: Simon and Schuster, 1944.

Epstein, Morris. *All About Jewish Holidays and Customs.* New York: Ktav Publishing House, 1970.

Fromm, Erich. *The Art of Loving.* New York: Harper & Row, 1956.

Homer. *The Iliad,* trans. William Bryant. Boston: Houghton, Mifflin, 1870.

Malinowski, B. *Argonauts of the Western Pacific.* London: Routledge and Kegan Paul, 1966.

Marcus, J.R. *The Jew in the Medieval World.* Cincinatti: Union of American Hebrew Congregations, 1938.

Marts, A. *Man's Concern for His Fellow Man.* Geneva, NY: W.F. Humphrey Press, 1961.

Muller, Max F., ed. *The Sacred Books of the East,* vol 27. Delhi, India: Motilal Banarsidass, 1976.

Payton, Robert L. "Major Challenges to Philanthropy," Paper presented to Independent Sector, Washington, DC, 1984.

———. "Philanthropic Values," paper presented at the Wilson Center Colloquium, Princeton, NJ, October 2–3, 1982.

———. *Philanthropy.* New York. ACE/Macmillan, 1988.

Pickering, Danby. *The Statutes at Large,* vol. 7. Cambridge, England: Cambridge University Press, 1763.

Plutarch. *The Lives of the Noble Grecians and Romans.* New York: Modern Library, 1932.

Simic, Curtis R. "The Role of the Board, the President, and the Chief Development Officer," paper presented at the Association of Governing Boards of Colleges and Universities, Washington, DC, 1984 Annual Meeting, San Francisco, CA.

Yang, L-S. *Studies in Chinese Institutional History.* Cambridge, MA: Harvard University Press, 1961.

3

THE ETHICS AND VALUES OF FUND RAISING

Robert L. Payton

The President's Situation

For presidents of all sorts of institutions, fund raising is an inescapable fact of life. In an increasing number of cases, fund-raising effectiveness is the key to the office—to both getting in and staying in. Intellectual and moral leadership seem to have yielded to the effective marshalling and management of resources. The career path to the presidency is now open to those who enter it from the development function. Like it or not (and I must say that in many respects I *don't* like it), fund raising is now at the center of the president's responsibilities.

There is a way of thinking about these grim-sounding assertions that may save the day for all of us—that, is for presidents and for the rest of us who want their leadership. While "fund raising," narrowly considered, may be the threat, "the philanthropic tradition" may provide the most effective response. In the early parts of this chapter, I will deal with the president's situation, and the extent to which fund raising and public relations influence it. In the last part, I will try to put it all in the proper context.

There is no function of the office of president that puts that party at greater risk than the development function. Not only must the president perform effectively in measurable ways—most particularly by achieving a balanced budget with the help of gifts and grants—but he or she must also guard the institution's integrity.

There are countless other actors, buffers, and shared guardians on the *academic* side: Each faculty member is expected to meet high professional standards. The duties to be performed are familiar to everyone. The standards of performance are very imprecise, but the lack of a clear bottom line is an accepted reality. In other words, in the academic performance of the institution, *numerous* individuals share responsibilities. But no one bears responsibility for the *ethical* standards of the institution more than its president.

The development function, in contrast, focuses responsibility *at the top*. There is no clear consensus about what spells success in fund raising, other than the funding total at the end of the year. The consensus is that fund raising is ethically ambiguous, at best. And people watch for signs that the president has strayed from the moral path in an effort to succeed at the bottom line. Although others are involved in fund raising with the president, there is little sense of shared responsibility. For fund raising, the buck stops with the president, like it or not.

Success in fund raising is much more complicated and problematic than inexperienced presidents would like to believe. Simplistic bottom-line measures in dollars raised in a particular year or in a particular campaign often mask fatal damage to presidential leadership. Pyrrhic victories are common. Presidential reputation is a frequent casualty: Presidents who have been successful in meeting fund-raising goals often are denigrated for having made unacceptable compromises of personal or institutional integrity (or both) in reaching those goals.

Presidents from diverse backgrounds have come to recognize these sobering but usually tacit conditions of the office. Some abandon the idea of repeatedly serving as a college or university president because of the burdens of fund-raising. For those who still believe that educational leadership is one of the benefits of being a president, fund raising usually is looked upon as a painful but unavoidable necessity. Organizations such as CASE try to enlighten the relationship between the president and his principal development officer, and the Association of Governing Boards gives special attention to the relationship between the president and key trustees and fund-raising volunteers. But it is the president who suffers most if fund-raising efforts fail or if fund raising is conducted in a way that detracts from the institution's dignity.

In spite of the importance of fund raising, there are important and instructive exceptions. Some presidents learn to lead the development function so effectively—carry the burden so lightly—that recognition of achievements is widely shared. The development effort is seen as a common effort in which everyone participates. Even disappointments are distributed fairly. Everyone seems to have a valued sense of making a personal contribution to a community effort—and the president receives credit for making it happen that way.

The president's situation has changed in recent years. There is too much emphasis on fund raising and other material indicators of progress and success. Presidents have been cautioned away from educational and moral leadership roles and left with a managerial assignment that no one else wants. In some cases, trustees and faculty members have been content to let the president do the work, only to second-guess performance at almost every step along the way. (A philosophy professor left his teaching role to become president of a college. When he went back to the campus to visit with his former colleagues, one of them asked: "John, when you become a college president, do you lose your integrity all at once or does it just dribble away?")

The most serious diminution of the office will be sacrifice of the educational and moral leadership it once called for. We can't afford that. Thus we must manage the development function in a way that lets the president put the stamp of individual ethical and overall administrative standards on the fund-raising function without becoming the chief development officer. (Chapman's Law says that under stress the executive seeks to fill the role of the person immediately below in the hierarchy.) Properly understood, fund raising rises to its rightful role as institutional development. The development function integrates with the academic objectives of the institution. It is as honorable and useful and important as any other function in achieving institutional purposes. It cannot be thought of as separate, or judged by a different (and lower) standard.

The dimension that is most critical, and yet often curiously neglected, is the ethical one.

Ethics and Values

There are several aspects of the "ethical dimension" that I should spell out. Some writers would approach the subject in terms of principles, even rules, of ethical fund raising. Other writers would emphasize the benefits to be gained by all of those affected by the fund-raising effort. Still others might write about the personal qualities called for in the effective fund raiser. Moral philosophers have technical terms to describe these various perspectives (and there are well-known authorities to turn to).

My own approach is shamelessly eclectic and borrows from all of these. It also places heavy emphasis on the need to talk about ethics and values in settings in which presidents and their key allies and associates can learn from their continuing shared experience. My role in this book, such as it is, will be to plant questions in the reader's mind that can be asked of each of the other chapters (as well as this one).

Ethics is concerned with relationships. A moment's reflection will call to mind how diverse and numerous a president's relationships are: with trustees, faculty members, students, alumni, wealthy donors, journalists, development staff members, business leaders, legislators, foundation executives. . . . To be "ethical" means to be serious about one's concern for all of the others involved in those relationships—and to be "serious" means that lip service is not enough. We have different obligations to different others (we often use the sociologist's term "significant others" loosely to mean those people of special importance in our lives). There is also a widely varying intensity in the relationships: Some become very intimate and personal; others are arm's-length and disinterested; some are conducted by mass communication designed to *seem* personal and direct. At one level we speak of "constituencies" (e.g., students), while at another level we speak of "special friends of the institution."

In listing significant others, we begin to appreciate that our obligations to some often conflict with our obligations to others. At times even our constituencies come into conflict. One of the reasons that ethical reflection can become compellingly interesting as well as important is that undeniably good things can be in conflict. Resolving those conflicts, as Chester Barnard wrote 50 years ago, is what the responsibility of an executive is all about.

"The president is commonly thought to be virtuous and a guide to the good life. The president is expected to be an exemplar for virtuous behavior whom young people can follow, and a person of professional integrity who provides a moral reference point for faculty and administrators." These words (made up by way of example) may sound quaint in a world where private life is distinct from public virtue, and where even words like "virtue" and terms like "the good life" are intellectually suspect. Yet I believe they still carry great weight in the common morality, and that college and university presidents are judged by them whether or not they consider this fair. I also believe that thinking about virtue and what it means to be virtuous is intellectually defensible as well as useful. As for trying to live the good life, the private lives of presidents are on constant public display. In fact, one of the reasons it is so difficult to be a president is that you must be smart, efficient, decent, and honorable all at the same time—all the time.

Because development pulls the president into an arena where material values predominate, and uses the perquisities of office to increase effectiveness, and because development activities so often are public occasions, presidential virtue most frequently is measured in that context. All those lonely, private struggles with tenure decisions and research contracts and budget compromises may in the end do little to off-set the impression that the president makes as the chief development officer.

Thinking about presidents as virtuous persons has its advantages (in case this painfully high standard has made you uneasy). It requires assessment of the whole person rather than of a single skill or quality. And it requires assessment over time, rather than on the basis of a single act. Because society has drifted from thinking and talking about virtue, there is a tendency to judge performance more narrowly—hence the bottom-line mentality. Among the authors contributing to this volume are some who have been very closely involved in passing judgment on presidential performance. They would agree, I think, that presidents should be judged on their character (personal and professional) over a reasonable period of time; that presidents are expected to be virtuous, but not without flaw. The recent experiences of presidential candidates Hart and Biden and others suggests that assessment of character will rest on a single act only if that act is thought to be revelatory of suspect traits of personality. The public usually is much fairer than it is generally given credit for being.

In development, the values of character given greatest weight—the prime virtues and vices—are those thought to reveal pride and humility. For instance, there are several well-known scandals of excessive expenditure for presidential residences. The lesson to learn is that the development rationale (sumptuous residences or offices are necessary to meet and entertain wealthy donors and prospects) can be stretched too far. Since we assume that Aristotle's *Ethics* is part of the cultural literacy of college presidents (whether it is or not), it is difficult to claim ignorance of the mean between magnificence and meanness. The burden for these matters rests with the trustees: Presidents should be appropriately housed and officed, but the trustees should know the difference between ostentation and good taste. If they don't, the president should err on the side of modesty and restraint.

If moderation in personal matters is important, your attitude toward others should reflect Kant's admonition that we always treat others as an end in themselves and not as a means of reaching an end. To think of donors as ends in themselves pulls you up short, because the initial reason for interest in a donor is the prospective gift rather than the donor as a person. Nonetheless, the interest of the individual must be paramount, even at the expense of the gift.

Many people see these relationships as mutually manipulative. It is better to be cynical about them, they say. Play to the pride of the donors, massage their egos, flatter and pamper them. Alas, all too often this works! In some cases, *nothing else* will work. Indeed, in some cases, only the award of an honorary degree or some other important institutional praise yields a gift. In other cases, gifts become bribes: Off the record, under cover, a donor will propose a gift in exchange, say, for admitting someone to the school.

We must consider, at this point, the responsibility for weighing the integrity of the institution against its need for financial support. The taboo line to be crossed, as Kenneth Boulding warns us, is likely never again to be drawn at the same place. Ethical compromises tend to be permanent. When the president is asked to make an unacceptable compromise, the institution's integrity as well as the president's is at stake.

The president needs allies in these situations. Institutional integrity is not a one-person matter. The trustees are most important, both because they are the judges of presidential performance and because they are expected to represent the public interest (that is, to be "dis-interested"). Because presidential judgments of "appropriateness" of compromises often affect the heart of the institution's educational in-tegrity (that is, admission), you should bring into the discussion faculty members considered to be people of good character.

Eventually, of course, the day comes when the advisors, colleagues, and trustees cannot themselves agree, and the buck stops here—with the president. (That saying, and the advice to stay out of the kitchen if you can't stand the heat, are only two of the reasons we are indebted to Harry Truman.)

The President and the Good Life

I've argued that the development function has come to be so important that it is perhaps the most important presidential activity. (By the way, I include legislative relations in my definition of develop-ment, however it is organized. There is nothing in this chapter that exempts the presidents of public institutions.) My second point is that the development function exposes the president to public view and assessment more dramatically than any other activity, and thus adds to presidential vulnerability. The third point is that the development function, because it is based on personal relationships between the president and so many other people, is ethically charged. Not only the president's competence but his or her character will be judged. Finally, I suggest (drawing on personal experience) that the development func-tion can be a Slough of Despond which the president should not enter alone.

Under the circumstances, then, why would a person of good char-acter and strong intelligence want to be a president?

In my opinion, the president has three roles to play: *manager, moral exemplar,* and *educational leader.* The first two are inescapable; the third is optional. The president as manager will be judged first on economic performance, second on academic administration. Neither task is easy. Balanced budgets achieved by careful control of expenditures as well as by effective fund raising are essential. At the end of the day, academic administration is about balancing economic and educational budgets and avoiding deficits in each.

Of course, the president is more than manager and administrator. He or she will be judged by all constituencies as a person of virtue— perhaps as a person of easy virtue. There may be intellectual reasons for arguing against such judgments, but the common morality won't accept those arguments. Presidents of colleges and universities may even *survive* and *prosper* as persons of dubious personal integrity, as successful exploiters of the weaknesses of others, as clever manipulators and "con men." Some will find allies who exhibit the same qualities. But of these, many will know the truth, and many will think the truth more important than the deception.

The president as educational leader is different from both of these. The notion that educational leadership implies some national reputation is not what I have in mind. I refer only to the role of the president as a leader of the intellectual life of his or her campus community. It seems obvious that most presidents can have the first two qualities and lack this one: There are others who can pick up the slack.

The reason I give the matter such importance is that *presidents may find in the study of philanthropy itself the avenue to educational leadership.* This is the argument:

1. Presidents are immersed in development.

2. Development is one aspect of philanthropy, but not the only one. (Voluntary service and voluntary association are the others.)

3. Philanthropy is an ancient tradition, but it is little known and less understood. It is rarely taught.

4. Presidents are in an unusually good position to observe the workings of philanthropic activity in all its positive and negative aspects.

5. Presidents who become knowledgeable about the philanthropic tradition will be able to present it as a rich and complex field of intellectual inquiry.

6. Philanthropic behavior touches the lives of every constituency,

every person associated with a college or university; philanthropic behavior is a common experience and a common value. It is, in fact, a major source of the common morality and of the public agenda.

7. The president who is a scholar of philanthropy as well as a practitioner has an opportunity to become engaged directly in the intellectual life of the campus. The topic permeates the disciplines and professions, yet it is no one's sacred precinct.

Even preliminary study of the history of philanthropy will bring out the role of philanthropy in shaping American higher education. An excellent book by Robert Bremner on the history of American philanthropy has been issued in a new edition (see note at end of chapter). It brings out the ways in which education and other philanthropic purposes have been served by "public–private cooperation" since long before that became a political slogan. Reading such vital materials will raise important questions about your own institution's philanthropic history. And at last the names on buildings and professorships and scholarships and prizes will come alive.

Inquiry into the origins and development of philanthropic behavior and values will lead back (in the Western tradition) through classical authors to and past the Bible. The Old Testament is a rich resource: Certain of the prophets remind us that philanthropy, religion, and social reform have enjoyed a tremendously long history of cooperation. Aristotle, Cicero, Seneca, and others bring the ethical reflection central to the values we still associate with benevolent action for public purposes. Maimonides and Thomas Aquinas offer medieval summaries. (Maimonides' hierarchy of the levels of giving reveals remarkably the forces at work in benefiting others, as well as the values of anonymity.)

Study of the history of philanthropy gives evidence that some communities have held fund raising in high esteem. Many have learned that seeking resources can be an honorable activity and should not be denigrated as "begging." More commonly, in recent years we find, however, that people apologize in asking for financial support and often feel embarrassed about it. Just what is "the philanthropic relationship," and how can it be sustained at a level that protects the dignity of those involved? Psychologists and sociologists should be able to help us with this one, but thus far they haven't given it much attention. William James's *The Varieties of Religious Experience* may provide some insight into thinking about the problem. Presidents should attend very carefully to the varieties of philanthropic experience, their own and others', if they are to understand them and be sensitive to their complexity.

There is a case *against* philanthropy, of course, and American colleges and universities are in the middle of the controversy. The question of who should pay for higher education—what balance of individual, public, and philanthropic resources—appears on the front page of every campus newspaper, and often in the public media. Economists and political scientists, weak as they are on philanthropic values and practices, offer little help. Yet presidents are expected to have a grasp of the relative importance of each factor.

What is the rationale for philanthropy in the support of higher education? Where can a president read about it? There are some sources available, and more coming. For the most part, however, the resources are thin, and presidents will have the opportunity to lead the campus discussion if they can be educational leaders.

Philanthropic activity is not always placidly benign. For example, the continuing controversy over divestment illustrates the tensions arising because people presume that voluntary initiatives are for the public good. Some people would suppress student and faculty action to divest; some students and faculty members would simply bend the institution to their own political will. (In an essay published elsewhere, I have raised the question of whether corporate earnings from South Africa are "tainted" and thus rejectable when offered as philanthropic contributions.) Another example might be the conditions that donors put on gifts. To what extent is the president letting outsiders determine the institution's goals when he seeks and accepts restricted gifts? If the vice president for development comes in with a prospective contribution that falls outside the goals of the institution, is it up to the president to turn it down?

The history of philanthropic support of higher education provides many illustrations of the problem, and of different solutions. The problems themselves, however, are philosophical, organizational, and managerial. They cut across the specialized disciplines. They call for reflection that combines theory, practice, and contrasting values.

Philanthropic studies might become a special field of presidential interest. No one in the institution will bring more experience to bear, so the president can speak with the authority of the practitioner. No one else will be an expert on the theory of the subject, and the president thus faces an undeveloped field of intellectual opportunity. The president will rarely (if ever) find a better point of entry into the intellectual life of the campus. The subject is important; it is interesting, and it defies being reduced to a neat and tidy package. Philanthropic values and issues are the sort that encourage exploratory discourse. They reveal and shape the institution's character and purposes.

The development function, thought of in so small a way at the beginning of this chapter, is a threat to presidential well-being. Thought of as a powerful and often ennobling set of ideas, development can be transformed into an asset of great value.

Bibliographical Note

A handy starter set for an overview of the study of philanthropy would include Merle Curti's essay "Philanthropy," in the *Dictionary of the History of Ideas* (Scribner, 1973). If your library has a copy of the eleventh edition of the *Encyclopaedia Britannica* (1910), you should read Charles S. Loch's justly famous essay "Charity and Charities." Robert Bremner, now emeritus professor of history at Ohio State University, has published a second edition of his *American Philanthropy* (University of Chicago Press, 1988). Merle Curti and Roderick Nash published *Philanthropy in the Shaping of American Higher Education* in 1965 (Rutgers University Press). It is out of print but indispensable.

James Douglas's *Why Charity? The Case for a Third Sector* is a special favorite of mine. Walter W. Powell has edited *The Non-Profit Sector* (Yale, 1986), and various essays that, among other things, add depth to one's understanding of Douglas's topic.

We are witnessing the emergence of a field of inquiry after decades of useful, sometimes brilliant, but always isolated works of scholarship. Many recent books, articles, and essays will come to your attention as you explore the subject.

II

THE NECESSARY
FOUNDATION:
POSITIONING
THE INSTITUTION

4

THE VALUE OF FUND-RAISING COUNSEL

Barbara W. Snelling

With Jim Fisher's ringing comment in Chapter 1 on the necessity of a bottom-line focus for your advancement program fresh in your mind, you should apply the same measurement criterion to the value of fund-raising counsel. Simply put, the primary purpose in hiring a consultant is to help your institution raise more money.

Fund-raising consultants can provide assistance in a variety of special services, all of which you can ultimately measure by improved results in your fund-raising programs. Among these options, the service of most importance is guidance to the president, the board of trustees, and the vice president for development, in making critical decisions in a timely fashion. All other services relate to providing ongoing advice and assistance on how to effectively implement those macrodecisions.

Why Hire a Consultant?

The obvious question for you as a new president is why you should need an external consultant's guidance if you have a vice president for development and a functioning staff of institutional advancement specialists. Your institution may be starting to raise private funds or adding programs and staff. Or it may have a dependable, sound, and mature program with all of the essential elements. Rarely is a new president knowledgeable or experienced in evaluating the effectiveness of institutional advancement staff and programs. Nor can the new president recognize the programs' relative maturity levels. Many institutions with high potential are doing poorly in mining that potential, and yet they appear to be doing well because the dollar results seem high. Similarly, many institutions with relatively low potential are achieving a fine donor record, but to the uninformed observer may appear to be below expectations.

Determining your institution's place on this scale, and knowing which steps to take thereafter, requires a degree of professional sophistication in institutional advancement that you may not have. The unbiased and knowledgeable assistance of someone not intimately involved with your program can give you the insight and understanding to take the right steps. In this context, you should know that using consultants is common, and considered valuable, even for those prestigious colleges and universities with long traditions of generous private giving. Too many incoming presidents assessing their awesome new responsibilities turn quickly to those areas they understand. They do this with the thought (or hope) that once the academic and administrative aspects of the institution are shaped and functioning smoothly, they can attend more fully to an area—fund raising—that they do not understand.

Avoid this mistake. The selection of fund-raising counsel, and your initiation into the intricacies of fund raising, should come early in your administration. This is because rarely can an institution afford to lose time with less than the most appropriate effort to obtain private support. If you put your consultant on the task early, you will have answers and direction available when you can take advantage of them. Similarly, access to a consultant will protect you from errors of fund-raising omission and commission during your early months in office. Presidential honeymoons are too short-lived, even with the best of performance, to lose the special fund-raising opportunities that accompany them.

Selecting a Consultant

Because the advice of a fund-raising consultant can help determine your ultimate fund-raising success, selecting the firm and the individual should be *your* responsibility. However, remember that the consultant may be involved in helping you present your rationale for program improvement to the trustees. These recommendations might involve changes in personnel, budget, or even trustee behavior. So, at that point, make certain that the consultant is someone trusted and well regarded by your board. Including a few key trustees in the selection process should ensure a good relationship and be well worth the extra time.

Similarly, you should include the fund-raising vice president in the selection process, because the consultant will be working closely with this person. This is true even if you have not yet made up your mind about the effectiveness of your vice president. There is no need to heighten the vice president's anxiety over your relationship by not including him or her in the consultant selection. Development vice presidents know well that their careers depend on the president's confidence and that new presidents frequently make changes for both valid and nonvalid reasons.

While you should involve trustees and the vice president in the selection process, do not trust anyone other than yourself to make the final decision on the consultant. Also, make it clear from the beginning that the consultant will report to you. Frequently, such institutional representatives as trustees and directors of the annual fund hire consultants. In different situations each of these arrangements can work, but if you are to use this consultant as your confidential and trusted advisor, make it clear from the start that there will be a direct reporting relationship to you.

In selecting a consultant consider the type of firm, the individual with whom you will work, the legal stipulations of the contract, and your expectations. Consulting firms range from single individuals operating from their homes to large firms with staffs of over 100. Different firms have different philosophies and specializations. These differences will affect your working relationship with the firm, and might even have an effect on the advice that you receive.

Some firms are comprehensive and can provide you with almost any fund-raising service, while others specialize in certain aspects of institutional advancement. Consequently, you should know enough about the options to assess each firm's strengths and identify the services they can best provide. Some firms specialize in program counseling and will happily (and effectively) work with clients who are, and will be for several years, unprepared for a capital campaign. Other firms primarily handle the sequence of events leading directly through a capital campaign: capital campaign planning, the feasibility study, and campaign management. These firms tend not to be as ready or willing to provide in-depth management audits and program counseling separate from capital campaigns. This is especially true if your institution is small. (You probably will not pick up this nuance in the firm's advertisements and other materials.)

Because you need immediate advice on long-range strategy, and an evaluation of current performance, you probably should not choose a campaign consulting firm. On the other hand, you may want to engage such a firm later, when you are ready to consider a *capital* campaign. Increasingly, these distinctions among firms are becoming blurred as many firms opt to provide all services. Nevertheless, a thorough inquiry into relative strengths and experience will help. Ask which type of service is predominant among current clients, and what kind of experience they have in each area. Although a list of available firms can be found in the *CASE Membership Directory,* the best information on their reputations and performance will come from talking with your colleagues who have either worked with them or heard about other institutions' experience.

Whereas you might initially have up to eight firms on your list, you should be able to narrow this to approximately three through telephone interviews and reference inquiries. Actual face-to-face interviews with these firms should be sufficient. You may decide early that you need a comprehensive firm, and eliminate all others. Or, similarly, you may have such good early feedback on a particular one-person operation that you decide to include that firm. It usually makes sense to interview different types of firms so that you can hear which distinctive strengths they bring. Provide them with adequate advance information about your institution and its fund-raising history, and your immediate need for counsel. Allow two hours per interview, and ask for a formal written proposal from each firm right after it. (You will do yourself a disservice if you ask for proposals before the firm fully knows your requirements.) You will hear some discussion about whether you should meet, during the firm's initial presentation, the person you will work with. If you think you will make your decision on the basis of this interview and the proposal (and this is the most common procedure), the assigned consultant should be present at the interview. If there is time for a second round after you receive the proposal, you can interview the assigned consultant at that time.

Characteristics of an Effective Consultant

Selecting the right type of firm is important because from this firm come the individuals you'll be working with, and the support services available to you. Nevertheless, you will ultimately rely on the individual consultant. The firm, no matter how good, cannot make up for any serious inadequacies. The key criterion in your final selection should be the caliber of the individual who will work with you. You must act on the basis of this person's advice and even accept, on occasion, risks based on your consultant's judgment. The value to you of that advice will rest squarely on your faith in the consultant's knowledge, experience, objectivity, and integrity. You must believe that the consultant, as your trusted advisor, will give you the advice you *need* to hear, not necessarily what you *want* to hear. The honest objectivity of a knowledgeable, experienced outside observer is a consultant's greatest contribution.

Besides integrity, intelligence, and experience, a good consultant should possess the analytical skills to identify both the similarities and uniqueness of a client, compared to past clients. A consultant often persuades people to make the right decisions and to make changes in practice. Consequently, effective counsel must have good interpersonal skills and a high level of both oral and written communication ability. Then, you must consider the elusive chemistry in the client–consultant relationship: Does the consultant fit your expectations fully enough so that you will be comfortable taking advice, confident that this person can be effective with both staff and volunteers?

Writing the Contract

Once the initial selection process ends, you should review the contractual relationship. Be aware that some firms require three-year contracts, and some a fixed contractual relationship only for management audits, feasibility studies, or the most critical months of a campaign. Other firms allow flexible, month-to-month periodic counseling, providing time as needed. There is no preferable arrangement, but be certain of your comfort level with a firm, and of your exit options before signing on for an extended period. While the most common notice period is 90 days, it would not be excessive to ask for a 30-day notice for terminating a contract.

Frequently, trustees new to using consultants will suggest that consultants should prove their bottom-line effect on the institution's fund-raising by being paid on commission. This suggestion implies both a misunderstanding of the way in which consultants function, and of the way to raise funds. Commission payments are contrary to the ethical codes of all professional associations working in educational advancement (CASE, American Association of Fund-Raising Counsel, and the National Society of Fund-Raising Executives). Reputable firms charge for their time and will not agree to payment on a commission basis. (The most common daily rates range from $750 to $1,500.)

In the contract define the work to be done, and indicate the amount of time and charges. There are no standard contracts in general use because individual firms design their own. And the contract tends to relate to the requirements of each client.

You should be certain to define clearly your expectations about the topics to be covered in the consulting relationship, the form of reporting, the schedule of action, and how much detail the consultant should provide with recommendations on how to proceed. This request should not present a challenge to an experienced consultant. You should ask: What do you plan to do? Who will be interviewed about which topics and with which objectives? In which areas will I receive guidance and recommendations? If you recommend new policies or programs, will you provide written policies or program plans as needed, or will you subsequently work these out in future consulting time? And will your report be in writing so that I can share it, if appropriate, with other staff or volunteers? Will you provide a separate confidential report either orally or in writing if you address sensitive personnel matters?

From the answers to these questions you should be able to define the services you expect to receive. The consultant will appreciate clear instructions on the objectives and the assigned tasks. After you have firmly established the working relationship, you can be more flexible in defining assignments. But it is always valuable to have clear agreements based on your objectives. When you're going to measure results in dollars, a consultant's plan of action needs to be specific and to provide outcomes that are measurable.

Your First Assignment

Although there are many different tasks that you might assign your recently acquired consultant, two will be the most helpful to you during your months as a novice. First, you need advice on your short-term strategy—on how you should use your available time to take advantage of the enthusiasm and momentum of a new presidency. Second, the consultant should assemble and analyze for your mutual deliberation the clearly identifiable (to a consultant) collection of information about your institution's fund-raising capability that will help determine your long-range strategy. In order to provide you with sound advice in both these areas, your consultant will need to become familiar with your institution. As you explore the workings of the decision-making and governance processes in your new setting, the consultant must understand both the institution's fund-raising climate and the institutional culture. In the broadest sense, this culture is a collection of attitudes, opinions, formal and informal policies, and practice formed over the years through the exposure (or lack of exposure) to fund-raising programs.

The consultant will need to talk at some length with all of your senior staff; with those in charge of the academic curriculum; with staff in admissions, student life, career planning and placement, finance and administration, alumni, development, and public relations. Also include several deans or department chairs. Among the institution's volunteers, the consultant should visit the chair of the board of trustees; the development committee chair, and probably one or two other active trustees; the president of the alumni association; and the chair of the parents' association. Meetings with a few small groups of students would also be helpful. These interviews are not casual conversations, but carefully and systematically designed meetings to elicit the information that you will need for both short- and long-term fund-raising strategies. The consultant should have available, *before* the interviews, several years of president's reports, annual reports, planning documents, alumni magazines and tabloids, recent campus newspapers (student and administration, if both exist), the most recent accreditation report, any development case statements, and feasibility studies or audit reports.

The combination of the structured interviews and analysis of the institution's publications will enable the consultant to give you sound advice and guidance based on an assessment of the fund-raising culture and status of your institution. This information gathering is the most valuable portion of an in-depth performance audit of your institution's fund-raising programs. And your consultant should conduct it promptly if you are to receive valid advice tailored to your circumstances.

The second portion of an audit is also valuable, but relies on more concrete measurements and does not necessarily require your consultant's services. It concentrates on examining and evaluating the institutional advancement office itself: the development, alumni, and public relations programs. Your consultant, or a team of CASE colleagues, can manage this portion. However, your consultant should perform that portion of the audit requiring the best available combination of experience and judgment, because it will serve as the foundation of all of the consultant's subsequent recommendations.

While it is possible to contract with CASE for the full audit, the members of the CASE audit team would rarely be in a position to provide the ongoing counsel that a consulting firm provides and that a new president should have. The slight additional cost of hiring a consultant to conduct the evaluation for a new president is a sound investment! The in-depth exposure to your programs places this professional in the best possible position to help implement recommendations.

There are other times in an institution's history when the CASE audit can be an appropriate alternative to the use of a consultant. For example, an audit might be useful to an experienced president who wants a periodic evaluation or benchmark of performance, or at the end of a capital campaign, or possibly before conducting a search for a new vice president. These all are occasions when an audit, by either a consultant or a team of advancement colleagues, can provide valuable information.

An Audit vs. a Feasibility Study

You should be aware of the distinctions between audits and feasibility studies. Frequently these are confused by those not close to fund raising, even though the purpose of each is quite distinct. A management or performance audit, as the name implies, focuses on determining the internal capacity of an institution to mount fund-raising programs that will achieve the maximum potential. A feasibility study, while including some assessment of internal capacity, centers primarily on assessing the attitudes, opinions, and intentions of the institution's external constituencies, and interprets their responses to the institution's projected fund-raising plan. A feasibility study is usually reserved for determining the institution's potential goal in a capital campaign once there is consensus on the list of objectives. It also provides guidance in the ways to conduct the capital campaign. Consequently, it is a performance audit, not a feasibility study, that you need as your immediate guide to action.

Determining Short- and Long-Term Strategies

Armed with the information gathered from the audit, the consultant is prepared to help you with both short- and long-term strategies. The consultant's first and foremost duty is to educate you about the critical elements of fund raising so that you can use your orientation period to become knowledgeable, comfortable, and competent in your role. The consultant's analysis of the circumstances at your institution will provide the curriculum for this education. The audit report should include comment on the climate for fund raising and what institutional behavior supports or obstructs an optimal climate. It should cover the following points: clarity of mission, soundness of the long-range planning process, trustee leadership, availability of other volunteer leaders, institutional policies, organizational structure of the advancement staff, the president's willingness to provide time and personal leadership, and the president's willingness to ensure commitment to institutional cooperation and advancement in budget and staff. The discussion should focus on all of these elements, with background on the way in which comparable institutions behave and the fund-raising results that they achieve. The consultant should help you become conversant with realistic expectations based on these comparisons and the recommended changes. Once a full audit is complete, the consultant should also make preliminary personnel recommendations regarding current staff, and a recommendation on the vice president's performance.

In this effort to expand your knowledge about fund raising and your understanding of your institution, the consultant might help you analyze your own skills for building the critical relationships that will spell success. You could review the kinds of social situations with which you are most comfortable and that you find most productive. The consultant can then help you to design an action plan and schedule for initiating the relationships with trustees, important donors, prospects, volunteer leaders, and state and community decision makers.

Perhaps, during your selection process and early introduction to your new position, you have formed a sense of immediate, highly targeted funding needs whereby contributions would serve as a catalyst toward your goals. The consultant can advise a strategy to help you capitalize on your popularity and translate the impact of your arrival into heightened prospect cultivation and fund-raising accomplishments. Your attention, early in your tenure, to major donors and prospects will be the highest possible compliment to them, and a visible recognition of their value to the institution.

The consultant, on the other hand, while advising on immediate cultivation activities and even some solicitation, can help you fend off premature engagement in extensive solicitation. Frequently, trustees push a new president toward a capital campaign, eager to take advantage the chief executive's popularity even though not all of the planning and preparations are in place. It is far better to plan over the next two to three years to engage actively in the cultivation and preparation that will guarantee resounding success.

One of the areas that the consultant will explore in the audit is the institution's long-range plan to implement its mission, and the process that created the plan and keeps it current. Analyzing this plan and process may well be part of your own most urgent agenda. The consultant will be able to advise you on how extensively you can translate the plan's objectives into viable fund-raising objectives, as well as how familiar the principal constituencies are with the plan and whether they give it their endorsement and support. Possibly, through an institution's publications and constituency meetings, groundwork already has been laid for a campaign, subtly or overtly. This information is crucial to designing your long-range strategy for institutional leadership and fund-raising. If, indeed, the planning process needs revitalizing, the consultant might help with this process, or advise on appropriate ways to use the process most effectively for fund-raising purposes.

Working with the Board

Another area in which the consultant can help directly with long-range strategy is work with the board of trustees, to help them recognize their roles and responsibilities in the field of advancement. These responsibilities run the gamut from devising a thoughtful trustee selection and nomination process, to providing personal leadership in giving and asking, to participation in alumni and public relations programs, to adequate investment in staff and budget for advancement. The consultant, as an outsider and observer of the behavior of many other boards, can give strong advice and direction to the board—advice that might be difficult for you to give, or even damaging to your relationship with the trustees.

The right action on all of the important areas covered by a performance audit will set your fund-raising strategies for the future. The audit recommendations and subsequent discussions should lead to a master plan with a schedule. This plan should include specific direction to all advancement programs, with recommendations on all necessary institutional changes and activities. Once the plan is established, the consultant can help further in implementing it.

You may also require executive search services, which can be extremely helpful in efficiently identifying and recruiting the right staff. You may eventually need strategic-planning or annual-fund specialists, telefund consultants, planned-giving, or marketing and public relations expertise. All of these and more may be available through your original firm, or you may contract separately. In any event, these are all areas in which consultants, when used wisely, can be valuable. Bringing in this type of short-term, targeted assistance can provide you with expert knowledge that you can't possibly afford, or even use, on a full-time basis.

If you have defined your objectives carefully in advance, you will be in a strong position to evaluate results. If you have selected the right initial consultant as your personal advisor (and there are many good ones), you will have brought valuable and critical assistance to both yourself and your institution.

5

THE CASE STATEMENT
Robert L. Stuhr

In a major capital campaign or an annual fund with challenging goals, you should give priority to preparing and communicating the case for the support of the institution, its program, and its service to society. The president should play a leadership role in seeing that the institution's strength and service in its many programs are portrayed forcefully, and that the institution's publics are intimately involved in reaching the fund-raising goals.

What a Case Statement Is

A case statement outlines:

- The institution's programs and objectives, what it must do to sustain, improve, or change its activities and aims, and why the institution is valuable to society.
- The goals of the fund-raising program to support the institution. How will the institution use the funds? How will a successful program strengthen the institution? Why should attaining the goals be vital to society and particularly to the publics served by the institutions?
- Ways in which the institution can remain significantly productive in the next decade—through both the generosity of its supporters and its own efforts to operate more efficiently.

The case statement should be not just a catalog of past achievements but a compelling statement interpreting the importance of the institution and showing the institution's full potential for future service. It should do more than announce a campaign. It should state the case for the institution's aims, purposes, and mission. It should present the case for the current program. It should make the case for the new programs envisioned, and show how they will enrich and benefit the lives of many. And it should forthrightly and dramatically show the institution's impact on its publics—*economically, culturally, educationally, spiritually,* and *aesthetically.*

It is logical and necessary that the president appoint the members of the case statement team and work closely with it. The public relations and development staffs will help write and plan it.

How a Case Statement Will Be Used In A Campaign

A case statement serves as an internal document and as the basis for an external sales publication. You use it to:

Obtain Consensus. Particularly during the early phases of institutional and development long-range planning, the case statement helps obtain from the institution's major publics—faculty, administration, trustees, alumni, parents, donors, and prospective donors—a consensus about the institution's priorities, the directions envisioned, the resources deemed most crucial, and the avenues of services to be emphasized and opened up. In its early stages, the case statement goes through many drafts. At this point, it is an internal document. Representatives of key groups in the institution read and revise. Through repeated versions, a general agreement should develop concerning institutional priorities, aims, and financial goals.

Recruit Volunteer Leadership. The case statement helps to recruit key leaders for the development effort. This must be done early in the planning phase, even before any brochures are printed. The case statement, which shows specific reasons for the institution's goals and objectives, helps answer questions of prospective volunteer leaders and workers, and gives them confidence in the planning and direction.

Test the Market. You can use the case statement to determine how the potential major donors feel about the proposed development goals. It provides a vehicle to bring prospective major donors into the planning process, and enables them to react to the proposed objectives.

Obtain Major Gifts. The case statement, even in draft form, helps major donor prospects, especially if it has a personalized cover and a personalized approach keyed to the particular donor.

Form a Basis for the "Sales" Brochure. Finally, the case statement, once your leadership reaches consensus, serves as the basis for solicitation materials and a resource for subsequent news stories, features, videotapes, speeches, proposals, and brochures for use in reaching potential donors.

How to Create a Case Statement

Base your case statement on continuous long-range planning, at least five years into the future. You should assign one person to write the first draft. The writer should:

- Be knowledgeable about all aspects of the institution and its long-range plans
- Be authorized to talk to administrators, faculty, students, trustees, alumni, donors, and others who use the services and facilities
- Understand the publics that the statement addresses and be aware of their expectations and interests
- Relinquish pride of authorship
- Ask for a review committee representing the institution's key publics
- Rewrite . . . rewrite . . . rewrite

The consensus reached through the various drafts of the case statement, incorporating ideas from such key groups as trustees, faculty, administrative staff, alumni, and parents, will enable the program to have credibility, a sense of direction, and a definite plan.

What a Case Statement Should Include

A sample table of contents for a case statement might include:

Institutional Aims

Educational goals and program
Important heritages and distinctions that have endured
Factors that appeal to:
  —trustees and volunteers
  —prospective donors
  —past donors
  —friends and community
  —potential leaders
  —faculty and administrators
  —clients, patrons, and those who use the institution's program
  —students and their parents

Institutional Accomplishment

Academic growth (regular and special programs)
Role in teaching, research, policy
Students (meeting their needs)
Faculty and administrators
Alumni
    —further education
    —careers (achievements)
    —civic leadership
Professional growth
Community service
Improvements in campus and physical facilities
Financial viability
    —annual operations
    —capital (current and endowment)
    —methods used to finance accomplishments
Philanthropic support (distinctive gifts and bequests)
Where the institution stands today compared to similar institutions

Directions for the Future

Existing programs that must continue
Changes in programs
New directions (new programs)
Students
    —number to be served
    —nature of student body
    —qualifications
Parents
Visitors
Faculty and administrative requirements
Governance requirements
Financial policies
    —tuition and fees
    —investment management
    —business management
    —private gifts and grants
Physical facilities
    —campus
    —buildings
    —equipment
    —renovations
Community services

Urgent Objectives in Fund Raising

Priorities and costs
Endowment for
    —financial aid for students and clients
    —faculty chairs and professional staff
    —library
    —laboratories
    —operation of buildings
    —campus maintenance
    —general purposes
    —strengthening specific areas
New buildings
Renovation of present facilities
Property acquisition
Debt reduction

The Plan of Action to Accomplish Future Objectives

Goals
Proposed programs
    —to support current operations
    —to support capital expansion
    —to support special programs or projects
    —to provide support through estate planning and deferred giving

What the President Does in Developing a Case Statement

First of all, the president appoints the committees that may begin preparing the statement of the case for supporting a major campaign as many as five years before the campaign officially begins. Committees to be appointed far in advance of the campaign include:

1. Case Statement Committee

2. Committee on Academic Blueprint

3. Committee on the Physical Plant

4. Committee on Charges and Additions to Curriculum and Academic Planning

5. Committee on Growth and Development of Specialties and Services

6. Committee on Finances

The president is responsible for the articulation of these committees. He or she must see that the specific planning committees are represented at meetings of the Case Statement Committee. As plans are made, the president reports to development committees of the trustees, associates, faculty, alumni, patrons, and other publics.

The president bears much of the responsibility for creating understanding and enthusiasm for the campaign. (Somebody must really *want* the campaign!) Trustees must not only approve, but also be enthusiastic about, the "grand plan." Faculty members must be part of the planning that produces the objectives, so that they are committed to help make the plan work. Major prospects must be prepared for the coming campaign. Again, the president must involve them in precampaign planning. The president must "sell" the campaign to the key governing boards and institutional participants.

What a Checklist for Your Case Statement Should Check

Does your case statement emphasize the all-important aims and purposes of your institution?

Donors these days are more and more "mission oriented." In your case statement, you must clearly spell out how your institution serves society, and why it deserves support.

Does the statement emphasize the programs of your institution?

What is there about your program as well as the economic impact of your institution that merits a donor's interest and major investment?

Does the statement indicate the relationship of your institution to its founding organization and to its publics?

Private institutions, church-related institutions, and those committed to a community, state, or region, all have special appeal to different donors. Do not overlook the origin and essential nature of your institution. It may be your strongest selling point.

Does the case statement forcefully reveal the impact of your institution on the community—economically, educationally, culturally, spiritually?

You should update economic impact studies every few years. An educational inventory showing the groups, communities, and segments of society that your institution serves can make a compelling case for supporting your institution.

Does the case create confidence and credibility?

You must convince donors of major gifts that an institution is well managed and that it has a competent administration and trustees of integrity. Especially these days, donors of major gifts are interested in an institution's viability—its chances for survival into the twenty-first century.

Does your case show your prospect the most advantageous ways of giving?

Cash gifts, payments over a period of years, estate notes, bequests, annuities and other life income plans, and gifts of property all have important advantages for various donors. While studies show that forms of giving or tax incentives are not the main reason *why* donors make major gifts, they do influence greatly the *time* and *size* of gift.

Does the case statement provide recognition and appreciation to your donors?

Some institutions create a climate in which the donor feels appreciated. Other institutions do not always appear grateful. Remember that past attention which donors have received and/or the promise of future attention, can deeply influence them.

Does the case show measurable results of the institution's programs and service?

Many business executives are asking pertinent questions about measurable achievements of philanthropic institutions. For instance, here are the comments of James F. Bere, chairman and chief executive officer of Borg–Warner Corporation:

> Philanthropy is not expected to show a profit, but is supposed to have results. Inefficiency and unclear purpose can develop in both profit and nonprofit sectors. But in business, we are held to account. If less money is available, we must cut costs and do things better. In the future, business will be asking for similar accountability from philanthropy. . . . Frankly,

the more we are asked for, the harder we must look at the requests. Grant seekers must go beyond simply asking in the name of a good cause. . . . Philanthropic or business organization, we face the same rule: Become more productive or be prepared to fade away.

The Process of Creating the Case Statement Is as Important as the Final Document

A case statement provides direction and a means of institutional communication, particularly in the important formative days of planning and setting goals. An effective one serves as more than just a brochure for prospective donors. It is the rationale for the very existence of the institution, as well as for its growth and strengthening. It shows the institution's productivity and how it benefits society. It presents clearly the ways the institution wants to improve its service to society, and the new resources required. And, of course, it serves as a first step in launching a major fund-raising program.

6

THE FEASIBILITY STUDY

Mary Helene Pendel and David M. Thompson

Sooner or later you will feel the need for, or will be asked to consider, a feasibility study. Sometimes the idea for such a study may arise because you, your board, or your development officers know that you need development counsel for significant financial needs and do not know other ways to ask for it. In this chapter, we try to clarify the feasibility study and give you guidelines for deciding when it will be profitable, what you should expect, qualities to look for in professionals who will conduct the study, why you should look to outsiders to conduct the study, and approximate costs.

What Is a Feasibility Study?

Think of the feasibility study as a market test. Essentially, it is an assessment of the degree of acceptance and enthusiasm that exists or can be generated among your constituents for a given plan or program. When handled properly, it can also be a powerful cultivation tool, and an instrument for identifying kindred souls to be developed as potential constituents. It can also be an effective diagnostic device yielding important management information.

The feasibility study has come a long way since its earliest version. At one time it resulted in a simple, summary "go" or "no-go" for a capital campaign at an identified dollar level, depending upon the answers to interview questions about who might give what. Estimating the potential success of a program is still the reason for conducting a feasibility study. But practitioners have become far more sophisticated in the interview process itself, in analyzing and synthesizing the information acquired, and in translating all this into a plan of action designed to advance you toward meeting your designated institutional needs, even if there is delay and remedial work to do.

Those conducting your feasibility study present your program to selected prospective doners, key volunteers, and others whose actions and influence can (and probably will) have an impact on the program's success. They present it in a written case statement that profiles your college or university by identifying the skills and resources that your institution has acquired and/or is noted for. It also shows how you can, and intend to, develop these skills and resources to address identified educational and/or community problems. And it points up your track record of success in the past in using and applying such resources, and details what you will require now to develop them for optimal results.

If properly prepared, the "case" will present in a reasoned, comprehensive, and persuasive way a directed look at your institution, designed to catch the attention and interest of thoughtful people, some of whom are outside your current circles of constituents. In a coherent statement written so that it will attract and hold a reader, the case will offer pertinent information on your institution that the respondent would not usually find in so useful a format or would not normally bother to pursue. Note that the case statement is *not* a campaign brochure. It is *not* a painstaking history of your institution. While it reflects the total college or university, it is *not* painfully constructed to afford equal play to every institutional component. A case statement *is* a comprehensive look, with details selected to show why and how your college or university is an effective agency for achieving the results promised in the programs chosen to be presented for philanthropic investment.

In intensive, confidential interviews, those conducting your study will explore the response to, and critique of, your program by these selected respondents. The powerful prospect-identification and donor-cultivation aspects of such interviews, when conducted by sensitive, knowledgeable, and informed interviewers, has prompted some colleges and universities to increase the lists of respondents beyond those deemed adequate to provide the required overall, general information.

The study directors weigh comments and insights of respondents— and the attitudes and environment of acceptance that these reveal— along with other pertinent information, to give you a report. This document details exactly where you are in terms of achieving your specified goals, what can affect your success, and how you can bring favorable influences to bear on the outcome.

Traditionally, your advisor might call for a feasibility study as a final check of your preparedness for a campaign or a capital gifts program. It is customary that, when embarking on such a study, you know what is needed. You might feel that you are ready, with prospects identified and cultivated, volunteers set, and arguments for the needs well documented. What might you have overlooked? To whom could and should you look for leadership? How realistic is your dollar goal? Should it be phased? Or could your constituents be convinced to stretch in response?

Presidents, working with their fund-raising counsel, increasingly have found the feasibility study useful also in earlier stages of preparing for a campaign. The diagnostic aspects of the technique, the possibilities for donor and advocate cultivation, and the opportunity to "fish" for potential new constitutents in a serious, studied way, can contribute to the preparatory period, long before you could claim to be "ready." You diminish the chances for false starts. You can gear staff efforts and budgets for greater return by getting a reading of the market they must sell. The discipline and expectations engendered by a well-written plan of action, approved by the board and understood and agreed to by staff and volunteers, can generate momentum.

Why and When Should You Consider a Feasibility Study?

Let's look at some of the different kinds of situations in which you could profitably turn to the feasibility study as a tool for developing useful information. To illustrate our point, we offer examples from our own client experiences.

A Study Tests the Readiness You Feel You Have Achieved

Suppose your college or university has a long tradition of successful fund raising

Your alumni and parents are well organized, convinced that there is a tie between philanthropic support and the standards of excellence they expect of your institution. You can expect to raise their sights to generous levels. You have established their commitment in previous successful campaigns. What can you learn from a feasibility study? Why not just go ahead?

One danger here can be taking things and people for granted. The feasibility study is designed to listen—*really* listen—to these close, committed constituents. It probes for any serious questions or misgivings that may be developing beneath the surface, to make certain that the relative ease of fund raising has not allowed you to let communication slip into something that is more rote and routine, less sharply focused and intense, less intimate and persuasive.

Example: A client, a prestigious private college on the West Coast, discovered in such a study the depth of a growing concern of key major donors, alumni, and trustees over the heightening costs of high-quality private institutions. These respondents were not questioning the college's identified needs. They were asking a more fundamental question. They needed assurance that college goals and operations, while pitched at a level of standards well beyond the ordinary, were based on a studied cost-effectiveness and not on an easy assurance that the money was there and would be easy to raise. The president had been in frequent personal contact with most of the respondents. Before the feasibility study, they had not voiced this concern forcefully.

Example: Here is another and related example that underscores the need for listening and communication. It is different in the degree of success that the institution in question had already achieved in fund raising.

A once-threatened private college in the Midwest had experienced an exhilarating turnaround and a successful capital campaign thanks to the drive, commitment, and esprit de corps that the president had awakened in the board. Coming soon on the heels of this high, a feasibility study, anticipating a second campaign, warned the president of how fleeting this success could be. Board spirit was too fragile to allow him to decrease his communication effort. Board-building had to start all over.

Another danger can be moving out too far in front of your board, key volunteers, and constituents—failing to bring them along with campus plans, failing to test campus planning in its formative stages against the more objective (and sometimes more realistic and informed) insights of these committed friends outside the campus community.

Example: A leading Eastern private university, an international pioneer in a professional field, discovered in a feasibility study that deeply committed trustees and donors would not indulge its plans to develop *the* definitive international library in that field if the plans meant attempting to gather under a single roof *the* definitive collection. They gave the go-ahead to *a* library, but one designed with full awareness of the advances in computers, data access and management, and telecommunications which, they argued, made the concept of a comprehensive collection under a single roof archaic.

Suppose your college or university stands on the brink of its first comprehensive capital campaign or has not had a successful one for 10 to 15 years

You've been preparing for several years. Failure is unthinkable. But you are not sure.

In today's world, there should be no instance of not meeting your goal. A goal is set so that you can achieve it. This does not mean that there is no connection between your goal and actual needs. It means tacit acceptance of the never-ending aspect of fund raising. A campaign is a blip on the screen. There will be recurring blips on your screen. A campaign usually has two important outcomes. One is the dollars raised for designated projects and programs. The other is a development in your constituents—strengthening, deepening their commitment, enlarging their numbers, and readying them for the next effort. Success contributes to the latter.

You can translate a feasibility study of *needs* later into campaign *goals*. Your counsel may recommend delaying the goal-setting. It is unnecessary until the campaign "goes public"—that is, until you announce it publicly and rally the total constituency. At that moment, you have achieved the major gifts and at least 60 percent of your goal is in hand in the form of gifts or pledges. What remains is the clean-up phase. While these dollars may be the more difficult and expensive to raise, they are known to be accessible.

The feasibility study gives you and your counsel the tool to strategize and pace your campaign for the greatest possible return. Sometimes the feasibility study results are definitive, unmistakable. More often, they may suggest possibilities that your counsel will help you play patiently to reap not only the largest dollar return but a genuine shot of adrenalin for your constituents.

For instance, consider a small private university on the East Coast, less than 40 years in existence but with a dynamic and growing reputation that belied its youth. It had had successful minicampaigns in the past, targeted to specific small goals. Now, through the campus planning process, leaders had constructed a long-range plan with definite and comprehensive large-scale needs that would have to be covered by fund-raising efforts. Obviously the university had not identified, much less cultivated, the numbers of prospects it would now require. Feasibility-study interviewers uncovered a decided lack of excitement over the long list of difficult-to-relate needs, but a depth of genuine affection and pride in the university. In a specially constructed plan of action, counsel divided the advance-gifts phase into two parts, allowing the urgency of the campaign to engender excitement in prospects already deeply committed to the university. They became part of the Nucleus Fund. Intensive prospect research identified additional prospects for Leadership Gifts in the second part of the extended advance-gifts phase. Thus was achieved a successful campaign that a feasibility study of the past would have deemed impossible.

A Study Guides Your Continuing Preparations for a Campaign or a Capital Funds Program

Suppose you know your college or university must make major changes in habits or attitudes that characterize your constituents' ideas of fund raising

Your institution may have received a gift from one significant major donor for so long that your history of fund raising misled you about the future. Constituencies very easily become accustomed to "Let George do it." But George will not always be around.

Yours may be a public institution that has yet to bring its constituents along to the extent of some state-assisted colleges or universities, which must depend on private support for essentials such as programs and facilities. Your constituencies must feel a sense of ownership and responsibility for your college or university. How can a feasibility study help?

Obviously you must raise sights and instill a sense of urgency. You don't need a feasibility study to tell you that. You do need to identify the proverbial "group of willful people," the project capable of enlisting them to run with it, the concepts and arguments that can fire their enthusiasm, and the information and cultivational moves that should set the project in motion.

Example: A public university in the Midwest enjoyed the political advocacy and the personal giving of an elderly state legislator whose seniority made him both a power in the capitol and a resource that had to be considered short-lived. Yet the community had long been used to letting him control its future. A certain political naiveté kept residents seemingly unaware of the fact that they could control the strength and dynamism of their own institution, including the university. Unfortunate provincialism prevented the university from tapping the full power of its region. This feasibility study required informed interviewers who would listen for a new readiness among community leaders to assume active direction of the area's affairs. These leaders would also appreciate the difference that this campus's resources could make in their plans.

Example: A private college on the East Coast, with a name that led some to assume that it was a public institution, was further handicapped by a long-term relationship with a donor who had been making sure that there never was a budget deficit. This level of giving could not sustain the development plans of the new president. The magnificent mansion that served as the administration building dramatized the college's relationship to the donor. Through a sensitive feasibility study, the college found that certain respondents saw a thread of quality running through the new president's plans and the style of entertaining that he had introduced. The administration building reinforced this sense of quality. The thread of quality was strong enough to support aspirations for the college that the school could sustain real development activities.

Suppose the vision you have been formulating for your college or university calls for capital investment and advocates at a level never before achieved by the institution

You don't need a feasibility study to estimate your campaign readiness. You are well aware that you're still groping your way through campaign preparations. You need a feasibility study to help you devise a strategy to break your college or university out of the constraints it has traditionally accepted. You need to identify new allies and potential partners, and you need to know what it could take to enlist them.

Example: A public institution, newly developed into a university from a former teacher's college, is located in a state where private support of the leading (and much older) public institutions is well established. The university finds itself at a critical point in its development at a time when the state is drawing back somewhat in its support of higher education. Private support has become essential, but this university's constituents have seldom associated it with anything other than scholarship assistance—a "nice to have," but no real need. An educational program is called for, but such a program would take time to make the concept stick and to raise constituent sights. Feasibility study interviewers, alert to possibilities, sensed that reactions to the president's concept of a "great populist university" might be developed to create a statewide constituency for this single, distinct campus in a determinedly elitist state, even tapping into constituents for the older, more prestigious campuses. The president, his ideas, and his qualities of leadership, although figuratively bigger than his campus, nevertheless were capable of personifying the potential of this institution.

Similarly, another university was able to ride the coattails of its president into a far more visible and dynamic presence within its city. This president had distinguished himself, not as a recognized leader but as a concerned citizen of his metropolitan area.

Example: A private university of the South found itself being squeezed between a prestigious neighboring private university with a national reputation, and a growing public institution that bore the name of its city. What's more, it was associated with a religion not shared by community leaders. Feasibility study interviewers found that although community leaders had little enthusiasm for the institution itself, they individually voiced a sense of debt to, and respect—even affection— for, the institution's president. He had been distinguishing himself as a volunteer in community affairs and had willingly undertaken "the scut work," as they called it. These findings led to a plan that enlisted "movers and shakers," who would not formally associate with the university. They would serve as an anonymous, behind-the-scenes leadership group to launch preparations for a successful campaign while the university signaled its desire for partnership with the community by broadening the base of its board and investing it with real authority and responsibility.

A good feasibility study allows you to develop a custom-tailored plan designed to maximize the opportunities that your distinct situation presents, while dealing with any uncovered problems. Don't waste your time with those who concern themselves only with traditional or text-book styles. You need an *effective* plan. What other institutions have found successful may or may not have any bearing in your situation. You need professionals with the experience, confidence, and creativity to adapt proven techniques to your specific needs.

Example: A small private college in the Northeast had a long history of paying cash for campus buildings. It had done so on the basis of borrowing, stringent oversight of cost of operations, and inspired investment management by an unusually effective business officer. The board, except for the powerful chairman of buildings and grounds, had learned to leave financial concerns to the president and his staff. Now the college needed a new science building. The chairman of buildings and grounds, concerned about the mushrooming costs plus inflation, pushed to borrow as usual and begin construction immediately.

Looking ahead, the president saw increasing need for investment in program and faculty and other extras beyond regular operations, if his small college was to hold its own in admissions competition. Such needs could not be covered by borrowing. Philanthropy would have to address some of them. But the college's private support to date had been low because appeals went to its city and environs. A community foundation regulated giving in this city. While the foundation had accorded the college the largest grants to date, it kept the concept of college support at a level commensurate with other community initiatives.

Feasibility study interviewers had to develop a plan that would foster two breakthroughs. There would have to be a strategy to help break the college out of the confines of its community while identified potential major donors within that community were persuaded to make gifts at levels they had never before considered. This would break the college out of the pack of community charities and recognize its leadership role in the city.

What Should You Expect in a Feasibility Study?

These are the components of a feasibility study:

1. *An audit of your development, public relations, and alumni programs as well as personnel.* This will determine the capacity of your advancement staff to support a capital campaign or a major gifts effort.

2. *Guidance in developing and writing the case statement.* A member of your staff should do the writing. Gone are the days when a visiting expert breezed in to write the case for your institution. Unless the campus community "owns" the case it is no blueprint for development. It remains just an interesting idea. No outsider will have the depth of understanding and the knowledge of people, programs, and details of your institution necessary to bring the case to life, to invest it with the kind of emotion and excitement that attracts. But it is important that the inside staff member who writes the case be under the close guidance and review of outside counsel.

3. *Guidance in developing the list of respondents.* You should expect a custom-developed list for your college or university, and the specific institutional elements or programs to be presented for philanthropic investment. This last concept is important. The list must include major gifts prospects selected with knowledge of a potential compatibility of interests between the prospect and the program (or programs) showcased in the case statement. Of course, there will always be people included in the list for "political" reasons. These might include trustees who are not major prospects yet are influential, or who might create problems if not included; alumni or community leaders who could be expected to influence a campaign outcome; and/or outside people whose approval might be required to validate the case's claims about the potential broader returns to the community of your institution's programs.

You should choose these names jointly with counsel. To make selections, use prospect research findings and other evidence provided by your development office. You should also rely on your own experience, and the advice and counsel of key trustees and other top-level volunteers. In some cases, counsel may provide the names of key foundations and national regional corporations for your consideration. Time spent on this step is critical. The effectiveness of the study's results will depend on the appropriateness of the list of respondents. Remember, however, that this list is only a starter. You should add to it after completion of the feasibility study, as you receive other prospect research findings, both broad-scale and in-depth.

A standing board committee or a committee specially selected should approve the final names. Board leaders, or those who will expect to be responsible for fund raising, should be comfortable with the list and convinced that the study interviewers will be talking to the right people. You should see that these are in-depth profiles, or extensive dossiers, on every person to be seen, to ensure that the interviewer can pursue an effective line of questioning with each individual.

4. *Market testing.* Be alert to the quality of the person assigned to do the interviews. From our earlier assessment of what you can expect to get from the feasibility study, it should be obvious that the most accurate and productive readings will come from experienced professionals who not only know development but have a sophisticated background in higher education and in the political, social, and economic forces that are shaping it. How else can they extract from each interview the real story as far as your institution is concerned? Interviewers should go in, primed with background on the individual—how he or she has related to the institution in the past, and with some sense of what impact this individual can have on the environment that will shape your college or university's development. Most firms will assign two or more people to split up these interviews, to allow for a broader base of analysis and to reduce the influence of individual bias.

5. *The report and plan of action.* Be prepared to allow your firm sufficient time for analysis and creation of a strategic plan. This is where the time and talent you are purchasing pay off for you. This is what you really are buying. Do not expect even an oral report too soon, for while an early report may identify pervasive or obvious findings, it may be different from where your counsel eventually ends up after patient probing of findings.

Be prepared to listen to some negatives if the study is tough-minded and can provide an appropriate foundation for a plan realistically designed to move you toward your goal. There will be positives if the study has turned up opportunities and assets that allow you to move immediately and build. Understand that counsel will highlight the negatives because these are the things your plan must focus on at once to help you position your institution more favorably. The report is for management—you, and your board (if you are fortunate enough to have a committed, active, and involved board). The report should not mince words unless it needs verbal camouflage to increase its effectiveness as an education tool in your board's education program. You should receive a no-hold-barred draft, and you and your fund-raising counsel should decide where editing is in the best interests of both the institution and the project under consideration.

There may be a flat charge for these five steps. Or there may be separate prices for the development audit and for the case development. Counsel has only time and talent to sell. Costs will be based on the firm's estimate of the investment of time and talent that your program will require. This estimate is based on experience for most of the five steps, except for developing the case and the list of respondents. In the first instance, the time estimate will depend on the quality of the campus writer, the extent to which major decisions already have been made, and the extent of cooperation to be expected from faculty and administrators in developing the statistics and anecdotes to enliven the document. Some firms will price case development on a per diem rate. Don't pinch pennies here! The quality of your case, particularly if your institution is embarking on its first campaign or using the study in early stages of preparation, will be a major determiner of the value of the feasibility study.

In the second instance—developing the list—the time involved will depend on the quality of your files, the professionalism of your researcher, the time you are willing to expend in the painful process of collecting data, rating and screening, and the degree to which you can enlist the cooperation of appropriate trustees, other volunteers, and friends.

Could You Achieve Some of the Results of a Feasibility Study in Other Ways?

Yes, of course. There is never only one way in the people business of fund raising. But each method has its inherent assets and liabilities.

You could convene focus groups of alumni, friends, and donors with you, a staff member, or outside counsel as leader. But experience proves that people do not comment as freely in group sessions as they do in personal, confidential interviews.

You or a member of your development or public relations staff could conduct interviews with the selected individuals. But important criticisms or negative insights will not be as forthcoming if a member of the campus community conducts the interview. Remember, it takes effort and real commitment to criticize a program effectively. This effort becomes more difficult if the critic must address directly the person who has designed the program and/or is deeply involved with it. Tough criticism should be seen for what it is—a major contribution. You should create an effective structure and environment to foster that contribution. A good feasibility study offers that structure and environment.

You may retain a firm to do a development audit and broaden that audit to include some key alumni, parents, trustees, volunteers, and other friends. Using this technique, you would have the outside interviewer and the confidentiality. But you would not have respondents reacting to a case statement. Respondents would simply be reacting to an impression of your college or university, not to your institution's intent.

Choose your development counsel carefully: Some firms and individuals do not believe in feasibility studies.

What Should You Look for in a Firm Conducting a Feasibility Study?

Look for a firm that believes enough in the power of a feasibility study to assign their senior professionals to the task and to charge enough to ensure that these higher-priced professionals will give their time

This means more than a senior supervising one or more young or less-experienced staff. Remember, the raw materials of your feasibility study and plan are the findings gleaned from the interviews. The senior supervisor depends wholly upon the antennae, the insights, and the story-tracking abilities of the staff member who sat in the room, heard voice inflections, watched body language, picked up pertinent details of the respondent's environment, *and* had the understanding and knowledge to recognize and follow effectively any unexpected tangent that led to crucial evidence.

In the feasibility study, you get what you pay for. Beware of the bargain price, which sometimes is a loss leader for a firm that expects to handle a campaign. The feasibility study should stand on its own, with no strings attached.

Look for a firm prepared to custom-tailor the study to your institutional needs

Be on the lookout for boilerplate or programmed study reports. Telephone the presidents of other colleges and universities who worked with assigned interviewers in other such studies. You cannot ask the firm for copies of its reports because these are confidential and the property of the client institution. You might ask a colleague president to let you see what the firm delivered, but the nature of the report might make the president reluctant to share it.

If the firm you are considering handled development audits for several institutions like yours, you might ask colleague presidents for these reports. While these are not the same as feasibility studies, you can get a sense of how the firm has interpreted and responded to several different campuses. Watch for repeats. This does not mean that a consultant cannot use a technique, idea, or tool in more than one institution. It means that you should avoid the firm that seems to have only one technique, idea, tool, or way of organizing its plans—one that is not reshaped by each institutional situation.

A feasibility study is a major investment in the future of your institution as well as in the dollars it costs. Make sure that you retain a firm prepared to work with you to maximize all of the assets in your particular situation. More than likely, these are not exactly parallel to any other institution's assets.

What Will the Feasibility Study Cost?

While costs are likely to differ from firm to firm, in our experience a full-scale feasibility study, including all of the previously listed components, can cost anywhere from $15,000 to $50,000 (depending on the numbers of respondents and their geographic spread). The greater the number of travel days, the higher the cost. The more senior the professionals involved, the higher the costs. And so it goes.

A feasibility study that does *not* include the cost of developing a case statement can be reduced by between $3,000 and $7,000.

What Are Your Responsibilities?

You must use the authority of your presidency to expedite the study and assure its effectiveness by:

1. Assuring that the necessary planning is carried out to the point of decision-making. In some cases this may mean only identifying acceptable options, because the feasibility study is a test whose results may have to be fed back into campus decision-making.

2. Assuring the kind of faculty and administrative cooperation that will give the case writer effective data, statistics, and anecdotes and will feed important information to prospect research and development of the respondent list.

3. Planning for effective involvement of the board in engaging the feasibility study, and in planning and approval of the case before it goes to the marketplace.

4. Assuring that your development office has someone involved in collecting the required mass databases and the refined prospect profiles that the feasibility study must use and build on.

5. Enlisting the cooperation of knowledgeable trustees, key volunteers, alumni and parent leaders, and other friends in developing and refining prospect files.

6. Assuring that you do everything possible to prepare the interviewers.

7. Not shrinking from making tough decisions, if required, on the basis of the study report. The real payoff on some of the feasibility studies mentioned came through the strength, courage, and determination exhibited by presidents who involved their campus communities in considering and implementing decisions that went at times to the very heart of the institution and its self-image.

The feasibility study is *not* a panacea. But it *is* an increasingly effective method of amassing information critical to institutional development decisions. The hallmarks of its success to date are the thoroughness of the case statement, the appropriateness of the respondent list, and the quality of the interviewers. Use it with care and creativity.

7

ALTERNATES TO FEASIBILITY STUDIES

Arthur C. Frantzreb

We are well into the era of surveys, market testing, polls, consumer analyses, and philanthropic support feasibility studies. Products, services, and attitudes are constantly being tested and analyzed, eventually to persuade others to buy, use, share, invest, or give an opinion. Many claim that these procedures are scientific tests. I suggest that at best they are guestimates, regardless of opinions to the contrary by self-serving individuals and organizations. Eventually people must *do* something—buy the product or the service, change present attitudes, accept a request to volunteer personal services. *Actions* are the real test. Probability does not always predict reality.

Next to religious beliefs or prejudices, philanthropic giving is perhaps the most intangible attitude to test. The *real* test of philanthropy is the generous gift of volunteer time, signature on a check, a securities certificate, a gift transmittal form, a statement of intent, a commitment letter, a will, an estate plan, or a deed for the transfer of property or other asset. Verbal promises of commitment are as intangible as attitudinal analyses. Our cemeteries are full of people who promised to heirs and to charities resources that never materialized.

Fund-raising feasibility studies are similarly intangible. At best they reflect attitudes and impressions *of the moment*. Attitudes can change very quickly. Such studies can answer "Why not?" and "if you do, what constraints you can expect?"—but they cannot assess or prove realistic potential.

Experienced fund-raising professionals implement most philanthropic feasibility studies. But semiprofessionals untrained in the art of direct or implied interrogation or persuasive interrogation also conduct studies. Too many studies are implemented when the professional is unfamiliar with the breadth and depth of the client or respondent personality, or with the options of concrete market-testing devices.

Perhaps 90 percent of such studies are conducted when the organization is far from ready to implement the expected program. Thus, the "test" is premature and creates an attitude of expectancy on the part of the respondent. And, if the program does not seem mature, this can be counterproductive. Unfortunately, some professionals may press for immediate feasibility studies as a foot in the client door, for sequential retention, or to use unassigned personnel. Yet the feasibility study can be a useful device if properly timed, adequately prepared for, and conducted by a trained interviewer.

Thoughtful administrators can retain reputable, experienced professional counselors to assess *internal* conditions and preparedness before attempting to "test" probabilities with any *external* constituency. An experienced professional who has known the cold ashes of disappointment and the warm fireside of success can ascertain in two or three days' time management and administrative *pre-conditions* for increased private-sector philanthropic productivity. Such a preliminary audit—a state-of-readiness analysis—can be invaluable to administrators. It can also prevent embarrassing verbal and written reports of problems and constraints that undermine trustee/volunteer confidence in administrative competence. When accomplished and heeded, such an internal audit can accelerate the organization's preparedness to initiate a properly timed feasibility study, capitalize upon its strengths, and minimize weaknesses.

Given these vagaries of procedure, timing, and results, what are the preliminary requirements for a truly productive feasibility study? What are the study processes, and how can results be honestly, objectively evaluated? Are feasibility studies really necessary?

Preliminary Requirements

If a feasibility study is to result in an adequate test of volunteer and philanthropic potential, and that test is to be followed by a systematic, progressive plan of action, then the organization must have:

1. A studied five-year plan anticipating services and programs to be budgeted or funded

2. A financial plan of costs and contingencies for the approved plans and programs

3. Present on its governing board the kind of leadership that can serve as authenticators and leaders not only in advocacy but also in *personal* gift support

4. A person-sensitive, sales-oriented, production-oriented development staff

5. A comprehensive philanthropic resource development program for current fund support; a program project, physical plant, or equipment fund; a capital fund; and planned gift investment opportunities for endowment

6. Identified, researched, and groomed prospects apparently *capable* of providing the kind and level of gift support expected

7. A motivational case or prospectus for substantial philanthropic support meager on history, dynamic on services, and competent on projections for the future.

These are indisputable basic management requirements that should be in place before money or time is wasted on feasibility studies. You may require experienced counselors to help develop these internal preconditions. But external respondents should not have to judge the *unpreparedness* of the organization to progress in private sector financial support.

Study Processes

Assuming that the basic housekeeping requirements are in place, you should carefully select potential external respondents. Do not interview *all* potential large-gift prospects, because many such people are turned off by such procedures. Analyze each potential respondent with that in mind.

Interviewers must become thoroughly familiar with all research and resource data concerning each prospective respondent. Personal nuances, eccentricities, and prejudices are far more important to know than such administrative data as position, asset resources, and so on. Therefore, you should see that each interview is designed for each respondent to assure that he or she will be comfortable. The historic routine of asking each respondent the same five questions, and from there devising probability response charts, is antiseptic, impersonal, and insensitive. Potential deeper interests and positive comments may evolve from a custom-made interview strategy for each respondent.

Respondents should receive a response mechanism before the interview. This is a *real* test. A draft, informal copy of the case statement for private sector support can be sent seven to 10 days before a scheduled interview. You should ask the respondent to be prepared to discuss the case document confidentially. Respondents are impressed, intrigued to participate in such a specific response process. They feel they are making a definitive contribution by being invited to help in developing the sales arguments, designing the program, and formulating a plan of action. Expected complaints or other discomforts about the organization are turned into constructive recommendations based on prepared plans and on analyses of future financial requirements.

You can include gift support needs and gift opportunities with gift range requirements, time schedules, leadership requirements, and so on, to draw out specific responses. Too, most respondents can rate lists of proposed prospects and analyze them for crucial personal evaluations on a confidential basis. This adds further substance to a dull, routine attitudinal analysis. (Of course, you would exclude the respondent's name from such a listing.)

The study interviewer and analyst must be adept in order to guide each interview to achieve preplanned results. The interviewer must also offer to leave at the appointed time—after 45 minutes to one hour. Should the respondent request the interviewer to stay, so be it. The interviewer is then on the respondent's time. But the interviewer must use the time judiciously. No gossip. Nor rumor test. No feeder complaint questions. If such problems exist, they will come out in a relaxed, constructive atmosphere and environment.

The entire interview process is a cultivation, a sales process, even if the respondent is thoroughly friendly toward the organization, its leadership, its services, and its programs. The interviewer must never act as a prosecuting attorney or yearbook advertising salesperson. The desirable intangible stakes are too high.

Throughout the interview process, the interviewer must watch for body language, conflicting verbal expressions, comparative illustrations, tonal inflections of conversation, and other personal traits. No interview is ever a mere "yes" or "no" exercise. The feasibility study process is an art in both preparation and implementation.

Evaluation

Each client is at the mercy of the interviewer when it comes to analysis and reporting honestly each interview. The integrity of the interviewer is at stake from the beginning of the exercise, but even more for analyses and recommendations. It goes without saying that nearly 100 percent of those who conduct so-called feasibility studies intend to offer a constructive service for the organization and for themselves. Yet, many such people may be subject to personal pressures. For instance, many interviewers do not debrief themselves immediately after each interview, to record each detail while it is fresh. Many will conduct four or five interviews in a day and write interviews up at the end of the day, trying to remember intimate nuances and vital statements and impressions. Some will interview 10, 20, 30, 50 or more respondents and then write up interviews. You can imagine the integrity of these reports. And there may be other personal pressures that can affect reports and recommendations.

Organizations should insist upon a personal, on-site, immediate exit debriefing of the interviewer before he or she returns to the home or personal office for immediate impressions before they are "laundered" in a formal and sometimes formidable report document.

Feasibility study evaluations reflect the experience, the personality, the prejudices, and the impressions of the interviewer. Feedback from respondents to the president of the organization is vital *before* the official report arrives.

The respondent evaluation is difficult for any interviewer because of its vital importance to the organization. The organization should expect an honest, objective analysis; adverse criticism; doubts about future potential; concerns about leadership and so on; and constructive reports. An honest report will not whitewash interviews or respondents' true statements, and of course always will maintain absolute confidentiality.

Hence, the receptivity of an honest feasibility report requires the same regimen of integrity on the part of the organization as that expected of the study interviewer.

Is This Trip Necessary?

Carefully review the following condensed form of our discussion so far. If all of the conditions cited are in place and poised to perform, a feasibility study is not necessary:

- The planning process was thorough, involving key governing board leadership.
- The composition of the governing board has been designed and fulfilled with balanced influence as well as affluence and access among its members.
- The prospect research procedure has identified and thoroughly provided comprehensive documentation on the top 50/75/100 prospects, or 1–2 percent of the total constituency.
- The governing board and key constituents are confident of the administrative and development leaders' competence.

- The development program and process is thorough, comprehensive, and progressive.
- The proposed program(s) intended to be subjected to a feasibility study can be timed and phased on a progressive basis.
- The case for substantial and continuing support is well put together, highly motivational, and realistic.

All that *is* needed in this case is a plan of action prepared by people experienced and competent to analyze all of the above conditions and then to create an operational plan. If confidence in administrative leadership exists, then get on with the job!

An Alternative: Chief Executive Consultations

For Princeton University's recently completed $330 million asset-building program, there was no feasibility study. Rather, there were a large number of *Presidential Consultation Conferences (PCC)* among alumni and friends, area by area, where the case or prospectus was explained and discussed. In these sessions, it was not a question of *should* we proceed, *can* we proceed, or *how shall* we proceed. Rather, the sales proposition was: here we are. We have designed our future; here is how we see our destiny. This is what our destiny costs—and this is how we intend to proceed.

Those involved in these sessions saw the breadth and depth of planning, heard the positive rationale for unprecedented philanthropic commitment, helped design the process and the sales story, became owners of the process, and assured the results. The program failed to reach its goal (so to speak) because over $410 million resulted. What happened at Princeton and what happened with those clients whom I have served since developing this PCC process at Carleton College some twenty years ago can benefit from constituent consultations. A feasibility study at Chapman College may have suggested an asset-building goal of $25 million. Instead, step-by-step prospect cultivation resulted in a noncampaign result exceeding $54 million.

You can use the case statement as an internal consensus document, and then as a basic motivational sales document. You can also use it as an invaluable cultivational agenda for crucially important philanthropic gift prospects and volunteers. Seldom are any institutional publications market-tested as to their effectiveness or intended impact. Yet, the case document is the recommended precursor of capital fund/ asset-building programs as the basic sales story heralding the role, mission, status, plans, and goals of the organization.

Since it is clear that slick publications alone do not stimulate most large capital/asset gift prospects, why not use the case document in rough draft form to market test its validity and its ultimate productivity?

This *a priori* involvement technique can accelerate each prospect's interest, concern, and eventual commitment to the institution. Each person will be both curious and complimented by the unusual invitation to an intimate setting for a substantive response to an institutional idea, plan, or prospectus before he or she is invited to invest in it. But you must plan the setting to invite participation, to incite response, and to promote each person's identity as a *special* person.

Consultation meetings provide these benefits:

1. Feeling of close relationship to the president.

2. A new, basic understanding of the dynamics of the institution, its case, its costs, and its financial requirements.

3. Pride in being included in a small group to discuss the institution.

4. A new (or renewed) level of confidence in the administration, in its management, and its leadership.

5. An expectancy to be called up to help in the sequential implementation of the program.

6. A critique of the case statement in form, in substance, and, in detail.

7. A new level of advocacy for the institution.

Consider the following features and factors in a progressive series of presidential consultation meetings:

A. Involve Trustees

1. Seek a consensus within the governing board using the case document as a basis for consistent information and goals, documentation, and arguments as an advocate of the institution generally and the proposed asset building program specifically.

2. Market-test the case document among managers of the public trust as a truly persuasive institutional sales instrument.

3. Inculcate renewed/enhanced pride in the institution according to its utility, dynamics, plans, unrealized potential, and destiny, including costs and current and endowment investment opportunities.

4. Inculcate ownership of the proposed asset-building program in and among individual members of the board.

5. Stimulate active advocacy and support of the institution as never before and for the proposed program.

6. Build personal confidence in the potential of the institution in order to cause members to alter personal philanthropic priorities and to increase personal commitments to the institution.

7. Prepare board members to serve as hosts for similar sessions among key prospects, as an intimate personal introduction and cultivation device.

8. Engender a partnership relationship with the president to actively pursue the proposed programs goals.

9. Educate the board by participating in conference discussions and in developing its advocacy through hosting these conferences.

B. *Involve Key Prospects*

1. Introduce the institution—its history, its heritage, its status and its destiny—to those individuals who have the power to influence and to provide private-sector philanthropic gifts of *very* substantial amounts.

2. Create an understanding and appreciation of the institution even though it may be unheralded and grossly underfinanced.

3. Stimulate interest in and concern for the institution to become what it was created to become: a designed instrument for the social good of mankind; a philanthropy existing for the love of humankind.

4. Draw out individual interests and concerns that may accelerate or deter eventual program success.

5. Inculcate confidence in the institution's leaders and management.

6. Create a desire among these individuals to become major investors in the institution's future.

C. *Use This Format for the Consultation Meetings*

1. Initially, have a board member or key leaders host them.

2. Hold the meetings in a business, rather than social setting.

3. Indicate that the case statement draft is the sole agenda item.

4. Lead attendees through the evolving case, literally turning pages—not reading, but describing, projects, programs, personnel, services, and facilities with current and endowment cost elements, using simple charts and diagrams.

5. Allow for interruptions, always encouraging the interchange of ideas and comments

6. Request reactions by asking:
    a. Are we on the right track?
    b. What does this say to you about our potential?
    c. Are our plans worth fighting for?
    d. What motivational emphases are we missing?
    e. Are our arguments really persuasive?
    f. Are our goals logical, realistic?

g. Can we count on your help as we implement our program?

h. Whom do you know that we should begin to acquaint with our institution?

i. Would you be willing to host a similar conference for us?

7. Anticipate possible response/retorts:

a. I had no idea that you were doing all these things.

b. Your institution has certainly kept its light under a bushel.

c. Just who are your peer institutions/organizations?

d. Just where does your institution rate among its peers?

e. In what areas are you truly distinctive?

f. That goal is an awful lot of money. You must believe that it's possible.

g. Where do the trustees stand on this plan?

h. Do you have any top gifts lined up?

i. When does the program begin?

j. What can I do?

k. Are you going to consider estate gifts?

8. Use one staff person present just to "read" the attendees' response—body language, side talk, implications of comments, and so on—and to participate in the discussion only when asked.

D. Make These Points in a Presentation

1. We have been underplanned and underfinanced for decades, yet we have been a totally dedicated service organization for all who sought and qualified for our best assistance.

2. We have spent an inordinate amount of time in serious internal analyses of our mission, our history of service, our status, our personnel, our markets, our costs, and our unrealized potential.

3. The program/project costs are based on current economic levels.

4. We can wait no longer to announce our serious leadership role and the costs of sustaining that role.

5. We are in a total mobilization of resources effort for unprecedented, high-priority asset-building.

6. We need outstanding gifts of confidence in our mission, our proven service, our plans, and our social utility.

E. Implement the Program

1. Create an active ownership/partnership in the institution.

2. Identify, cultivate, groom, bring along, nurture those closest to the institution to a point where they see the relationship between

current fund needs, special capital requirements, and endowment for stability and security.

3. Expand the prospect list of those capable of significant gifts ($100,000; $250,000; $500,000; $1,000,000 and up).

4. Raise personal gift sights to suggest the investment gift idea and to show people diverse ways to accomplish unprecedented philanthropic ideals.

5. Test and study voluntary leadership potential in action.

6. Refine the case document continually.

7. Ascertain the nature of special presentations, special brochures, and support materials required for the program's success.

F. Stage the Meeting

1. Select a host to invite ten to twelve (expecting only five to seven to attend, no more) persons of choice for a presidential consultation conference to discuss a draft document of vital importance to the institution. The host pays for the occasion.

2. Have the host personally invite persons by telephone followed by a confirmation letter; indicate that the session will last not over two hours—breakfast or lunch, not dinners.

3. Have the host or the president send the numbered and dated draft copy of the case document *only* to those agreeing to attend the session, not earlier than ten days before the session, with the specific request that participants read, annotate, and be prepared to discuss it constructively

4. Study carefully the people so that they are as homogeneous socially, culturally, and economically as possible.

5. Invite a staff associate (who actually makes all arrangements).

6. Sit at the head of the table. The host sits at the center on one side of a rectangular table.

7. The staff member takes notes.

8. Keep the agenda fairly formal, with little side talk, because the main purpose of the meeting is to present and discuss the case of the institution's future.

9. Move quickly. You must proceed with the document discussion as soon as appropriate, to assure that each invitee remains to discuss the entire document.

10. Send out thank-you letters to each attendee immediately after the session, including a renumbered and dated draft of the studied document that includes approved ideas suggested at the session.

11. Make sure that the attending staff member schedules a personal interview with each attendee within one week to glean

confidential information concerning the case document and the entire program.

Most leadership candidates and wealthy individuals are tired of being the objects of the so-called feasibility studies and surveys. The conferences described herein provide respondents with a hands-on document to read and analyze, and an intimate forum for dialogue about it. To be asked for such advice concerning specific programs is unique and attention-getting. You must carefully plan the conferences. You must be sharp in your presentation of the case. And you should *never* allow the meeting to digress from its stated purpose. Properly conducted conferences, you will find, can be *most* productive in assuring the success of well-planned programs!

III

CONDUCTING THE FUND-RAISING PROGRAM

8

THE ROLE OF
PUBLIC RELATIONS
Richard W. Conklin

To begin: The purpose of public relations on any campus—
big or small, bucolic or urban, public or private—is to engender understanding and support for the institution. Note that the two nouns,
"understanding" and "support," are yoked. "Understanding" presumes
that a certain level of institutional self-identity has been achieved; that
the college or university knows what its educational mission is and has
some sort of plan in mind to enhance it.

Public relations, contrary to misconceptions throughout the years,
is amplification, not invention. Before public relations can do its job
of communication and influence, the institution must have gone through
enough self-examination to know what it is, and what messages it wants
to convey about itself.

And the messages must have some grounding in reality. It is futile
to attempt to convey the message that Old Siwash is breaking new
ground in the educational use of computers, when the fact is that it is
a late follower in terms of adapting that technology to the campus. It
is a mistake to try to make a junior college, whose real job is providing
the opportunity for two-year Associate of Arts degrees to minority
students, sound like Harvard. Sows' ears might be made into silk purses
somewhere on the planet, but not in the newsrooms of newspapers or
television stations—at least not those I've dealt with for twenty-five
years.

The word "support" is also important. When I advise people
wanting to get into education PR, I say, "I hope you have some facility
with the English language, and I hope you get along well with people
who raise money for a living." The way most advancement sectors of
colleges and universities are organized, PR people report to development
people, and the public relations function is presumed to support the
never-ending task of providing resources for the institution. I have no
quarrel with that; it's just that people entering the profession should
know up front that they will share a bottom line with fund raisers.

And they should. Public relations eventually seeks transactions—parents enrolling their children, alumni supporting the annual fund, the city relocating a road for campus expansion, *U.S. News and World Report* citing the institution in its biennial evaluation of American higher education.

The President and the Vision

The chief public relations executive of the institution, no matter who has the title, is the president. The institution's constituencies see him or her as personifying the institution. As the chief public relations officer, the president's most important task is to articulate the vision. You can have all the rest—the personnel, the budget, the feasibility studies, the screening committees, the campaign plan, the shopping list of specific needs—but without the vision, you haven't got the most important element.

The vision goes beyond the functional case statement. It paints with a wide brush, creating a compelling picture. The vision positions the institution for its alumni and friends as a place with a special sense of purpose. It is never a depiction of the institution as it is; it is always where the institution wants to be. The vision is never accomplished; the institution is becoming.

Rev. Theodore M. Hesburgh, C.S.C., president emeritus of the University of Notre Dame, took over at a time when the public perception (not necessarily the reality) of the institution was that of a school in the Middle West that played exciting football. The only people to attend his first off-campus news conference as president in 1952 were sportswriters, one of whom tossed him a football and asked him to assume the hiking position. "Seared" would be too mild a verb to describe how that incident was imprinted in Father Hesburgh's memory.

For the next thirty-five years, this president talked about a vision of Notre Dame that had nothing to do with autumnal games. Time and time again, before alumni, friends, trustees, benefactors, reporters, and foundation and corporate officials, he talked about Notre Dame becoming a world-class Catholic university, a twentieth-century version of the great Catholic universities of the Middle Ages that handed on the oldest intellectual tradition in the West. It was a vision that went beyond pleas for buildings, endowed chairs, scholarship funds, and graduate residence halls, it was a vision to animate people.

People get excited by visions—especially visions that reflect their own values and hold out the promise of perpetuating them. People excited by visions give money to realize them. So the president's main job is to describe his or her vision for the institution and get others to make it theirs. You needn't ever directly ask for a dime (most presidents are poor "closers" anyway). If you articulate the vision, you've done enough.

The Public Relations Organization

Smaller institutions, such as liberal arts colleges, have centralized public relations operations, unless a department head has run amok. When it comes to universities, with their fiefdoms of colleges, professional schools, teaching hospitals, and research institutes, public relations (at least on the level of media relations) is sometimes decentralized. This means that public relations activities exist outside Old Main, and sometimes even report to people other than Old Main vice presidents.

There are three types of universities: presidents' universities (fewer and fewer of these as the tenure of the chief executive officer on campus gets shorter and shorter), deans' universities, and faculty universities. Presidents' universities generally have centralized PR activities. Deans' universities, as you might expect, have decentralized ones. Faculty universities try to hide the PR operation, centralized or decentralized. All my years in educational public relations have been spent in centralized operations, and they have one great advantage: control.

When Old Main has what amounts to "the administration's public relations" while deans of colleges, heads of hospitals, and directors of research institutes have their own purveyors of news releases and directors of special events, there is ample room for jurisdictional disputes. If there are to be outlying pockets of PR activity, their personnel should report to an executive in Old Main who has oversight responsibility for institutional public relations. An institution-wide perspective is necessary for good public relations judgment, and that is not often found in someone reporting to an academic satrap, no matter how gifted he or she may be.

As important as having public relations centralized is the integration of *all* institutional advancement functions under *a* vice president. The most common example is a vice president for university relations under whom fall such areas as development, public relations, alumni, community relations, publications, alumni, and special events. As noted above, since development is the engine that turns the turbines, the captain of the ship will normally be, first and foremost, a fundraiser. To have separate vice presidents for such areas as development, public relations, and alumni is, in my judgment, to have a table of disorganization.

Institutional advancement areas are interwoven, and when there is a major project ahead, such as a capital campaign, there must be one vice president capable of commanding everyone's attention. It is critical that everyone be singing from the same songsheet. (You can see the influence of marketing in higher education today in the fact that some campuses now have a vice president for marketing, under whom comes the traditional advancement areas plus admissions and financial aid and placement.)

Public Relations Activity

A sound public relations program in support of development goals does not start when campaign solicitation starts. It has to be an ongoing activity—one that precedes the campaign, accompanies it, and follows it. A useful basic exercise in doing an inventory of campus public relations is to list in one column all the institution's constituencies—faculty, students, parents, alumni, benefactors, local townspeople, trustees, news media, and so on. In another column, list the ways in which the university now communicates with each constituency: publications, special events, audiovisual presentations, newsletters, letters, and personal contact, for example.

In a third column, list the focus of messages that predominate in the communications received by each group, such as excellence of teaching, financial need, pioneering research, or value overlay to instruction. This serves to clarify some crucial questions: Have you identified all your constituencies? Have you adequate ways of getting information to them? Are the messages they are receiving the ones you want them to receive? Are there any conflicting messages? (Is the president emphasizing that athletics should be kept in perspective, whereas the athletic department has just arranged for the annual sports review to be sent to all alumni, and a trustee has just gotten the basketball coach to talk at the dinner for his professional association?) What is the reaction to the messages? What do you hear? Lastly, how can you evaluate the effectiveness of what you have done: How do you know whether or not you've communicated well?

A public relations program must have focus. What are those specific things about the institution that you want its constituencies to know, and how does their knowing them affect the bottom line? At Notre Dame, three years before we were to launch a multi-million dollar campaign (that included, for the first time, substantial outlays for graduate education and research), we were already sending this message in various ways to our constituencies: Notre Dame is the only Catholic university positioned to join the nation's first-rate research universities.

This communications story also illustrates why it is important to listen to how your target audiences react to your message. Our feedback said this: "O.K., but please don't destroy an outstanding undergraduate educational program when you start emphasizing research and advanced studies." So we altered our message to reassure people that this would not happen. We stressed continuity and emphasized that we were building upon undergraduate excellence in our reach for distinction in post-baccalaureate education and research.

The Faculty—A Special Constituency

Most educational public relations activity is geared to influencing the opinions of external constituencies, especially where the goal is raising money. Little of that comes from within. It is, however, crucial for the faculty to support the larger message: the vision of the president, and its embodiment in a campaign. The reception will never be unanimous; a faculty member is by definition one who thinks otherwise. But substantial backbiting by the very people who have to implement the academic future will have a chilling effect on those asked to believe in it. There is a pertinent story of a Missouri institution in the middle of a capital campaign that planned a sesquicentennial celebration to boost fund-raising activity. The faculty objected: they had received no raises that year, and had other ideas for the anniversary budget.

I recall overhearing a chairman of one of our departments while he was giving a campus tour to a potential faculty appointee. In front of Notre Dame's famous "Golden Dome" he pointed skyward and said, "People throw money at that, and most of it sticks." Conversational hyperbole to be sure, but nonetheless revealing. The most effective response to a fund-raising drive from the faculty should come long before there is one.

At this point a faculty-dominated committee should plot the academic future of the institution, reporting either to the president or to the chief academic officer under the president. One of the first things this committee does is survey faculty members, through middle management, about what they think is needed to fulfill the institution's mission. A smaller group scrutinizes this report after the committee has vetted it once. (This smaller group most often is comprised of the chief academic officer and his or her advisors.) On the skeletal framework of academic needs that emerges eventually hangs the case statement and the accompanying "shopping list" of price-tagged priorities. The shopping list either is then matched against a previously commissioned feasibility study about development potential, or becomes itself the touchstone for such a study.

At some early point, the faculty itself needs to be solicited for campaign contributions, on the principle that all internal constituencies ought to be committed before the campaign seeks outside generosity. This usually is done gingerly, and is eventually justified as an educational endeavor.

As is the case generally, internal faculty public relations ought to begin long before there is concentrated development activity.

Public relations practitioners in a university ought to be people who understand both ideas and those who toil to disseminate them. This means keeping the lines of communications open. It means treating with a sympathetic ear a faculty member who has just finished the definitive work on, say, Portuguese grail manuscripts. It means appearing before college councils or faculty senates for periodic give-and-take sessions. It means clipping newspaper stories that deal with areas of specialization of faculty members, and sending such to them. It means lunches with deans and department heads, to go over the changing academic landscape.

All these things help prevent campus public relations people from being labeled as the personal press agents of the president. They are also a wise recognition of the vulnerability of the public relations practitioner in academe. As one university president put it, "Public relations people are the nonphysician in hospitals, the nonsinger in opera companies, the nonacademician in institutions primarily committed to academics. Without support from the president, such people can become completely isolated, easily seen as irrelevant, misunderstood, overlooked, rejected." Amen.

Athletics, PR, and Money

Repeat after me: There is no empirical evidence demonstrating a correlation between athletic achievement and fund-raising success. A number of researchers have explored this putative relationship, and they all have concluded it does not exist. The myth persists, however, aided by anecdotal evidence from sports reporters who apparently spend more time in bars than in development offices.

I recall that a couple of years ago the highest-paid television sports anchorman in the country reported that Notre Dame trustees were about to meet to discuss the fate of a losing football coach, and that a major factor was declining contributions. I called the news director of the Chicago station, to point out that the trustees did not even have a committee dealing with sports, and that the university had raised more cash than ever in the past fiscal year. He, like the anchorman, hadn't known the facts.

One talks against the wind. Is it more pleasant to raise money in good athletic times than bad? Certainly. Any development person will tell you that he or she would rather not spend the first fifteen minutes of a solicitation interview explaining away dismal athletic records. And in the larger PR sense, sports provides a point of unity for alumni and friends that rarely is matched by any other aspect of campus life (a fact tacitly admitted recently by a group of front-rank academic universities which formed a conference to get more competitive visibility for their programs—and more alumni interest). These are all pluses in creating a climate in which to cultivate persons who might be willing to share their wealth, but they don't bear that heavily on decisions to share. As noted above, major benefactors are not motivated by the play of a quarterback, but by the vision of a president. In the long run, the integrity of the athletic program is more important to public relations and development goals than are season-to-season basketball and football records. A president interested in the interplay of athletics and fund raising would do well to pay more attention to the campus credibility of the compound-noun student–athlete than to win–loss records.

Bad News and PR

For more than a decade I have taught the "bad news" class in CASE's annual Summer Institute in Communications. I observe early on in those classes that university presidents often come to their jobs woefully uninformed about how news media people work, and how public relations practitioners interact with them. For example, I think that many neophyte campus CEOs presume that the media can often be manipulated, that stories can get printed regardless of their newsworthiness, and especially that there is some magical way to keep unfavorable news out of the newspapers or off of TV news. Too many PR officers must continually do remedial educational work on this issue.

It is important for presidents—and development personnel—to remember that bad news is like rain: inevitable and passing. Overreaction is counterproductive. The news media have a transitory interest and a short attention span; that is why the quick hemorrhage is better than the slow bleed. Get the bad news out as quickly and fully as possible—otherwise, the story builds as each new fact comes to light. (It is especially dumb to hold back information that is bound to become public knowledge, as NASA did with launch-time weather reports immediately after the Challenger disaster.) Wise presidents also anticipate when unpopular decisions on tuition increases, tenure refusals, tighter rules on campus alcohol use, requests to relocate a city street and such are likely to stir controversy. In advance, they seek public relations counsel to minimize the damage.

An even better idea is to involve the public relations director in the decision-making process. Stephen Trachtenberg, president of George Washington University, once noted:

> I think that a public relations director should sit in on top-level policy meetings. He or she doesn't necessarily have to speak a lot, and he or she doesn't have to vote, but I have found in the course of my administrative experience that an awful lot of presidents go through a process of making a decision and then calling in the public relations director to tell them. I just think that for the kind of bucks we are paying for a public relations director, I want twenty-four-hour input; and if there is some wisdom to be had, that sort of talent in on the decision-making process.

Some campus officials are wont to overemphasize the effect of bad news on fund raising. I am sure that some at Cornell University during the Great Days of Student Unrest, after seeing a wire-service photograph of rifle-armed students ending a building occupation, thought about closing the development office. But, the last time I looked, the place seemed to be doing quite nicely, thank you. The best advice for those prone to panic came from Edward Levi, then president of the University of Chicago, who found a bunker elsewhere on campus and outlasted a group of students occupying his office in the late 1960s. "Each day we would discuss the worst thing we could do and then we would decide not to do it" was the way Levi explained the strategy of patience.

Public Relations and the Capital Campaign

In the words of my mentor, James E. Murphy, associate vice president for university relations at Notre Dame:

> Public relations can get along without fund raising. After all, there are many organizations and agencies that have sophisticated PR programs but that don't raise money. But the opposite is not true. Fund raising—particularly at colleges and universities—does need considerable PR support. You do not conduct a development campaign in a vacuum. Inevitably, a campaign exists within the environment of what people think of an insti-

tution, organization, or cause. The role of PR, then, is to create the most favorable possible context for the campaign.

Ideally, the public relations officer sits on the highest councils planning the campaign and prepares a master public relations plan that maps out communications strategies for each phase of the campaign. A lot of work is done in the preannouncement stage, when there is the task of communicating the campaign prospectus to trustees and other leadership gift prospects. Publications get involved in creating campaign materials—the vision statement, the case statement, and the various brochures to be used by volunteers. Public relations surrounds the announcement of the campaign, and follows it off the campus. For example: Everywhere that the president, top officers, or faculty appear on the campaign's behalf, the PR officer considers trying to get media exposure.

A campaign in and of itself, however, is a tough sell to out-of-town news media. In the middle 1960s, when the nation's major universities launched multi-million-dollar campaigns, they attracted national media attention. More than two decades later, capital campaigns in higher education are so commonplace that they are not usually considered newsworthy outside an institution's local area. The campaign usually has to be sold on the road in an indirect fashion, meaning that the administrator or the faculty member out in the hustings can only attract the news media by relating to what is currently newsworthy.

Father Hesburgh's lifelong activity in civil rights, world hunger, and nuclear disarmament could usually guarantee a news conference anywhere (no more sportswriters in attendance). Seldom was the day when one or another of those issues was not in the news, and fewer yet were the days when Notre Dame's president did not greet the news media with a few words about why he was in town.

Another thing that has changed over the years is the public perception of higher education: There has been an erosion of confidence in colleges and universities. As George N. Rainsford, president of Lynchburg College, put it:

> Directors of public relations now need not only to sell their own individual institution, but also to understand and sell all of higher education at the same time. They have to overcome obstacles and questions in the public mind about higher education as such before they can talk about their own institutions.

Educational public relations people often do exhibit a creativity to match challenges, however. At Wittenberg University, for example, a key element in public relations for a recent campaign was the formulation of a communications advisory committee composed of media-related professionals with some relationship to the university (alumnus, parent, trustee). Members came from areas important to the campaign's success, and often were able to open doors and lend credibility to campaign public relations efforts.

Campaigns are wartime. Everyone from the president on down must continue to fulfill the normal activities of an academic year while shouldering the additional burden of campaign responsibilities. All advancement professionals must pull together, which is why it makes things a lot easier when they report to the same vice president. For example, the vice president should not dictate to the editor of the alumni/ae publication how he or she should communicate the campaign. Instead, the vice president should make sure the editor understands that the magazine must do its part in helping the campaign, and then ask the editor to consult with his or her staff and propose how the magazine can best go about the task.

Togetherness of purpose not only is essential, but for the entire length of the campaign must remain everyone's No. 1 priority. One of the ideas that became an enormously successful staple of Notre Dame fund raising—the "fly-in"—came not from the development office but from some brainstorming and subsequent refinement by all advancement area department heads. Years later, the flying-in (on donated executive jets) of a small number of couples to campus as guests of the president for a weekend (in which they are steeped in the needs and vision of the university) still yields an average gift of $300,000 from each couple. While the capital campaign represents the treadmill test for an institution's public relations personnel, the rules are the same. What messages about the institution do you wish to convey to further campaign goals? To whom do you wish to convey them—who are the key target audiences? What do these audiences now think about the message—do you wish to underscore or change their opinion? What are the most effective means to do this communicating? What is the feedback? How can you evaluate your efforts?

To end: The purpose of public relations on any campus is to engender understanding of, and support for, the institution. Historically, it has been a function closely linked to development activities and perceived as creating a positive climate in which to enjoy success in seeking needed resources. The messages that public relations practitioners in higher education convey to an institution's various constituencies must be grounded in a mature sense of institutional self-identity and must be honest. The president is the chief public relations officer, and he or she must articulate the vision for the institution and convince others to share it as their own. A campus organization in which public relations is centralized and in which it and other institutional advancement activities are integrated under one vice president leads to less internecine combat. At the heart of public relations activity is the identification of constituencies, the choice messages you wish to convey to them, and the selection of the most effective means of doing so.

It is also imperative to listen for target audience feedback (and be flexible enough to adjust the message if necessary), and to evaluate the effectiveness of the communications plan. Among constituencies, the most important internal one is the faculty, and wise is the public relations practitioner who makes sure they know that he or she is at their service as well as the president's. Presidents would do well to pay more attention to the integrity of their athletic program and less to their dubious role in fund raising. Bad news is like rain—inevitable and passing—and its effect on development should not be overemphasized.

9

THE ROLE OF
THE GOVERNING
BOARD
Robert L. Gale

No president or chancellor, whether he or she heads a public or independent institution, has enough time or staff to raise the amounts of money the institution needs. Outside help is a must. This can come from many sources, but certainly no individual or group has a stronger reason to help than the governing board. Without substantial help from that group, institutions cannot be expected to reach the sizeable fund-raising goals they set for themselves. The chief executives simply cannot do it alone.

Should governing board members feel responsible for helping to raise money? It is my contention that indeed they must. Administrative staff members, in most cases, are the wrong people to ask to solicit funds, and other volunteers often are too loosely tied to the institution.

Basic Governing Board Responsibilities

Before turning to the fund-raising role of the board, I will point out the overall responsibilities of members of governing boards, whether public or independent:

1. Appoint, support, and assess the performance of the president;
2. Review regularly and approve the mission of the institution;
3. Approve long-range plans;
4. Approve the educational program;
5. Ensure the well-being of faculty, students, and staff;
6. Ensure adequate financial resources;
7. Ensure strong financial management (both budget and investments);

8. Maintain the physical plant;

9. Preserve institutional autonomy and academic freedom;

10. Enhance the public image;

11. Interpret the campus to the community and the community to the campus;

12. Serve as a court of last resort;

13. Assess the board's own performance;

14. Be informed about the institution and higher education.

Different institutions will pay closer attention to some of these responsibilities than to others, but in general this list covers the spectrum. Surely under number six, "ensure adequate financial resources," comes a very strong mandate to act in a fund-raising capacity.

Differences Between Public and Independent

I should make a distinction here between the roles of public governing boards and independent governing boards with regard to fundraising. The independent board as a group should be responsible for raising funds, and members of such a board should be picked for their ability to do so. Generally, a development committee of the board of trustees supervises this function.

On the public side, most trustees and regents are not picked for their ability to give and raise funds. In most cases, a separate foundation must be set up to raise and receive funds. In this respect, the board of the foundation should serve much as the development committee of the board of an independent institution. Nonetheless, public governing board members still must take responsibility to see that an effective foundation is operating and that, whenever possible, governing board members themselves identify, cultivate, and (when appropriate) call on prospects.

Why Boards Must Raise Money

Let's look for a minute at why boards *must* both raise and give money. Obviously there is a financial crunch everywhere. Cuts in federal, state, and local aid; an unsure economy; and unprecedented competition from other nonprofit institutions all make the need for help from trustees undeniable.

Too, since presidents and chancellors are overloaded with other duties, they cannot spend great amounts of time cultivating and soliciting gifts. There just must be a spreading-out of the responsibility, and the governing board logically must assume some of it. As a matter of fact, certain trustees often have more clout than CEOs, and should be able to cultivate and solicit their peers of great means.

What Kind of Board Is Needed?

The board needs top people in the community with clout and money, carefully chosen, properly cultivated and enlisted. They need to be trained to their roles and responsibilities both as trustees and as fundraisers. (Of course, board members who prove not good at solicitation should not be involved in it.) What is needed minimally is a few good troops who can carry the flag high. However, *everyone* on *both* public and independent boards *can* be involved in the fund-raising process—by identifying prospective donors and by cultivating them.

How do you revitalize your board for better fund-raising support? The following comments pertain almost exclusively to independent boards and the boards of public foundations, although I suggest that older board members and chief executives of public institutions use all the influence they can muster to see that new members prove helpful in the fund-raising area. The most important step to take is to improve board composition through the use of a nominating committee. You need a strong, active nominating committee made up of some of the most powerful members of the board. Too frequently, key board members are put on other (seemingly more important) committees, and the least effective members are left to control the future composition of the board. Only the strongest people on your board have the ability to identify, cultivate, and enlist the kinds of people needed to bring in substantial funds from the outside.

A nominating committee should develop a board profile that indicates the skills and backgrounds of current board members, which skills are needed, and how the necessary compensatory changes can be carried out. Obviously there should be special emphasis on developing such a profile to leave space for people who have an ability to give and to attract money. In general, the board of a public foundation should include only those who can give and get money, or who can help in public relations.

Once there is such a profile it is then incumbent upon this committee, working closely with the president and the staff, to identify, cultivate, enlist, and orient board members who have appropriate financial clout. Such committees frequently aim too low, not realizing that membership on the board is a sought-after honor, even though the person in question seems to have no particular connection to the institution.

Some obvious choices have close ties, and you can ask them immediately. For others, it is worth spending as much time cultivating them for membership on the board as you do to cultivate a major gift prospect. Pick those on the way up, what I call "comers," who have not yet reached the top but quite obviously are on the way up. Once someone has reached the top, you will find him or her hard to enlist. Someone else will have asked first.

One other suggestion here is to check volunteer references on anyone about to be asked to join the board. Sometimes those who look good on paper turn out to be those who just lend their names to boards and do not work or give. A call to a staff member of a board the person has served on will usually determine whether that party produces or not.

Improving the Current Board

There also are ways to improve the fund-raising performance of current board members. Make sure you have developed a case statement for all fund raising so that everyone understands the needs and the goals. Frequently, board members are unsure of just why they are supposed to be raising money. It is also important to determine the commitment of current board members to work and to give. Often no one has asked them to do anything, and they are considered to be deadwood. Sometimes a luncheon to discuss their commitment to the institution, particularly in the fund-raising area, brings out some amazing offers to start work. You, the president, can do this through individual sessions with an appropriate trustee (probably the chairman of the development committee) or, if appropriate, the development officer.

This brings up the necessity of establishing an active development committee to help spearhead the fund-raising effort and to bring along the rest of the board in the entire fund-raising program.

A retreat, with emphasis on the fund-raising role, may prove helpful. Trained facilitators and effective backup materials (including videotapes) are available to help make such a workshop effective.

No one should forget that volunteers don't produce well unless staff work backs them up. Effective staffing can make board members much more productive, save them time, and make them feel more comfortable in their role as fund-raisers. Feeling comfortable with fund raising is especially important, and in this regard it is usually helpful to teach board members how to ask for money. Most people have a dread of making that first call, but once they have had a successful "hit" they will be hard to stop. A great philanthropist and fund raiser has said that the greatest thing he can do for people of means is to get them to invest some of their wealth in a worthwhile project, because this will make them feel much better as they look back on their life.

The Board's Roles in Fund Raising

Assuming that you now have a board with an appropriate number of people with financial clout developed and trained, what then are the board's roles in fund raising? Here are some of them:

1. See that planning is conducted—both institutional and fund raising;

2. Be involved in that planning;

3. See that an adequate development budget is established;

4. See that top staff is enlisted—the chief executive makes the decision, but the board should make sure that the institution is not "saving" money by paying below-market salaries;

5. Set the example for others by giving—both annual and capital—commensurate with their means;

6. Talk up the institution to all of their contacts, especially to potential donors;

7. Identify potential prospects;

8. Cultivate prospects as directed by the development staff;

9. Solicit prospects—alone, with the chief executive, with others—as programmed by the staff;

10. Take volunteer leadership roles in annual and capital campaigns when asked;

11. Help motivate and direct other volunteers;

12. Thank donors to the institution—in person, by phone, or by mail—as asked to do, but also spontaneously. No one can be thanked too much.

To flesh out these roles a bit: It is clear that you must do institutional planning, that you must establish fund-raising goals and the planning to reach those goals to help carry out the institutional plan, and that you must involve boards in that planning if they are going to "buy in" to the development program. Obviously, staff and faculty should do most of the planning, but the board should ensure that it is done, and should have enough involvement to feel a sense of ownership.

You must invest to raise money, but too frequently in these difficult times it is almost impossible to put together a development budget that is adequate to the task. Without an adequate budget you cannot recruit the proper staff needed to carry out the program, be it annual or capital. In addition, the research necessary so that board members can feel comfortable when making calls does not come cheaply. In other words, you must invest money to make money, even though the faculty may object.

If members of the board do not give according to their means, why should others? This question is raised more and more frequently by major individual donors, foundations, and corporations. Board members must give as they can, and should be prepared to talk up the strong points of the institution to all of their contacts. Unless they show total support, few others will step in to help with gifts of their own.

Many board members feel very uncomfortable in the role of fund raiser, but no one can duck the responsibility to identify prospects and to help cultivate these prospects, and others, as directed. Once they have identified and cultivated these prospects, others can move in to make the "ask." Obviously, a certain number *must* be prepared to solicit prospects.

Board members should also show enthusiasm and involvement beyond just attending board and committee meetings. Often, taking volunteer roles in the fund-raising campaigns can be especially helpful in motivating others. It means a great deal to interested alumni and friends who are working as volunteers to find that a member of the board is in there working with them, whether it's the governing board or the foundation board. Such action speaks much louder than words.

Board Selection: An Important Task

What are some final thoughts for presidents or chancellors in the fund-raising arena? You should get involved in the board's selection process if you have not already done so. In fact, you should orchestrate it. Generally, the chief development officer can be of great assistance in coming up with names of people who could be helpful, but it is too important to the future of the institution to allow the nominating committee to function without great input from the chief executive officer.

You should also work with the nominating committee to see that new board members are properly oriented to their tasks. All of this starts when the nominee is invited to join the board. And no one should be allowed to join the board who has not been told verbally and in writing what is expected of him or her.

You should continue to cultivate board members who have financial clout *after* they have joined the board. You should look upon them just as you look upon potential major outside donors. Far too often, strong members join the board and then are expected to give and get without further attention. The chief executive, plus some key board members and the chief development officer, can best continue the cultivation process.

You also need to make sure that appropriate staff backup is available to the volunteers. It is better to have fewer volunteers with good staff backup than many volunteers with faulty staff support. Volunteers do not function by themselves, particularly in the fund-raising area.

You must make sure that proper research is done on prospects and that good written materials are available for solicitors. Nothing can turn off a dedicated board volunteer more than making a call with erroneous information about the background and the giving potential of the prospect.

You should always remember that more than 90 percent of the money comes from less than 10 percent of the donors. And that most of these donors are individuals. Most of you shouldn't have your development staff wasting time on foundations and corporations unless you have particular "ins," either through your research capabilities or through geographic location.

And finally, you should be aware that building a strong board—whether it's a governing board of an independent institution or the foundation board of a public institution, is the chief executive's responsibility—obviously with appropriate goading by the chief development officer. Too many chief executives prefer not to play this role. But it is a role that one *must* play to have a successful development program.

Properly enlisted and trained, the board can help enormously to reduce the pressures upon the president or chancellor as the chief fund-raising officer for the institution. Only by spreading the load can we raise the necessary resources to keep our institutions great. Your board should be there with you, shouldering the load.

10

THE ROLE OF
ALUMNI RELATIONS

Robert G. Forman

Many university presidents view alumni as adversaries rather than as potential resources. It is not that presidents do not appreciate alumni financial support. Instead, they are troubled by possible alumni involvement in other institutional matters. Furthermore, presidents often see alumni only as frequent communicators of bad news: "Why wasn't my son or daughter admitted?" "Why can't I park on campus?" "How come my tickets are in the end zone?" And in addition, alumni have the peculiar trait of looking upon the institution as their own. They exhibit a vested interest in the affairs of the university, college, or school, whether public or private.

Despite whatever trouble the occasional alumni remark may cause, alumni are, without question, the single greatest resource a president has. They not only provide needed funds but recruit students, offer new and innovative ideas, and communicate to various constituencies. And they provide all this support in a loving and caring manner. The enlightened president understands this resource, cultivates and nourishes it, and uses it wisely to support the institution.

The alumni role in fund raising is multidimensional, yet its potential is barely being used. Although alumni financial support dates back to 1792, when Yale established its class officer system, it has only been in recent years that we have begun to contemplate and implement the means to fully enable alumni to financially support private and public institutions.

Understanding Alumni

To use alumni as a resource for fund raising, you need to understand them and how we have traditionally worked with them. First of all, don't forget that alumni are the products of the educational enterprise. They are yesterday's students who have tested the advantages of their education in the marketplace. Their accomplishments and successes are the measuring sticks for the quality of their alma mater. No institution can be recognized for its quality if the institution's alumni are not successful examples of its educational process.

Alumni traditionally act in two ways that on the surface may seem frivolous but actually provide the basis of the strength of their support. The first is exhibiting an almost sophomoric attitude about their alma mater. They are the fans at sporting events, the eager beavers at homecoming reunions, and the ones who unabashedly shed a tear during the singing of the old school songs. The other type of such behavior by an alumnus is seen in the individual who views the institution in the manner of a proud parent—basking in its accomplishments, lamenting and grieving over its disappointments.

While these attitudes may appear immature to the president, they are the qualities that set alumni apart from any of the other publics to which a president must appeal for institutional support. And such support is meaningful enough to rend negligible the modest liabilities of such alumni attitudes.

Organizing Alumni

To maximize the use of alumni as supporters and advocates of the university, college, or school, the president must establish an environment conducive to good alumni relations. Historically, this has been done in one of two ways: by organizing an alumni relations program integrated into the institution's overall advancement program, or by establishing an independent alumni organization.

Each approach has its merits. In general, an alumni relations program integrated into the advancement office provides for better communication, allows the smaller organization to use limited personnel in a variety of jobs, and of course, keeps control of alumni activities within the institution's organizational structure.

The independent approach often is more cumbersome, and frequently has serious limitations with respect to institutional control. As educated people, alumni have a tendency to think independently, and although many support the same mission and goals as the executive officers of the institution, their approach may be, on occasion, dramatically different.

A third alternative is a highly-bred organizational approach whereby the university provides financial support and organizational maintenance. But an alumni policy board or council largely handles policy and decision-making.

Presidents need to examine the history of alumni relations at their institution, and try to work with alumni volunteer leaders to form the type of organization deemed most appropriate for the needs of their particular institution.   In general, the independent approach seems to work better at large universities.   At such institutions, alumni can run major alumni relations programs as largely self-supporting.   Income from membership, service, and entrepreneurial activities supports a large and diverse alumni relations program.   One of the concerns that many administrators have about the independent alumni program is whether membership dues for such groups detract from annual giving income. In fact, alumni who voluntarily pay membership dues outperform non-members dramatically with respect to their support of annual fund or alumni fund programs.

Membership organizations provide alumni with the feeling that they are "stockholders" in the organization.   Alumni are more inclined to respond to invitations from their "own" organization to participate in alumni activities.   Regardless, you as the new president should look charitably upon any organizational format that allows the alumni to feel that they play a major role in governing their own organization, whether that organization is independent or dependent.

An additional advantage of the independent organization is that it bears much of the cost of alumni cultivation.   Activities such as continuing education, alumni family camps, educational travel programs, and group life and health insurance not only provide self-supporting income, but provide evidence to the individual alumnus that the institution, through its alumni organization, wants to provide services that benefit the individual.   Thus the message is not "How much are you willing to give?" but "Here are services that may be important to you.   In return, we would like your continued support for your alma mater."

Building a Program

Alumni involvement in institutional service areas such as student recruitment or merit scholar awards provides an opportunity for alumni to identify with students.   As those students pursue their educational careers, the alumni who have helped recruit them will also respond to requests for financial support.   This is particularly true when such requests are to provide for scholarships and other forms of student assistance.

A well-rounded alumni program starts with several building blocks: an alumni records system, a club or chapter outreach program, a reunion program with associated educational activities, and a first-rate communications vehicle such as a tabloid, magazine, or newsletter. This basic infrastructure ultimately allows more sophisticated and advanced programs to be carried out.

The new president should immediately survey (preferably by using outside consultants) the extent of the institution's basic alumni programming. You should determine the adequacy of record-keeping, the extent of organized alumni activity, and the level of alumni understanding of institutional concerns and challenges.

A comprehensive database is key to building an alumni relations program. Alumni usually are quite willing to share personal data with their alma mater, and most alumni databases are replete with both institution-related information (class year, field of study) and economic information (current job, donor history).

Because most alumni bodies are geographically dispersed, it is important to develop clubs and chapters that provide for outreach programs. These not only are important vehicles for transmitting and communicating information, but also provide the cornerstone for student recruitment, public information, and (if appropriate) government relations. Local alumni clubs often take on community projects—for example, local educational issues, pollution, drug-abuse clinics, and other projects. Such activities not only provide needed help, but send a message to local communities about the parent institution's values and services.

Reunions are fundamental building blocks for bringing people back to campus. They provide an opportunity for the hands-on experience necessary to understand what is currently happening at the institution. Perhaps the main value of returning to campus is in the area of continuing education and enrichment programs.

The publication vehicles used for communicating with alumni are extremely important for carrying both the message of the university and the happenings of the alumni organization. Those publications that not only provide a better understanding of campus happenings but also take seriously the role of continuing education and enrichment serve the needs of both alumni and the institution.

Creative Programming

Using this basic infrastructure, there are many more creative programs that can help cultivate alumni as both donors and general supporters of the institution. Many alumni organizations, particularly the independent ones, have invested in facilities for conducting alumni family recreational and educational programs. The University of California–Berkeley, University of Southern California, University of California–Los Angeles, Brigham Young University, Stanford University, Indiana University, and the University of Michigan are among those that operate such off-campus programs. Using a facility and site that maximizes the advantages of the environment, these programs have been unqualified successes not only in providing excellent social, recreational, and educational experiences, but also in reuniting alumni and their alma mater.

You can say the same for the extensive alumni travel programs developed by most alumni organizations over the past decade. Again, records show that participants in alumni tours give more generously to university development needs than do nonparticipants. There is evidence of enhanced giving after each individual's travel experience.

Many of the entrepreneurial activities of alumni associations may seem suspect when such operations are performed within an integrated, dependent, advancement program. Independent alumni associations are able, since they are membership organizations, to provide such services without casting doubt as to whether the resources to support them came from the operating budget of the institution itself.

Perhaps the greatest service that a program can provide for alumni is in continuing education. Education is the main responsibility of universities, colleges, and schools. For these institutions to take seriously the role of alumni, continuing education is a plus that ultimately helps both the individual and the institution.

The Alumni Investment

The bottom line of fund raising is that donors must have a strong commitment to the cause, and a means of responding to that cause that allows them to feel they are doing something worthwhile and that the recipient recognizes their efforts. Through alumni relations programs, donors have the opportunity to be recognized in front of their peers. Alumni publications are most helpful in providing recognition of donors and gifts.

Although most alumni may be capable of giving some of their resources to the institution, perhaps an equally valuable role they can perform is to serve as volunteers in soliciting others. Alumni are excellent person-to-person fund raisers and often are excellent contacts with corporations and foundations.

The president who wishes to maximize the return on his or her alumni investment needs to start that investment process *while students are in school.* A former president of the University of Michigan, Alexander Ruthven, wrote what he entitled the Michigan Creed. Here is its introduction:

> We believe that the student should be trained as an alumnus from matriculation: He enrolls in the university for life and for better or worse he will always remain an integral part of the institution.
> We believe that the relations between the alumnus and his university should be beneficial to both, and that the mutual assistance provided by the graduates and by the institution should be limited only by their powers of services.
> We believe that to the person who has obtained what he should from his alma mater, Michigan is the factual expression of a practical idealism—government, religion, and state-supported education being inseparable;
> We believe that to the university the alumnus is a member of a brotherhood bound by the spiritual tie of faith in the ideals of education.

As President Ruthven appropriately indicated, the relationship between alumni and their alma mater is one that endures for life, and the obligation begins upon matriculation. Thus, student-alumni programs are very important in transforming students into alumni leaders. Student leaders turn out to be alumni leaders. The ranks of alumni volunteer leaders invariably include people who have held positions in student government, fraternities, sororities, and other student organizations.

The president who cares for a viable program of private support needs to think of alumni as members of the campus community. In a very real way, the role played by alumni equals that of students, faculty, and administrators. You need to acknowledge that alumni, in addition to their altruistic views about their alma mater, have another, more selfish, vested interest. They understand that regardless of when they received their degree, its value is almost always measured by a current interpretation of the institution's quality. Thus, it is in their best interest to assure that this quality is both sustained and increased in the future. Appeals to alumni on that basis are sound, and bring results.

The Alumni Administrator

The president must understand that the person on his or her professional staff who manages the alumni relations program must be recognized as an individual with opinions worthy of consideration at the upper echelons of institutional management. For a competent alumni administrator not only is responsible for the outreach program to alumni, but is viewed by alumni as the person to whom they can address their concerns, questions, and counsel.

The alumni director wears two hats: institutional administrator and alumni leader. Although volunteer leadership by definition provides the policies that drive alumni activities, the senior alumni administrator is viewed as the individual who manages alumni affairs in the manner of chief executive officers of other organizations. Quality alumni professionalism is necessary to create the kind of resource that you as president need to successfully conduct an advancement program.

Alumni feel that the relationship between the alumni director and the president indicates the president's view on the importance of the alumni effort. If you view alumni as an integral part of the university community, like faculty and students, then a senior alumni administrator should have a role which equals that of those individuals responsible for leadership in other areas of the community.

The analogy of cultivation and harvest, although trite, directly relates to successful fund-raising activity. The professional fund raiser and the professional alumni relations person have expertise in different areas. To treat them as equals helps the president's fund-raising program. In recent years, alumni relations activities have tended to be subordinate to those of fund raising. Surveys have shown that alumni administrators are not as well compensated as their fund-raising counterparts. Perhaps even more unfortunate has been the subordination of alumni relations activities to fund-raising organizations. This latter practice not only severely handicaps the alumni administrator's role as a professional, but it sends a message to alumni that their activities are not viewed with the degree of importance afforded other advancement areas—or that they themselves are seen only as sources of financial support.

Looking Forward

It should go without saying that alumni are educated people. As such, it is important that they play a societal role not only in advancing the cause of education but also in addressing the challenges that confront the world around them. Some look upon the educational mission as the training of problem-solvers. After training people to think critically, many educational institutions assume that they have discharged their responsibilities. But educated people *never* are without the need to better understand both themselves and the world in which they live. Thus it seems grossly unfortunate that the continuing education and enrichment of alumni, long a part of alumni relations rhetoric, has not received emphasis. In fact, perhaps there is no greater service that an educational institution can perform than to take seriously the mission of alumni continuing education.

By using the infrastructure developed by the alumni relations program, continuing education can be incorporated into club, reunion, travel, constituent society, and other programs. Such activities allow the educational process to continue, and provide credence for alumni relations programs. Alumni brought back into the educational process are more likely to respond favorably to requests for support of that process.

By making the educational process lifelong, we tie alumni into the institutional mainstream. As students, alumni are then always able to view their alma mater with the enthusiasm normally reserved for the halcyon days of their youth. Alumni continuing education also opens the doors to for-credit and degree-granting programs for alumni, which could help provide an answer to the continuing problem of declining enrollments.

The Presidential Asset

Developing a sound and diverse alumni relations program is essential to a president's fund-raising aspirations. Such a program takes advantage of the great affection that alumni have for their alma mater, and the vested interest they have in maintaining institutional quality.

Alumni need to be treated as full and equal partners in the educational community, and should be appreciated for their ideas and volunteer work, not just their financial support.

A viable alumni relations program is a mix of service opportunities for alumni to their alma mater, and services provided to alumni themselves. Such programs can largely be supported by the alumni and administered under policies they develop, regardless of the specific organizational structure.

Alumni continuing education is a direction in which all alumni relations programs should move because it provides another direct link between the institutional mission and the alumni body. Making the educational process a lifelong experience serves the alumni, the institution, and society itself.

Presidents and alumni have the same mutual objective: the well-being of the institution. If alumni believe that they are viewed as full members of the educational community, appreciated for their talents, leadership, and counsel as well as their financial resources, they can become an extraordinary presidential asset.

11

THE ANNUAL FUND

William R. Lowery

When, as president, you think about the annual fund, you probably think of it as a useful budget supplement, something whose size you inherited along with your office furniture. It's larger than you'd find at some institutions, smaller than at others—certainly it's smaller than you'd like it to be. Whatever its size, you think there's not much to be done about it. Obviously, there's not much *you* can do about it.

While I won't argue that you ought to start personally training phonathon callers, there are things you *can* do to improve the operation of the annual fund at your institution *and* increase its size. And the place to begin is with your own imagination.

First, let's define the terms: *Here* we'll be talking about gifts for operating support from alumni, parents, and friends, either directly or through their foundations or their privately owned companies. You'll read *elsewhere* in this book about support from larger foundations, and from corporations.

Let's begin by imagining what it's like to be a donor. We have to remember, first, that no one *has* to give. Even in this country, where philanthropy flourishes, individuals *choose* to give—or not to. And while their choice has something to do with their sense of duty and responsibility, it finally boils down to how they imagine themselves. That is, it depends on how they picture themselves—how they see themselves in relation to others, and to the world in which they grew up.

One bright young woman I spoke to, a hard worker who gave generously of her time to her collegiate employer, said she couldn't imagine *giving* to that institution: It just wasn't part of her heritage. A second-generation Asian–American, she said that organized philanthropy wasn't part of her upbringing. Perhaps she stated more openly than most what many Americans feel. They don't see themselves as among those who give support, even though they know intellectually that *someone* provides it. Maybe they weren't trained by parents, church, or synagogue to help the less fortunate. Maybe they didn't breathe an atmosphere of giving out of privileged responsibility (*noblesse oblige*). For whatever reason, they can't imagine themselves doing it.

Now, there are many reasons why people won't give to their college or university. For some it's bad memories, a weak major, a sense that time has passed them by. Others think that we embrace the wrong mission. Some feel shame because they think they can't give what they should, so they give nothing. Some simply think that providing support is a task that belongs to others, not to them.

And so on. But if there are dozens of reasons *not* to give, the reasons why people *do* give are few: They give because they believe in what we do. They give because they believe that what we seek to accomplish is like what they hope their lives will accomplish. They give out of pride, affection, love, respect. They give small gifts, that is, for much the same reason that they give large ones: because their hearts tell them to. (To be sure, some will give because they think they *should*. But those gifts, unlike the ones prompted by the heart, rarely grow with increased resources and the passage of time. And while all of us depend to some extent on the gifts that are prompted by "oughtness," we'll spend more time here thinking about the gifts from the heart.) What it all boils down to is that reasons, negative or positive, are really only outward reflections of individuals' pictures of themselves. The difference is in the way people imagine themselves.

You and I know, of course, that operating support must come from hundreds or thousands of persons. We see those donors as a group. But it's not the group that gives. It's individuals like you and me who give, one at a time. Some voice has to prompt each of those persons, some nudging whisper that says, "Yes, you are a supporting, creating person. You are coming closer to attaining your life's goal by helping this institution, whose goal you also embrace."

The task of your college or university, then, is to make individuals— alumni, parents, friends—imagine themselves to be supporters of your institution, to imagine themselves as integral to your success, to see themselves as among the loyal believers, the inner circle, the fortunate ones who are as useful to society as your institution is itself. To see how that might be possible, we ought to see what the characteristics of an annual fund are, what has to happen to make a fund work, and who might be involved and how. Finally, we ought to see what you as president can do to foster this process, and perhaps to aid it yourself.

The Characteristics of the Annual Fund

Unlike most capital support, operating support—what the annual fund provides—comes mostly in small gifts, from many donors. (Both "small" and "many" are relative terms. Small may be $25 or $2,500; many may be 300 or 150,000.) And again, unlike capital support, annual-fund support comes in the form of gifts that repeat fairly regularly, if not every year.

Whereas it's a tenet of major-gift development work that every potential donor is unique and must be approached as an individual, annual-fund workers know that certain mass appeals are effective. This is true as long as these appeals recognize that there are categories of potential annual-fund donors. (For instance: alumni, friends, parents; old, middle-aged, young; rich, poor; near, far; enthusiastic, dutiful, grudging.)

Donors usually repeat the gift they made the year before, unless something happens to shift their image of themselves-in-relation-to-our-institution. If that happens, they may give more, or they may give less. For instance, John may see in the Honor Roll of Donors that Sam— a friendly rival during college days—has become a President's Society member. John, long a member of the Century Club at $100, has never thought of himself as a $1,000 donor, but if Sam can do it, maybe he can, too. His imagination begins to reshape his concept of himself in relation to his college. Within two years, he becomes a President's Society member himself.

Another example: Old Siwash begins to crow about the extraordinary intellectual accomplishments of most current students. Susan, comfortable with herself and aware that she and many of her classmates would never make it at Siwash today, sees little of herself in current descriptions, and decides that the college today and the college so vivid in her imagination are two different places. So she decreases her gift.

No matter how positive the donor's image of self-in-relation-to-institution, the donor won't repeat the gift—at least not many times— if he or she receives no attention. That attention has two crucial phases (though there may be others): You must ask the donor every year, and you must thank the donor for every gift.

Finally, for all that's necessary to occur as it must, the annual fund must calendar its plans many months in advance. It's more closely tied to the calendar than any other form of fund raising has to be, and that calendar becomes amazingly intricate.

What Happens if Your Annual Fund Must Maintain Itself or Increase?

For a start, you have to know where the people are and who they are: demography. More than a buzz word, demography tells your staff how they might segment their targets, the potential donors. To get accurate demographic data, you must have good records and flexible computer programs to ferret out answers to questions the original program designers didn't think of.

If we agree that our appeal must ultimately be to the potential donor's imagination, we also must agree that imagination is not a uniform faculty. That is, every person's imagination must work with familiar experience. We can use our demographic data to determine which experiences are common to the members of various segmented groups. For instance, you may know that classes that entered your university for a time after World War II started are fragmented, uncohesive, mostly female. Or that classes from the sixties feel disenfranchised because national fraternities disappeared in the seventies. Or that students from the fifties, aware that admissions standards were lower then, feel your college is "too good for them" now. (Every university or college has crotchets in its history.) So appeals to those groups may want to address their idiosyncrasies, directly or indirectly.

These principles, incidentally, apply to parents and friends as well as to alumni. Geography may dictate an appeal to local pride. Parents can see themselves as important recruiters for an institution they've come to believe in, thereby bolstering the significance of their financial support.

When we have some idea of how people see themselves vis-à-vis the college or university, we can figure out how to imply a relationship. (Remember: The potential donor creates the relationship. What we do is suggest the relationship's "shape.") If what we imply makes sense to potential donors, they can then make the imaginative leap to belonging. And when that's happened, they're on the way to being actual, not potential, donors.

A couple of examples. A few years ago, Pomona College sent a letter to alumni reflecting on the significance of Pomona, Roman goddess of abundance, generously distributing her largess to her subjects. Recipients of that letter could easily see how they had benefited from the gifts of the *institution* Pomona. And apparently they did make the imaginative leap to seeing themselves as children of both the institution and the goddess, for they responded with amazing generosity. (This happened, by the way, long after I had left annual giving at Pomona. I'm not beating my own drum.)

Even those who have never crossed Harvard Yard will find in David McCord's remarkable letters, reprinted in *In Sight of Sever*, frequent signals to make the reader imagine himself (for these letters were written when Harvard had only alumni, not alumnae) an active, receiving, and *giving* part of a great, thriving university.

Those are both general examples, depending for their success upon relative homogeneity among a constituent group. But our demographic analysis, coupled with knowledge of our institution's past and personality, lets us work up special appeals. There have been highly successful approaches to war-year classes, built upon the shared abnormalities of those times. Great campaigns have focused on single classes, in celebration of major reunions. (Not just Yale and Carleton have had spectacular twenty-fifth reunion funds, although Yale's Class of 1960 and Carleton's Class of 1962 set exceptional examples for other institutions.) Other kinds of segmentation lend themselves to success: based on age, on undergraduate majors or extracurricular interests, on athletic pride, and on unique shared historical experiences.

The point is that our messages have the power to establish or maintain a bond, a bond that can exist only in the imagination. Or they can destroy it.

But we have to remember that the annual-fund office does not control all messages sent. Lots of people send signals about the potential relationships between your target and your institution: the alumni office, all the people who sponsor events and send invitations, the staffs of the women's board, the athletic boosters, and the parents' council—what's done by the faculty, the career planning office, the dean of students, and the admissions folks. All of this has an impact on what our potential donors think.

Do I belabor the obvious to say that we must *ask* our potential donors? Although we all know that every person wants to be needed, both as an individual and for what he or she can create in the world, it's easy to forget this. Giving is a way to create. But only those with supremely active imaginations are likely to think on their own of creating by giving. We have to help them. That means asking, asking directly, asking for a specific amount.

As for your approach, remember that the potential donor usually wants to help you. But he or she also wants to do what's right. If the request is vague ("Won't you please give something?") the donor sees no guidelines, and—not sure whether $15 or $1,500 would be appropriate—may decline the opportunity for fear of being embarrassed. (If you think that only a gift of $100 or more is appropriate, then you feel embarrassed to give $10.)

While staff members may write the mail appeals or coach the callers, those ostensibly doing the asking must be credible: a classmate, fellow parents, an alumni leader, respected townspeople, perhaps even student leaders. And they have to ask in an effective, positive, upbeat way.

As supervisory professionals, you and I need to know the main ways to ask: via mail, telephone, mail and telephone linked, special campaigns (classes, parents, reunions, athletes in general, Coach Smith's best teams), and personal peer request. Even if we're not directing campaigns ourselves, it's useful to know the principal benefits of each method.

Mail helps most in explaining why gifts are necessary and how an institution will spend the money. Mailed messages, because they can command more time and thought from the recipient, can work hard to show how deserving the institution is. Personal contact by phone can produce increased gifts that rarely result from mail appeals. Phone–mail techniques help persuade recalcitrant nondonors, and special campaigns and peer requests work best at getting high-end annual-fund support.

We should also understand that perks generate some kinds of annual-fund support: better football tickets, the guaranteed opportunity to meet the president, invitations to all the art openings, the honor of belonging to the Dean's Circle. An individual who gives solely to receive perks will probably not increase his or her gift.

Finally, remember that stewardship completes the process. Appropriate thanks sent personally to the donor prepare him or her to give the next gift. Public thanks in your institution's Honor Roll of Donors, in the form of lists of names with appropriate honorific designations, can invoke competitive spirit among constituents, urging them to imagine themselves belonging to a new philanthropic category.

What People Must Do to Make the Annual Fund a Success

Some tasks belong necessarily to staff members. They must plan the basic marketing strategy. They have to figure out how to allocate the budget, how to segment their constituents, how to set up their eighteen-month calendar. They plan the mail campaign, including writing all the appeals or having them written. Ditto the phone campaign, including recruiting callers (paid or volunteer). If there are to be reunion campaigns, staffers must enlist chairs, make sure committees are appointed, set up campaign calendars, and run donor-evaluation meetings. Halfway through the year, they have to design next year's calendar and plan the next budget request.

But volunteers play an important part, too—at least at many institutions. They can nudge the staff, brainstorm with staff members, and maybe provide some of the best ideas. By expressing publicly their belief in what your institution does, they can provide the peer examples that will make the campaign credible. Some will do one-on-one soliciting for you; that's where annual-fund campaigning begins to resemble major gift work. They'll identify and recruit workers. And if your program is on its way to real success, they'll identify and recruit leadership replacements.

There's another reason to invest time, energy, and money to use volunteers, even if you think a staff person might do the job more swiftly and efficiently. The involved person will more likely imagine him- or herself as a philanthropic leader, and therefore give more. This simple lesson is as true for annual-fund donors as for board of trustees members, and its converse is equally true: The uninvolved person probably will give less.

Beyond your internal strengths—staff members and volunteers— you may need to enlist outsiders. At smaller institutions you may need to employ graphics specialists. (Creating and reinforcing your positive image is too important to be left to amateurs. Good design is breath-takingly expensive, but it's worth the money.) Sometimes you need to hire outside writers, though it's best to grow these internally if you can. You may hire experts to train your phonathon callers, or sometimes to run the whole phone campaign. And if you're working with a development consultant, perhaps one helping you with a major capital campaign, he or she may be able to give sound advice to the annual-fund staff, too.

Since the point of much of this, of course, is to keep the ideas flowing, this may be the place to say that it's good to give your annual-fund staff members, and maybe the lead volunteers, too, a chance to go to professional meetings—CASE meetings, of course: Special-focus national meetings help your professional staff, and both they and lead volunteers can benefit from district meetings. They'll get good ideas, both in formal sessions and in casual talk with newly met colleagues. Sometimes meetings of the National Society of Fund-Raising Executives (NSFRE) local chapter are useful. There may be a local group called Women in Development. Encourage staff to attend as many of these as you can afford, and urge them to build informal networks with colleagues at similar institutions.

What You Can Do as President

You can see that we've already begun to talk about how you can boost the process that generates your annual operating support. Let's look at other ways in which you can strengthen this part of your team.

It should go without saying that you'll urge your chief development officer to hire the best possible annual-fund staff members. The annual fund is a great area in which a person can begin a development career. What will your annual-fund chief look for in hiring a junior person? The same characteristics you want in the chief: persuasive verbal abilities (in both writing and speaking), spectacular organizational skill, great energy, friendly demeanor, excellent ability to get along with others, and optimism. Previous experience in other development tasks may not help as much as it hinders, because other development areas don't depend so much on calendars.

But even if the people you hire have no other development experience, you should still pay them as generously as you can: You'll keep them longer. (Experienced and successful annual-fund people are in high demand.) You may be training them for other positions in your shop. Many, if not most, senior development officers have had some annual-fund experience. Always remember that the lessons learned in managing a successful annual fund are basic to all development work. And if you're lucky, your junior annual-fund staff will have matured their leadership potential by the time your annual-fund chief accepts other responsibilities (ideally in your own shop).

Give the annual-fund staff the resources they need to cultivate and solicit. First, provide an adequate budget. What you spend will be repaid many times. Second, give technical support. No one can do an optimal job without modern computer facilities, flexible programs, good administrative computing help, and an excellent records setup. For a strong phonathon program, provide enough phones with easy long-distance access in one room so that callers can generate among themselves the heady enthusiasm that comes from hearing others succeed. To bring your institution up to speed, you may need to make a heavy front-end investment, but that, too, will repay you. Third, provide enough staff. Basic mail programs, and even simple phone programs, may not need heavy staffing, but the programs that bring the largest rewards (like high-end donor-support groups, person-to-person solicitation, and specialized campaigns for parents or reunion classes) are heavily labor-intensive, and you won't be able to mount them effectively if you skimp on staff.

Be available to help, insofar as you can and in accord with the careful plans you and your annual-fund staff make together. This may mean stroking lead volunteers (an invitation to an annual dinner?), thanking donors of gifts above a certain level, cultivating those who are capable of making large annual gifts.

Encourage everyone on your staff, not just those in the development office, to see themselves as development officers. Each can help make donors imagine themselves as ever more generous (and important) philanthropists.

Pay close attention and be involved—but don't overdo it. Too much attention to donors at too low a level may signal desperation, and thus can be counterproductive.

Having hired the best people you can find, let *them* do their work. Respect their ability. Involve yourself as they ask you to, but let *them* manage the details.

A Reminder of What This Is All About

The biggest gifts, both capital and annual, come from the heart. All our constituents, deep in their hearts, imagine themselves doing something useful with their lives. Like them, your institution has a life goal. If you can succeed in making donors and potential donors see that *their* life goals merge with those of your institution, you may capture their imagination.

Imagination, remember, creates personal reality. If that imagination-generated reality includes you and your college or university, then your imaginative, creative donors will bless you with an ever-growing annual fund.

12

CORPORATIONS
AND FOUNDATIONS
Mary Kay Murphy

There is a process of exchange which enables foundations to bring home to the universities ideas about planning for research projects, curriculum planning, and organization of activities which have made real contributions to the planning process, and even to the substantive organization of the university world.—*Adam Yarmolinsky, Principal Advisor to the Commission on Private Philanthropy and Public Needs*

As university president, you have many decisions to make about the extent of support that your institution seeks from corporations and foundations. You have much to say, as well, about the staffing and funding of these operations. In the end, your leadership and interaction with the power structure that drives corporate and foundation grant-making will be the key to the success or failure of your institutional experiences in seeking these sources of private support.

Overview and Assumptions

Whether you inherit a fully operating corporate and foundation program or have none in place at all, you should consider the following:

Do not assume that there will be or should be a corporate and foundation support program. Could the resources you commit to corporate and foundation support be better spent on individual giving programs, either annual or planned gift activities? Would these result in more bottom-line dollars? Do the academic and research strengths of your institutions relate directly to the interests and priorities of corporations and foundations? Do your trustees and faculty have a track record of securing corporate and foundation grants? You will treat fledgling and established grant-seeking programs of corporation and foundation support in very different ways.

Do not assume that corporate or foundation support will be continuous or that such support results from a loosely organized effort. Corporations

126

and foundations generally will not continue their support of an institution with the same grant over many years. Foundations want to support innovative programs and remain flexible in their commitments. Corporations look for strengthening the link between contributions programs and business goals. If your university has not sought such funds in the past, carefully determine which other sources of support might better be sought, including alumni, government, and special grants.

If you go into corporate and foundation fund raising, go for the long term. Expect it to take at least three years to get a program off the ground and to begin return on the investment you initially make in it. Also, expect it to take at least twelve to eighteen months to develop a successful program and proposal. Finally, expect one in seven requests from corporate and foundation sources *not* to be funded.

Do not overestimate the bottom-line dollars that can come from a successful corporate and foundation program. Even though corporations support higher education with more than three-fourths of the dollars they contribute to charitable causes, corporate support represents only 5 percent of total philanthropic contributions. Foundation support represents another 5 percent. Contributions from individuals account for 90 percent of all charitable dollars. Thus, corporate and foundation support represent a limited "market" for higher education. Your challenge is to target this market and carry through on a limited number of grant-making possibilities.

Do not look for short-cuts in establishing or fine-tuning a successful corporate and foundation program. Personalize your relationships with corporations and foundations. Do not be tempted to allow your institution to mass-produce proposals and send them unsolicited to corporate and foundation prospects. Develop a team approach to cultivating and soliciting carefully targeted prospects. The team will need the services of (1) a thorough prospect researcher, (2) a development officer with his or her peers on the foundation or corporate staff, (3) key volunteers or trustees who have high-level contacts on the corporate or foundation board, (4) faculty members with expertise related to the funding source, (5) select administrators of the university who will be accountable for the private grant, and (6) you as head of the team.

You will need to be sure that mechanisms are in place to control the institutional relationship with corporations and foundations. Get assurance from your development and academic administrators that they will present only the most appropriate and best campus project for funding. Require that they have a clear strategy in place to determine when, if ever, multiple submissions and multiple institutional proposals are approved. Make certain that they establish clear communication with corporations and foundations. These funding sources will look for evidence that similar organizations have funded your institution. Yet, be careful about seeking support from corporations and foundations for the same project without informing them of your pending requests with other funding sources.

The President's Role

Your leadership of the academic and research programs at the university puts you in a strategic position to initiate the planning process. This is vital to success in corporate and foundation fund raising. Early in your administration, you will likely set up a process to develop a strategic plan for the institution. Long-range goals will result from this management process. Without such a planning mechanism, your institution can expect to have little or no success in securing foundation and corporate funds. Such sources want to know the top priorities of your institution, and whether or not the projects for which you request funds are among those high priorities. Your leadership role will require that you set in motion a dynamic planning process that identifies changes in priorities over time.

There are several other areas in which your leadership will be especially important to a successful corporate and foundation support program:

Maintain Visibility. Your academic and research record and that of your institution will be on display every time you seek corporate and foundation support. Your track record and your commitment to future achievement in specific areas of the curriculum will also be important keys in your institution's ability to attract attention, submit competitive proposals, and secure corporate and foundation funding.

For your part, be ready and willing to go on calls to meet corporate and foundation officers. Go with the right team members at the right time. Be prepared with specifics about the program's goals, objectives, and evaluation. Do not go on the call unless you are needed. Do not go for an informal visit with the program officer. Neither of you can afford such use of time.

Promote Accountability. Your commitment to prompt reporting of the use and results of corporate and foundation funds will be essential to satisfying the requirements for receiving these funds. Even more important, your commitment to accountability will be essential to success in securing other grants from these sources. Make sure your development office and academic and research offices work together closely to prepare interim and final reports, and judiciously adhere to the purposes for which corporations and foundations make these grants.

Cultivate Networks. Your previous academic and research relationships will come into play as you look for key contacts on corporate and foundation boards and staffs. Your institution will look to you to find out whom you know among the country's top leaders of corporations and foundations. Cultivate this network and use your leverage and influence to help your institution gain access to compete for corporate and foundation support.

These contacts will come from a variety of sources, including higher-education associations, professional societies, and personal friends. Your leadership role in your institution and community requires you to take an active part in the influence network that drives corporate and foundation grant-making. People give money to people they know and trust. Your responsibility as a college president requires you to get to know these people of influence, to benefit your institution.

If you do not know these significant people, work closely with your vice president for development to find an alumnus or alumna, a trustee, or a faculty member who could help you with an introduction. You will be the *one* person from your institution whom many corporate and foundation officers will want to meet and know. Thus be visible, available, accountable, and willing to seek out influential people in corporations and foundations.

Coordinate Proposals. A successful corporate and foundation program requires that you as university president make a commitment to internal planning that allows the best and most competitive projects to be presented for corporate and foundation funding. Although you will want to honor the tradition of academic freedom as well as the spirit of entrepreneurship, you must face the reality that generally you should submit only one project at a time to each prospective corporation or foundation. The grant-making organization will look to you to select the top institutional priority for funding, and to communicate to the organization's trustees that it is precisely that. You will therefore need to work closely with your vice presidents for academic affairs, research, and development to ensure that an established process selects the best and most competitive projects that relate to your university's highest priorities.

Develop Creative Partnerships. Corporate and foundation support cannot save a flagging university, reverse financial decline, or substitute for a strong endowment. These funds can, however, provide opportunities to collaborate with some of the country's top innovators to create new academic programs, to strengthen areas of the curriculum that show promise, or to invest in an institution that will benefit the corporation and the community it serves. Your presidency will provide you with the compelling experience of creating partnerships with leaders in corporations and foundations.

Depending on the location of your university, its previous history in successfully securing such funds, and its potential for creating new funding successes, you might be a partner in these relationships, or you might be far removed from them. If your institution is or plans to be a major player in the corporate and foundation support game, look at the experience realistically. Enjoy it for its benefit in creating alliances and partnerships to benefit your institution. Do not count on such relationships to substitute for a balanced budget.

The Internal Environment

Chapter 1 outlines the staffing patterns of an efficient development office. In that model, the vice president for development has two directors with fund-raising responsibilities reporting to him or her: the director of the annual fund, and the director for planned giving. In this efficient/advancement area model, the vice president is responsible for prospect major gifts research and corporate foundation cultivation and solicitation. For many institutions, especially smaller, private liberal-arts colleges, this model is appropriate. If however you as president decide to augment this model with a formal corporate and foundation program, or if you inherit a large, structured, and segmented fund-raising staff, another model becomes appropriate (see Figure 12.1).

In this model, you must make several assumptions:

- Your institution has a curriculum, or can develop one, that will appeal to the interests of corporations and to the priorities of foundations.
- Your university has a faculty, or can attract members, whose work corporations or foundations will want to support.
- Your institution's financial resources are such that you can invest more money, not less, in order to raise money by structuring ongoing, full-time programs in the corporate and foundation area.
- Your university trustees, faculty, administrators, and you have developed, or can develop, high-level contact with decision makers in corporations and foundations.
- Your institution's location is an area in which corporations and foundations make grants. If not, your institution has connections

Figure 12.1. AUGMENTED FUND-RAISING PROGRAM.

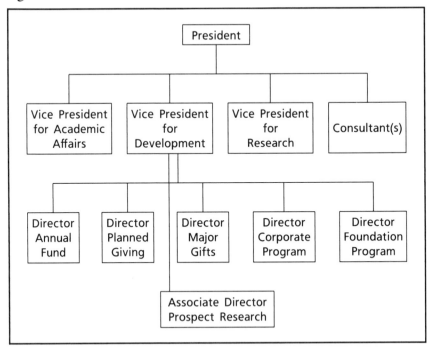

that span geographic limits or produce exceptions to the corporate or foundation guidelines.

- The external funding source sets priorities for corporate and foundation funding. Determining which campus projects to propose for such support will be the responsibility of the vice president for academic affairs or the vice president for research, either one working with the vice president for development.

With assurance that some or all of the preceding assumptions apply to your institution, there are several questions for a segmented fund-raising program and staff to consider.

Should you employ one person to direct the corporate and foundation program, or should you divide the job between two directors?

As you project your market, do you expect that you will have more corporate than foundation opportunities, or vice versa? Will the number of prospects be so great that you cannot cover the territory with only one director? Do you have funding available to set up operations for both a corporate director and a foundation director? Should you initiate both programs at the same time, or should you start one and delay one for a year or more?

After you answer these questions according to your institution's environment and profile, you can make your decision to move forward on the staffing. Or, if you have a corporate and foundation program that is not generating bottom-line income, you should consider eliminating that program.

Should you hire an experienced corporate and foundation officer or should you hire one who will need to be trained?

Experience in this type of fund raising most assuredly counts for a great deal. But then, of course one *can* learn the basics. That's where experience starts. The Council for Advancement and Support of Education, The Grantsmanship Center, and the National Society for Fund Raising Executives offer strong training programs in the techniques and issues related to successful corporate and foundation fund raising. However, the issue might not be that of experienced versus novice fund raiser for the corporate and foundation director's job. Rather, it might be finding a candidate with the right chemistry and character to mix and blend into the culture of your institution. At the core of the character of the person you seek must be integrity of the highest order. Your institution's reputation will go with this individual wherever in corporate or foundation circles he or she moves. You want someone whose word is law, and who does not hide facts or present the truth in any but the most direct way.

What characteristics should you look for in a corporate and foundation officer?

If you create two separate positions, look for individuals with somewhat different backgrounds and experience. The corporate director should have a working knowledge of corporate structure, culture, and product line. In addition, the director should be able to establish credibility with the corporate leaders and faculty members with whom he or she will have to interact. Also, the director will need to be a self-starter who can work the project through to completion, following up assiduously on details. In essence, the director is a broker between the corporation and the university. The success of his or her effort comes from the director's being able to access the highest levels of decision makers in the corporation, to benefit the university's support request.

The foundation officer will share many of the characteristics required by the corporate officer. Yet you will want to take into account the foundation's culture, and employees with whom the director will be interacting. Choose someone who can interact with trustees, bankers, trust officers, lawyers, and foundation staff. Rapport developed by your director with representatives of the foundation will pay dividends for your university in bottom-line foundation support.

If you select only one director to oversee both the corporate and the foundation program, choose someone who has the chemistry and character mix to relate to both corporate and foundation officers. If your program is structured more toward the corporate support side, you should select a director whose background will be compatible with the demands of that sector. The same will be the case if your program is more compatible with foundation funding and only one director can be employed to oversee this territory. Refinements of technique for working with either corporate or foundation officers can be developed as the program matures and the director's responsibilities become more focused.

How much attention should you pay to prospect research on corporations and foundations?

If you want to develop a successful corporate and foundation program, you will want to staff a strong prospect research office. You should employ an associate director for prospect research, as well as two to four full-time researchers, to support the efforts of your corporate and foundation office. CASE offers an annual conference on prospect research related to corporations, foundations, and individuals. A well-organized prospect research office can do much to undergird strong annual-fund, phoned giving, and capital campaign results. Do not underestimate the value and importance of thorough prospect research or the volume of such research required to support a successful corporate and foundation program.

How important are volunteers to the success of corporate and foundation fund raising?

Seek the most influential trustee, alumnus, alumna, and faculty member to help your institution present your case to the corporation and foundation, and involve them as advocates for funding your project. There is no substitute for the role of influence in gaining the attention of the corporation and foundation for a favorable hearing of your cause. However, influence alone will *not* produce grants. That will require excellence of concept, presentation, proposal, and personnel from your institution. Work with your vice president for development to identify those key volunteers already close to your institution who are in a position of influence in a corporation or foundation. This may be an alumnus or alumna who is CEO of a Fortune 500 corporation or a trustee who serves on a national foundation board. Identify these individuals and work closely with them to guide your project through the funding cycle, and advocate its selection over strong competition from other universities.

How much travel of staff and volunteers is there in a successful corporate and foundation program?

There is no substitute for personal contact with corporate and foundation staff and trustees. You should expect your directors to meet with appropriate corporate and foundation staff to establish close working relationships with them. Expect also that these early visits will lay the groundwork for you and the appropriate campus team for later visits with corporate and foundation officers and staff in order to make presentations and set up corresponding visits by the officers and staff to your campus. Budget funds for staff travel, and emphasize your commitment to involve corporate and foundation program officers. It is essential to work with these staff members and not ignore their role in your zeal to work with the corporate CEO or the foundation president.

How do you establish communication among members of the academic and development teams?

Ideally, your development officers are trained to write trip reports and schedule strategy sessions. These are the minimum levels of communication necessary for a successful corporate and foundation program. With your vice presidents for development, academic affairs, and research, establish a screening committee of key academic administrators in your institution to meet monthly with the corporate and foundation directors to review prospects and to suggest projects for preliminary development. Refrain from the temptation to develop full proposals and to complete projects before making contact with prospective corporate and foundation staff.

Collaboration is the watchword in corporate and foundation funding. Thus, have your campus team develop working papers that describe initiatives which your institution would like to explore with the funding source. Work with members of the campus team through the corporate and foundation directors to schedule meetings with significant people at the corporation and foundation. A process such as this, or a variation on it, generates genuine collaboration among campus personnel, and later between campus and corporate or foundation personnel.

Make sure you are included in this information loop, because you must review and approve projects and make visits as the leader of the campus team. Be an active member of this screening committee yourself, and make sure your schedule and your time commitments allow you to participate. During a capital campaign you will be a vital and necessary part of such an internal communication network. Your role in annual-fund and planned giving will also be important with major-gift cultivation and solicitation.

How much will a corporate and foundation program cost?
What return on your investment can you fairly expect?

If you are starting a new program, you can expect as a rule of thumb that about three years will pass before you begin to see a return on your investment. You should aim to keep your fund-raising costs at between 6 and 10 percent of the total raised. As with other areas of fund raising, you should carefully monitor your corporate and foundation program to ensure that the monies you invest in it are yielding the best results for your institution. You cannot make this decision in the first three years of a start-up program, but you can make it after that period has passed.

Corporate and foundation programs are not for every institution. You must have the right mix of curriculum strengths, faculty leadership, alumni and trustee influence, and a competitive profile for your institution. If you decide that these programs are not for your institution, redirect the resources to annual and planned giving, with increased emphasis on planned giving.

The External Environment

As strong and well-planned as your corporate and foundation program might be, there are several external factors over which you have no control and that will influence the success of your fund-raising effort. You must be aware and informed about these aspects of the external environment so that you can exert leadership when it is appropriate and possible. Here are some factors:

Motivation of Corporate and Foundation Philanthropy. In general, the motives of foundation founders and trustees drive foundation programs. But these programs tend to change over time. It is important to identify a university priority that does or will relate directly to these foundation interests if you want to successfully compete for funding. It is also important to monitor changes in these priorities, to ensure that your institution becomes eligible for funding, or to know in advance if it loses ground in its eligibility.

Corporate motives for giving are generally expressed in support for institutions that relate directly to the company product line, either through alumni, academic, research, or geographic connections. As in any exchange, it is important to understand the way your institution might most productively interact when seeking corporation or foundation funding. You should determine as much as you can about the motivation of corporate and foundation philanthropy and then relate to these motives as directly and forthrightly as possible.

Economic Forces. The strength or weakness of national and international business and industrial climates have a direct influence on the size and scope of corporate and foundation support programs. According to the Tax Reform Act of 1969, foundations are required to give away a percentage of income from their assets. Corporations are under no such mandated requirement. Yet many major corporations in this country give away on average up to 2 percent of profits (after taxes) to charities. In the past decade, more than three-fourths of corporate grants have gone to support higher education.

Both corporate and foundation support are closely linked to changes and performance in the stock market. Your director's knowledge of the timing of your proposals to corporations and foundations will be a key factor in the success your institution's experiences in the areas of corporate and foundation support. In addition, your corporate director should be aware of the advantage of stock gifts to your institution just before a private corporation goes public. A close network of influence between your institution and corporate and foundation leaders can benefit the bottom-line gift income that your institution generates.

Tax Reform Acts. When Congress initiates tax reforms, it generally takes several years after such initiatives to determine the results of the legislation. For example, the Tax Reform Act of 1969 for the first time imposed on foundations the requirement to disclose to the public information about awards, grantees, amount of awards, and assets and trustees of the foundation. The act also required foundations to make gifts based on percentage of assets owned by the foundation. Generally, foundations do not seem to have increased their level and percentage of giving to higher education since passage of that act.

The Tax Reform Act of 1981, conversely, established tax benefits for corporations manufacturing equipment that research universities would use. Several years after passage, the act appears to be a boon both to the university receiving the equipment gift and to the corporation manufacturing it and making the gift.

Some alarmists predicted that the Tax Reform Act of 1986 would initially decimate the total amount of private support from individuals to higher education. Perhaps it is still too early to tell, but it appears that these early negative predictions are unfounded. Whatever the case, you as the university president should seek the best legal and tax advice about changes in these tax laws as they affect charitable giving, and then map your institution's plan of action.

Commissions and Publications of Influence. There are specialized publications that will help you as you read and keep current on issues and trends in corporate and foundation giving. Classic foundation works by F. Emerson Andrews, Merimon Cunningham, John Nason, David Freeman, and the writings of Waldemar Nielsen, all should be on your bookshelf. (See the Bibliography at the end of this chapter). Also, you will want to read *America's Competitive Challenge: The Need for a National Response,* and *Corporate and Campus Cooperation: An Action Agenda,* both from the Business-Higher Education Forum. Another key reference for your attention is The Council on Foundations' helpful primer, *Corporate Philanthropy: Philosophy, Management, Trends, Future, and Background.* Must reading are the yearly reports on *Giving USA* from the American Association of Fund Raising Counsel, and *Voluntary Support of Education* from the Council for Aid to Education. You will want to read these and other similar sources, get to know the writers and opinion makers involved with these publications, and position yourself to use your experience as a college president to serve on committees and councils which will be formed to study trends and issues relating to philanthropy.

Trends in Corporate and Foundation Support. As you set up the process of evaluating your institution's corporate and foundation program on a quarterly and yearly basis, keep in mind the impact of issues and trends that will likely affect these philanthropic initiatives. These issues in the area of corporate contributions, identified in studies by the Conference Board, the American Association of Fund Raising Counsel, the Council for Aid to Education, and others, include the following:

1. The link between the contributions function and business goals strengthened.

2. Dollar amounts likely have plateaued and declines in giving levels are imminent. Thus there will be more attention on leveraging dollars and staffs as well as on use of nonfinancial resources.

3. Available dollars will come from medium-sized and smaller business, and traditional "big players" will take reduced roles.

4. There will be dramatic shifts in the industries which will stand out as future leaders in the support of higher education.

5. Cause-related marketing and similar programs probably will increase in popularity.

6. Globalization and an increased concern for the health of the community will greatly alter the flow of funds to other not-for-profit institutions. It is also predicted that there will be fewer new foundations to develop in the years ahead, resulting in a greater need to value the contributions of existing foundations. Finally, the impact of the Tax Reform Act of 1986 on foundation assets and funds with which to make grants is not yet clear.

Summary

As a university president, you have an opportunity to play a strong leadership role in the success of your institution's fund raising from corporate and foundation sources. Review your role in this enterprise carefully. Monitor the internal and external environments judiciously as to their impact on the bottom-line success of these programs. And continue to read and learn about the influence of these dimensions of the third sector on higher education.

In considering your role as university president who will provide leadership in successfully securing corporate and foundation support, remember the words of Franklin Roosevelt: "This is what the office of the Presidency is . . . a superb opportunity for reapplying and applying, in new conditions, the simple rules of human content to which we always go back. Without leadership alert and sensitive to change, we are bogged down or lose our way."

Attentive leadership on your part not only will guide your institution, but also will help you find your way to success in corporate and foundation fund raising as a part of a total fund-raising effort.

Bibliography

Andrews, F. Emerson. *Philanthropic Foundations.* New York: Russell Sage Foundation, 1956.

Chein, Earl F., and Theodore E. Lobman, eds. *Foundations and Higher Education: Grant Making-from Golden Years through Steady State.* Berkeley,

CA: Ford Foundation and the Carnegie Council on Policy Studies in Higher Education, 1979.

Corporate Philanthropy: Philosophy, Management, Trends, Future, and Background. Washington, DC: Council on Foundations, 1982.

Cunningham, Merimon. *Private Money and Public Service: The Role of Foundations in American Society.* New York: McGraw-Hill, 1972.

Edie, John A. *First Steps in Starting A Foundation.* Washington, DC: Council on Foundations, 1987.

Foundation Grants Index, 16th Edition. New York: The Foundation Center, 1987.

Freeman, David. *Handbook on Private Foundations.* Englewood Cliffs, Prentice-Hall, 1973.

Giving USA. New York: American Association of Fund Raising Counsel Trust for Philanthropy, 1987.

Heimann, Fritz F., ed. *The Future of Foundations.* Englewood Cliffs, Prentice-Hall, 1973.

Hodgkinson, Virginia Ann, and Murray Weitzman. *Dimensions of the Independent Sector.* Washington, DC: Independent Sector, 1986.

Koch, Frank. *The New Corporate Philanthropy: How Society and Business Can Profit.* New York: Plenum Press, 1979.

Nason, John W. *Trustees and the Future of Foundations.* New York: Council on Foundations, Inc., 1977.

National Data Book, 11th Edition. New York: The Foundation Center, 1987.

Nielsen, Waldemar A. *The Big Foundations.* New York: Columbia University Press, 1972.

————. *The Golden Donors.* New York: Truman Talley Books, 1985.

O'Connell, Brian. *America's Voluntary Spirit: A Book of Readings.* New York: The Foundation Center, 1987.

Odendahl, Teresa, and Elizabeth Boris. "The Grantmaking Process." *Foundation News,* September/October 1983.

Pekkanen, John. "The Great Givers, Part I and Part II." *Town and Country,* December 1979 and January 1980.

Renz, Loren, ed. *The Foundation Directory, 11th Edition.* New York: The Foundation Center, 1987.

Roisman, Lois. "The Community Foundation Connection." *Foundation News,* March/April 1982.

Rowland, A. Wesley, general editor. *Handbook of Institutional Advancement* 2d ed. San Francisco: Jossey-Bass, 1986.

Russell, John M. *Giving and Taking: Across the Foundation Desk.* New York: Teachers College Press, 1977.

Weaver, Warren. *U.S. Philanthropic Foundations: Their History, Structure, Management and Record.* New York: Harper and Row, 1967.

Whitaker, Ben. *The Philanthropoids: Foundations and Society.* New York: Morrow, 1974.

13

FINANCING THE DEVELOPMENT PROGRAM

Gary A. Evans

"You've got to spend money to raise money." College and university presidents and chief financial officers have heard that statement so often, usually from the chief development officer at budget time, that their eyes glaze over. They may even tune out the budget request under consideration. Although the saying is correct, their reaction is understandable—*if* the request for greater funding of development is based solely on the assertion that it takes money to make money. There should be a solid explanation appended of how added investment in development will yield desirable returns for the institution.

This chapter has two purposes: to encourage you, as chief executive, to be generous in funding your development effort; and to provide you with some guidelines to help you determine the reasonableness of your investment relative to the return. Before considering these guidelines, you should understand two broad principles of development as background for making budgetary decisions:

1. *You should know that good development programs grow over time.* If you are at an institution that has no development office or has a development program that has done very little, there are some fund-raising strategies that can generate positive results in a short time. If staff have used direct mail alone in your institution's annual-fund appeal, you can get a dramatic increase in giving by introducing a phonathon. Introducing a challenge grant into an annual-fund program can also bring significant increases. However, while you can get short-term improvements in giving by introducing new techniques for asking, the long-term dramatic growth that most colleges and universities need requires other solutions.

Substantial increases in private support from alumni, friends, corporations, and foundations come from cultivating *long-term*, mutually satisfying and rewarding relationships between potential donors and the

140

institution. Your development office must be the agent for building those relationships, with you as a key player. A relationship between an individual and an institution that results in a dramatic major gift seldom is one that matured overnight. Such a connection requires time to be germinated, cultivated, nurtured, and brought to fruition. When you invest in your development office you should expect results. But you should know that the best results take time and require consistent, not erratic, support.

2. *You should have a general understanding of the component parts of a full development program.* To be effective, your development program should include annual giving, corporate and foundation support, donor research, major gifts, records, and stewardship. For institutions with older potential donors among their alumni and friends, a planned giving program for bequests and trust commitments is important. For institutions dealing primarily with younger constituents, a planned giving program probably would not be a sound investment.

Knowing how many component parts there are to an effective development program, you can see why it takes time to build one. In allocating resources to your development program, you should make certain that the funds are invested in some approximate proportion to the potential for support from various sources, even if it will take time to realize that potential. Because major gifts will probably produce 80 percent or more of your gift results, you should make certain that the budget for the development office has a significant portion allocated for donor research, cultivation, and involvement of major gift prospects. And the budget should not be disproportionate in its support of annual giving programs, even though they may generate more immediate results. While your development office should include all elements of a comprehensive development program, the development budget should be apportioned according to your gift potential, and not based on the staffing distribution at other institutions.

With these broad principles in mind, what are some of the guidelines you might use to determine the appropriate level of funding for your development office? As you read these, you will readily understand that they are guidelines, not rules. Each may change according to the institution. Apply all with considerable flexibility.

Overall Development Program

If your development program costs you 20–25 cents per dollar raised, you are probably on the high side of an acceptable range. However, if your development program is new, and so trying some new initiatives, or if you are adding staff and new programs of donor cultivation, then a development budget costing 20–25 percent of funds raised is reasonable. For an established program, even one trying new initiatives but not necessarily making significant increases in staff, then 14–17 percent suggests an efficient operation and effective results.

If your development office costs you less than 10 cents per dollar raised, you can conclude one of two things. Either your development office is very effective, comprising experienced people and good programs producing maximum results for the investment, or you are spending modestly and benefiting modestly. It always seems desirable to minimize cost. But this can be a false economy if you are letting budgetary constraints keep you from tapping a potentially greater gift income. A careful analysis of gift potential should suggest whether an additional investment, though possibly raising the cost per dollar raised, would also yield increased gift income.

Specific Fund-Raising Programs

In addition to having some guidelines to evaluate your development costs compared to funds raised, you should know how much it might cost to adequately fund the component fund-raising activities within the development program.

Annual Fund. The cost of successful annual-fund programs can range from 15 percent to 35 percent of funds raised. In fact, an institution with a traditionally modest annual giving program but making a special investment to improve it might find the cost to approach 50 percent for a year or two! This is simply because the annual fund solicits large numbers of people who make modest gifts. And yet the budget for the annual giving program has fixed costs for staff, publications, and postage that may be nearly equal to the budget for major gifts. Yet the average return for major gifts is much higher. Remember also that the annual-giving program heavily emphasizes donor acquisition: It always costs more to attract a donor for the first time. As previous donors continue and new donors arrive, the fixed costs may vary little, but should decline as a percentage of gift income, since the annual-fund program costing 25–35 cents per dollar raised is reasonable.

Major Gifts. If the overall cost of the development program is about 15 percent of gift income and the cost of the annual fund runs as high as 25–35 percent, one of the fund-raising programs must be yielding support at lower cost. This program is *major* gifts. Typically, the cost of running a major gift program will be *below* 10 cents per dollar raised.

This suggests where you should make additional investments if you find gift potential high.

Corporate and Foundation Giving. The cost of corporate fund raising compares to the cost of major gifts and should be below 10 cents per dollar raised. The cost of a foundation program is even less, probably not exceeding 5 cents per dollar raised.

Deferred Gifts. It is very difficult to estimate the cost of a deferred-gifts program because time between when the cost is incurred and the gift received can be substantial. It may take effort and time, ranging from little to considerable, to negotiate a codicil to a will or to set up an income trust. Yet it may be several *years* before the institution receives a gift. An extensive study prepared for the Lilly Endowment, Inc., by Fink and Metzler, suggests that the cost of a deferred-gifts program, using current value of deferred gifts, is below 10 cents per dollar, and probably closer to 5 cents.

Capital Campaign

Your institution probably will want a separate budget for a capital campaign. You may fund it with an appropriation from quasi-endowment, to be repaid from unrestricted campaign receipts, or from earnings on restricted campaign gifts before use of the principal. In any event, a campaign will require up-front funding to be successful.

Basing their experience on a broad range of campaigns, fund-raising consultants advise that the campaign budget will be between 3 percent and 10 percent of the total campaign goal. For a $20 million campaign, this is a wide range for a budget estimate—from $600,000 to $2 million. The following factors will determine whether your institution is at the high or low end of the range.

The Size of the Campaign. The budget for smaller campaigns moves toward the upper end of the range because certain fixed costs have to be covered, even for campaigns with smaller goals. These costs include computer software and hardware, fund-raising consultants, promotional films, and so on. As campaigns increase in size, these fixed costs form a smaller percentage of the campaign goal.

Adequacy of Current Development Funding. If your institution has an adequately funded and effective development program, the incremental cost for a campaign will be less than if your campaign must cover expenses for activities not previously performed in the development office. For instance, if your ongoing development program has done a good job of donor identification and research, there may be only marginal cost for additional prospect research. However, if your donor list is thin and you need a major program of field research before the campaign, the budget must be higher.

Track Record in Fund Raising. If you are president of an institution with a good fund-raising history and previous success in capital campaigns, you probably have two things going for you to help you maintain the campaign budget at a lower percentage of campaign goal. First, your previous success probably suggests greater gift potential. This will allow you to consider a higher campaign goal, and the campaign budget as a percentage of goal will be somewhat less. Second, your previous success also suggests that you have experienced staff and volunteers. In fund raising, as in other activities, experienced people often can produce greater results with more efficient application of budget resources.

Centralized versus Decentralized Campaign. At an institution in which the campaign and associated development activities are managed by a single development office, the cost as a percentage of goal will be less than at an institution where campaign staffing is decentralized. Decentralization can bring redundancy of staff and services. However, you may *need* decentralization where alumni loyalty goes to units or schools of the institution.

Paying the Bill

Assuming that you have decided on an appropriate funding level for your development program, what sources are open to you to pay the bill? If you are in a private college or university, you can probably use the general income of the institution. Income from tuition, unrestricted endowment and gifts, campaign receipts and other unrestricted sources, all are available. Although these are the same income sources that must cover many institutional needs, there are probably few, if any, restrictions outside your institution's budgeting process to prevent using these funds for development.

At a public institution your situation may be different. At many public institutions you cannot use state budget funds for development and public relations purposes. However, you may have other sources. These include overhead receipts, unrestricted gifts, and income from unrestricted endowment. You may also find it possible to use state funds for record keeping in development.

More and more, both public and private institutions are seeking to finance the cost of fund-raising by applying an assessment against gifts raised. You can charge an agreed-upon percentage, say 5 percent, on each gift. Or you can hold gifts to the institution—its schools, departments, and programs—in a high-yield account until the gifts earn the agreed-upon return. The gifts can then go to their designated or undesignated purposes, and the 5 percent yield can finance the development program.

Some Helpful Hints

The *preceding* guidelines should help you to assess the appropriateness of your investment in development. The *following* hints are less specific, but should, when associated with the guidelines, help you make your budgeting decisions.

The most important resource in your development office is your people. Because donors rarely develop relationships with impersonal organizations, they usually identify with your institution through someone— often the development officer. After more than twenty-five years of successful development work at the University of Notre Dame, long-time Vice President Jim Frick said, "I never solicited a major gift from someone who wasn't a friend." A major gift results as often from the friendship and closeness between two people—the donor and the development officer—as from the relationship between the donor and your institution. You should compensate your development people adequately so they will not leave for salary reasons alone. It is a false economy to skimp on salaries and turn over staff. Turnover impedes building those relationships that eventually result in substantial support. When development staff leave, more than talented people are lost. Relationships end. And relationships are important to major giving.

Be sure to provide your development staff with an adequate travel budget, and then make sure they get out of the office. They do not need lavish expense accounts, but they do need sufficient travel funds to be where the donors are. You don't raise major gifts sitting behind a development office desk. If there are constraints on funding your development program, you are better off with a few good people adequately funded to travel than with many good people who can't leave the office. A successful development program is people-intensive, and development officers must get out where the people are.

Be prepared to put some money into special events. Banquets and convocations help build spirit and camaraderie. But do not fund large public events at the expense of small intimate occasions. For the most part, you cultivate more potential donors through small VIP occasions (with you there) than through large public events.

Don't cut costs on a consultant. Although you should expect your chief development officer to build and direct your development program, don't conclude that a consultant is unnecessary. As mentioned elsewhere in this book, consultants provide you with an objective viewpoint you cannot get from within, and can serve as both prod and cheerleader for your development staff.

Be wary of the argument that a $20,000 investment in a development officer who can raise $40,000 or $50,000 makes sense. After all, isn't even a 100 percent return a good investment? While this may be an adequate return the first year, projections should reflect a return of *tenfold or more* to justify the initial cost.

Although this chapter has focused on *financing* the development operation, the measure of your investment is your *results.* As the coeditor of this book, James L. Fisher, has said: "Be overly generous in budget; be lean and mean in evaluation." With adequate funding, your development office should measure up well in a lean-and-mean evaluation, and should justify the good judgment you show by investing in it.

14

ANOTHER LOOK
AT COSTS
Paul E. Wisdom

Is a development program expensive? If so, why? Obviously there is some cost to raising money. These costs can range from 8 to 10 percent for long-established programs with built-in appeals and well-to-do constituents (such as major private colleges), to well over 50 percent for some "charities" that rely on large mailing lists of people without strong ties to the cause or institution. These efforts yield a low response rate (1 to 3 percent), and low average gift sizes.

You'll also find that gift money of any magnitude comes in as the result of substantial effort, and consequently at some cost. Even in direct-mail efforts, three mailings will produce roughly triple the results of one, five will bring in five times as much as one, and so on, *up to a certain point.* Obviously, five mailings also cost five times as much as one.

The term "expensive," however, implies excessive—something that costs more than it's worth. With that in mind, let's look at why a development program requires expenditures, and try to gauge how much is appropriate and how much excessive. The largest single cost is personnel. A major reason is that people give to people, and the degree to which you can put that simple truth into action is the degree of success enjoyed by your fund-raising program. For example, direct mail is important in university fund-raising efforts, but primarily as an informational and educational device. It is costly, and does not produce much money. That's why we use phonathons: They produce more per dollar spent. Direct mail may have less than a 3 percent positive response rate; phonathons sometimes exceed 50 percent. That more personalized touch of one person talking to another increases dramatically the percentage of responses and the average gift size.

As important as direct mail and phonathons are to a program, they will raise less than 10 percent of the money in a good program. They are by far the most expensive kinds of fund raising, typically costing over 30 cents per dollar raised. Most of the money, more than 90 percent, will come from only 5 to 10 percent of individuals and organizations contacted. Phonathons, telemarketing, and direct mail are useful in identifying that small number of major prospects—but funds will come only after enough extensive research on that 5 to 10 percent to give a development officer the knowledge to map out a strategy of personalized cultivation. Therefore, all good development programs require time, a great deal of personal attention from fund raisers, and the efforts of faculty, staff, alumni, friends of the institution, and others.

For these reasons there is a high correlation between the number of development staff and dollars raised. However, you cannot simply continue adding staff and bringing in more dollars without hitting a limit. After a development officer covers the basic areas of fund-raising concentration he or she can handle successfully only 50 to 70 major donor prospects. The number of staff should relate to the number of major donor prospects that a program is able to produce.

Development is not only contact-intensive but paper-intensive. Prospects must learn a good deal about the institution, its programs, and its people before they will support it. They need to know what it is, why it's important, its quality, what it will do for them and for others, and why the institution needs their support. Conversely, the fund raiser also needs to know a great deal about prospects in order to maximize chances of success.

You should target much of the consequent information-gathering on discovering whether or not an individual qualifies as a major donor prospect (MDP), someone having the capacity to make a one-time gift of $5,000 or more. Once a person is identified as a MDP, the research efforts and contacts accelerate. Development officers need to find out as much as possible about each individual, in order to devise and develop a successful cultivation strategy. Ultimately each prospect will be asked for a major gift, ideally at the right time for the right purpose in the right amount at the right location and with the right person or persons asking.

A recent national survey of senior development professionals and consultants suggests that an average of nine separate cultivation activities should take place before a major solicitation. The cultivations can take place in a variety of ways and settings. They may include such things as a personal letter from a faculty member, an alumni volunteer, a dean, a development officer, a vice president, a department head, or the president; a phone call from any of the above; a personal visit at home or at the office; an invitation to lunch or dinner; attendance at an athletic event or play; a visit to an art exhibit; or even a suggestion for a golf match or a fishing trip. The event may not even be university- or college-related, as long as an institution-related person is involved.

The nature and style of these events depends on the ongoing research that determines the interests of the prospect, what he or she might or might not attend, what might entice an interest and what would not. All of the events are designed to develop a good person-to-person relationship that ultimately will bring success.

All of these cultivation activities cost money that you have to spend if the gift is to materialize: "It takes money to make money." But how much should you spend?

How Much Does a Development Program Cost?

Private Institutions. While I was at Lafayette College (2,000 students, liberal arts and engineering), I conducted a study of successful development programs among private colleges and universities in the Northeast. The costs of these programs varied a little from year to year because sometimes exceptional costs, such as for start up of a new program, feasibility studies for a capital campaign, or adding new staff to upgrade a program throw a program's budget out of kilter for a year or two. However, taking all those things into account, the best mature programs cost around 8 cents per dollar raised. These institutions all had well-established development programs (at Lafayette, 54 percent of the alumni contributed annually) and wealthy and successful alumni to support them. Constituents of good private colleges understand clearly that these institutions require substantial and regular infusions of gift dollars in order to exist, and especially to thrive. Consequently, raising money for a private institution is considerably easier than at a public one, and costs less. It also is easier to attract unrestricted gift dollars, because people understand why a private institution needs them.

Public Institutions. These colleges and universities are another story. Recently one of the major fund-raising consulting companies, Brakely John Price Jones, Inc., conducted a survey that concluded that at major public universities the average cost of raising money was 12 cents on the dollar. All studies I have seen show a high correlation between number of staff and dollars spent on the development program, and the amount raised. They also show pronounced dips and peaks in funds raised, following decreases or increases respectively in either dollars or staff. One of the reasons why capital campaigns generally cause big increases in institutional fund raising almost immediately is that, invariably, the institution increases numbers of staff and operating dollars substantially a year or two before the announcement of such campaigns, in order to gear up.

Obviously, well-established programs cost less to run than newer ones. The reasons are clear: An established program has better relations with industry, with alumni, and with other donors. So the institution must merely maintain those relationships, rather than create them (although new ones are generated, too, of course). An established program has most of the necessary donor data in place, and must simply update rather than establish it. A new program will have little constituent data, and must begin almost from scratch to create it.

In a new program it is necessary to persuade prospects first that they should give. Publics have to fight over and over the old battle of why you should support with gift dollars a "tax supported" institution. And, although they are diminishing in number, there are a few corporations and foundations that still give only to private colleges and universities.

So what should a public college or university development program cost? For an essentially new one, 12 percent for the first several years is probably unrealistic. The cost also will vary depending upon the quality of the institution's programs, the attitude of alumni and other constituents toward the university, their financial capacity, and many other factors. Business support depends upon the nature of programs offered. Corporations invariably look for a *quid pro quo,* a rationale for giving to one institution rather than another. A university with engineering, business, and computer science programs, for example, plus strong research programs, will attract corporate dollars more easily than a liberal arts college. Consequently, this approach has an impact on the relative cost of fund raising at these two types of institutions.

A new program at an institution with a good image and a healthy range of programs might shoot for a range of 12–14 percent. Over the longer term, the program might be run at a 10 percent cost level if managed superbly.

What Is Required to Have a Strong Program?

Solid Data. To have a strong development program is to have a cost-effective one. All of the following factors, which make up a strong program, have cost implications. The lack of adequate data can be your biggest problem. Here are the data you need, and why:

1. *Alumni records.* Almost every institution has records of its alumni, incomplete though they may be. Even the most sophisticated programs, with elaborate alumni records, have "lost" alumni—alumni files without an accurate current address. You should make considerable effort to maintain accurate addresses, including a mailing system which ensures that forwarding addresses will come from the postal service

regularly, plus an internal system that enables updates of address changes. Because about 25 percent of an institution's alumni may move in a year's time, the potential for losing alumni is great. The *cost* of losing alumni is even greater. When you consider that even in a mediocre program perhaps 10 percent of the alumni contribute annually, the potential for losing present and future gifts is substantial.

The second most important piece of data necessary in an alumni program is alumni telephone numbers. These numbers obviously are useful for fund raising, but they also provide a way to gather additional data.

You should periodically send out a well-designed questionnaire to find out such information as employer, position, title, income range, interests, degrees and activities, spouse and children, and so on. Such questionnaires are relatively expensive, but you can't afford not to have this information. Also important is a computerized alumni record system that can accept and make readily accessible this information, plus staff to input and update it promptly.

2. *Nongraduate alumni.* Fund-raising experts have found that nongraduate alumni frequently are among the best donors. They are grateful to be included, and sometimes are flattered. The numbers of nongraduate, unrecognized alumni an institution might have depends on a number of factors, including how long an institution has been in existence. But I have found it common for institutions to double or even triple their alumni rolls with a concerted effort to obtain names and addresses of nongraduate former students. Adding these alumni to a system is not easy, of course, but once the names of a substantial number are on a system, you should start communicating with them in every way possible. This will incur costs, especially in postage, extra copies of alumni magazines, and other mailings. But the financial rewards will be more than worth the initial expense.

3. *Parents.* Given the costs of an education at many private institutions, it is difficult to imagine many parents willing to contribute even more to the alma maters. However, parents *are* concerned about the quality of their children's education. And some *can* afford to pay even more than they are. If you approach them correctly, they *will* contribute. Generally, you involve the largest and most regular contributors in a parents' organization.

4. *Corporations and foundations.* You can read more about developing effective corporate and foundation programs elsewhere in this book. Basically, however, no institution can be successful without up-to-date and accurate information.

Let's say your institution and a corporation have had an effective relationship for 10 years. A corporate officer comes to campus to conduct a site visit and discovers that you do not have accurate records concerning the corporation's gifts and the alumni who are employees. That's embarrassing.

Foundations can be more difficult. You must conduct research to discover foundations with funding interests that match a program's nature and needs. After that, you must conduct an effective cultivation program. Unlike federal agencies, most foundations do not make gifts to institutions unless they know them quite well.

5. *Profiles.* These data summaries are necessary in order to develop effectively each MDP. A profile consists of research data that must provide to both staff and volunteers the kinds of information necessary to cultivate, and ultimately to solicit effectively, a major donor prospect. The amount of data necessary for each prospect can be substantial, because frequently the success of a solicitation will depend on how much one knows about the prospect.

6. *Nonalumni individuals.* You might be amazed at the number of nonalumni individuals—people who have had no educational connection with an institution, people we categorize as "friends"—who are donors to an institution. Nonalumni giving nationally is almost as large as alumni giving: 2.066 billion to 2.346 billion dollars in 1986–1987.

It is important to develop data banks for friends of an institution in the same manner as you do for alumni. Consider as potential friends anyone within sight who has the financial capacity to be a major donor. Once you develop lists of these potential friends, gather information and take steps to cultivate them. Get them involved in activities that can ultimately lead to financial commitment.

Effective Cultivational Efforts. Because, as a rule, 5 percent of donors give 90 to 95 percent of the total dollars, how you cultivate the 5 percent is crucial. Cultivation activities should involve the president and members of the institution's leadership, such as governing or foundation-board members, university officers, and alumni volunteers, to be effective. The development staff must orchestrate all efforts. It is easy to make the mistake of cultivating the same people over and over while ignoring others who need attention but are more difficult to reach initially.

After you have completed a successful solicitation, cultivation must continue. Development professionals call this "stewardship" rather than cultivation, because the best prospect for a future donation is a present or former donor.

Strong Alumni Programs. Essential to most university or college development programs is a strong alumni base. Even though alumni have a natural tie to their alma mater, that is not enough to guarantee their interest and support. They must continue to learn about it, to hear from it, and to be involved with it. Although others may send gifts to an institution, only those who are involved with it are likely to support it in a substantial manner.

The best alumni development programs generally have very strong alumni volunteer networks, and that networking is the key to their success. The only way to establish such a network is to identify and involve larger and larger numbers of interested alumni. That process can best take place initially at the grass-roots level. For that reason, strong alumni clubs or other geographically oriented organizations are important. Once club organizations are established and leadership identified in a number of geographic areas, those leaders will become involved and interested.

Alumni participation in overall fund raising is also crucial. Many foundations and a growing number of corporations inquire, when considering a gift proposal, about the level and percentage of alumni participation. They ask because they believe that one of the best gauges of the quality of an institution's programs is the degree to which it is able to generate alumni support. They also maintain that if those closest to an institution do not support it, why should they?

Effective Donor Recognition. Since the best prospect for a future gift is a present donor, you must recognize and reward present donors. They may be even more generous in the future. Spend some money recognizing them, honoring them, and entertaining them, because it will be money well spent.

Financial Support. It is easy to understand, especially in difficult times, why institutional leadership may find it difficult to fund a development program adequately, given faculty needs and other priorities. However, not to fund it adequately is extremely short-sighted because that limits the overall resources that the institution can generate.

How Much Staff Do You Need?

There is no easy answer. There are successful programs staffed by a single individual, and there are others with more than 100 staff members. The determination depends at the very least on several factors, including the potential dollars a university or college might raise, the number of prospects it has, and the development functions that you must cover.

If a college determines that a million dollars a year, for example, might be a reasonable potential dollar target, then that has a significant impact on staff numbers. You know immediately that the total budget to raise that million dollars should be somewhere between $100,000 and $200,000 (10–20 percent), much of which you must reserve for mailing, phoning, data collecting, travel, entertaining, and other operational matters. The staff will be limited, but you'll certainly need more than one.

As for major donor prospects: My experience, its conclusions corroborated by others, has proven that a single development officer can effectively handle fifty to seventy major donor prospects. Keep in mind, however, that some development officers might not be able to spend their full time dealing with MDPs if they have other duties.

The best way to determine the effective number of staff, however, is first to look at the functional area you need to cover. Then decide whether a single individual is required, or more, at a particular institution to cover each area, or whether one person can handle the several functions. Those decisions, of course, depend on the size of your institution, the size of the prospect base, and similar factors.

Here are areas that professional staff need to cover:

Gift Acknowledgement and Data Processing. They must compile data, maintain it, update it, manipulate it, publish reports, run mailing lists, and obtain other information from your development office databases. When gifts come, staff must record and acknowledge them. Because the best future donor is a present donor, staff must acknowledge accurately, cordially, and in a timely manner.

Prospect Research and Management. This function assures that staff establish, maintain, and update profiles on all major donor prospects and on corporations and foundations. It is necessary to have specially trained people performing much of this work because you need information above and beyond that normally found in constituent files. The staff must have access to, and the knowledge to use, various types of research materials, including Standard and Poor's directories, foundation directories, metropolitan or regional society publications and lists, Dun and Bradstreet publications, the Taft directories, and other research vehicles. Generally, staff also regularly screen business magazines and certain newspapers for new information on MDPs. Depending on the number of these prospects and the size of the institution, a lone part-time professional can handle this function at some campuses, while on others, staff in the double figures is necessary.

Major Gifts. Tied closely into the prospect research and management function is the major gift area, staffed by an individual or individuals with responsibility for identifying, cultivating, soliciting, and maintaining major donor prospects, and for their stewardship. Included in this responsibility would be establishing means and devices for identifying major donor prospects, researching them, and developing cultivation plans and seeing that they are carried out.

A major gifts officer also is responsible for determining when it is time to solicit, and then to develop the solicitation strategy. This includes determining the purpose of the gift, size of request, and who will solicit. In smaller development programs the chief development officer can handle the major gifts area, but at larger institutions you may need one or more major gifts staff members.

Annual Giving. This area is generally the most active, hectic, and expensive of all development offices. The current-giving office must deal with mounds of paper, tens of thousands of prospects, mailing schedules, deadlines, hundreds of volunteers (you hope), and many details. This function frequently costs more than 30 cents per dollar raised. But it is also one of the most important. Not only does it develop the habit of giving in an institution's clientele, but it also is the best means for identifying future MDPs.

Corporations. Such functions as cultivation, maintenance of relationships, and stewardship are as important for corporate giving as for individual fund raising. It is important to cover corporate relations, whether through the part-time efforts of a chief development officer at a small college, or through a centrally staffed office at a major university.

Foundations. It is fairly common for a single individual or office to handle both foundation and corporate giving. But at larger institutions the areas often are divided. The degree of staffing for a particular institution should depend on the number of foundation prospects it is able to develop, how many proposals are likely to be submitted in a period of time, and the degree of effort that these will entail.

Planned Giving. A planned-giving effort ultimately should be one of the most productive in almost any institution that has individual constituents. Planned giving is almost entirely a one-on-one proposition, with someone very specially trained in planned-giving techniques doing the calls. Less specifically trained development personnel can open doors and help with prospecting, but when it gets down to the end result and negotiating for the gift, you need a trained officer.

Even at a very small institution, when a program becomes able financially to hire a second development officer, I usually recommend that this person be a planned-giving officer. It is extremely difficult for a part-timer, no matter how well trained, to handle a planned-giving effort successfully.

Constituent Programs. Larger institutions and sometimes even small ones may need a constituent-based officer—for example, a development officer in charge of athletic fund raising. At universities having many colleges, a college-based officer enables that college to pay particular attention to its own alumni and to communicate with them about matters in sync with their interests or professional involvements. With programs that depend heavily on corporate and foundation support, a college-based development officer can establish a rapport with faculty, and as a result be better able to help develop good faculty and corporate relations.

In a large institution with a large prospect base, it is necessary to cover fund raising for individual units, so whether you assign an officer to a unit or to a central office, the function must be covered.

What Are Internal Concerns in Funding Your Program?

A principal problem that presidents have to face when trying to start a development program or revitalize an inefficient one is the difficulty of engendering internal support for, and understanding of, the program. Generally, a motivating factor for making changes in the development area is an inadequacy of funds to support the programs that the institution already has. To take large chunks of revenue off the top to fund a development program can create a major internal public relations problem. If you make an adequate effort up front, however, to explain development and sell faculty on the program, you can usually obtain initial support, or at least acceptance. The story is a good one, and there are ample statistics to convince even a skeptical faculty that development is a good investment.

Even after you accomplish that initial step successfully, internal problems can surface. For example, a development program not only has, but needs, high visibility. It's also one of the easiest programs in the world to second-guess. It's almost like the football program: The scores are up there for all to see regularly. A development officer either raises money or doesn't, and it is tempting to evaluate a program purely, solely, and too quickly on the basis of dollars raised.

Similarly, once a president determines to put substantial new funds into a development program, the initial results usually are impressive— sometimes too impressive. Great beginnings can cause totally false expectations which, when unmet, can create an impression of failure for a program that has been immensely successful. To illustrate: There are programs that have grown from $3 million one year to $6 million the next, and $9 million the following year, following an increase in staff and budget. It is very understandable that observers might feel that with that sort of success the program ought to continue jumping in regular increments to $12-, $15-, and $21 million in subsequent years. The likelihood of that sort of progression without intermediate base-building is extremely unlikely. And it is a tragedy for a program that has increased by 200 percent in two years to be considered a failure for remaining at that level during the third year.

Another problem that can contribute to a feeling of faculty discontent with a new or revitalized program is a question of "credit." Who gets the credit? Who really raised the money? Was it the new development program and staff, or was it really the faculty?

The answers to these problems are not simple. Successful fund raising is not a matter of a development officer or any other individual simply going out, contacting an individual or organization that has financial resources, asking for a gift, and coming away with a pocketful of money. That sort of thing does happen occasionally, but it is certainly the exception rather than the rule. It is also true that *occasionally* a totally unsolicited or unexpected gift will surface. What really happens in successful fund raising is that 90–95 percent of all the money raised comes from approximately 5 percent of the prospective donors. That money comes as the result of relationships that have been built over a period of time, and usually because they are asked for gifts in ways that make the donations likely.

If this is true, then how do you explain the unusual growth in gifts that sometimes occurs early in a new or revitalized program? When I went to Colorado State in 1985 to try to revitalize that program, the university had been "stuck" at the $4.5–5 million level for four years. We jumped to $8 million the first year, and $11.8 million the second. Was all that money "in the pipeline"? Did the new development effort have anything to do with the generation of that money, or were there simply fortuitous circumstances for which the development organization took credit? The fund-raising history of that institution (Table 14.1) suggests that there must have been a substantial correlation between the development program and the rapid increase in giving after plateauing for four years—but why?

The explanation is that faculty, alumni, and others over the years had built a number of good relationships that had created a *climate* with a number of individuals and corporations conducive to fund raising. There was also a charismatic new president, who had been in place over a year, and a number of programs worthy of support.

Actually, however, fund *solicitation* there, with some notable exceptions, had not been done well. Any number of donors were annoyed

Table 14.1. FUNDS RAISED VERSUS FUND-RAISING COSTS, COLO-
RADO STATE UNIVERSITY 1980–81 to 1986–87

Year	Fund-Raising Costs	Funds Raised	% Fund-Raising Costs
1980–81	$ 485,214	$ 2,480,452	19.56
1981–82	651,265	5,225,914	12.46
1982–83	743,534	5,324,903	13.96
1983–84	742,582	4,614,185	16.09
1984–85	844,108	4,992,231	16.91
1985–86	1,155,301	8,049,969	14.35
1986–87	1,542,240	11,816,361	13.05

by what seemed like hoards of individuals asking them for money. They were troubled to the point of telling me, the president, and others, "Until you can get your priorities straight and your act together, we are not inclined to support you." In other cases, individuals who knew faculty or staff at the institution, who liked what was going on, and who were inclined to support the institution were not even asked to give, or were not asked appropriately. So the difference that caused the quick increase in giving was a combination of the good relations that had been created over the years, and then suddenly a new development program that was highly visible. That program publicized its intention to coordinate fund raising and protect donors from multiple solicitations. It also began to see that gifts were solicited properly.

Then who raised the money? The increased funds could not have been raised without the new program. By the same token, the new development program could not have generated the gifts without the quality of the academic programs, the faculty, and, even more importantly, the reputations and relations that had been established over time.

How Do You Monitor and Evaluate a Program?

Very easily: dollars raised versus dollars spent. In the best private institutions the costs of raising money are in the 8 percent range; in the major public universities the average cost is 12 percent. Less well established programs will not prove as efficient, and probably should not be expected to compare. But these figures give a gauge.

A better way to evaluate your program is to make sure that your staff accurately, regularly, and consistently record fund-raising costs so that you are able to compare accurately on a year-to-year basis what it is costing to raise money. Doing so enables you to (for one thing) match costs with comparable institutions. It is important, however, to make sure that you take other factors into account—especially short-term discrepancies such as gearing up for a capital campaign. There are definite cause–effect relationships in fund raising. But they are not always short-term. And they certainly do not always fall into our arbitrary fiscal years.

15

DETAILS YOU
SHOULD KNOW
William P. McGoldrick

While you will want to remain as broad-visioned as possible, there are details of your institution's development program that you, as president, should know. Through your knowledge of these details you will develop greater confidence in your development program and the staff. You will be better informed for conversations with your vice president and development officers.

Your success may depend in part on your familiarity with certain terms and definitions (see the "Development Glossary" at the end of this chapter), with methods of planning and evaluation, with a basic understanding of development programming, and with the signs of success. You will be more certain of the information you should review. You will also be more certain of when to be satisfied, when to be concerned, and when to be alarmed.

In this chapter you will be advised of how to evaluate the people on your development staff, and how to direct their activities. You will learn more of the basic programs that must be part of every development operation. This chapter proposes ways to focus those programs on the most important elements of your institution, and addresses the various topics that you should address in your day-by-day discussions with your vice president.

First, Look at the People

Your ability to rely on the judgments and actions of your vice president will be based on your confidence in the staff's level of experience and expertise. Start by reviewing the credentials of your development staff. Read them carefully, and prepare to interview these people personally. Ask them to describe their mission, the mission of your college (which may prove different), their understanding of your external constituencies, and their plans for the coming year. You will quickly learn the level of their skill, drive, and potential. You will also learn their philosophy of development and management, as well as their approach to leadership and problem solving.

As you evaluate your staff, look closely for drive and initiative in their behavior. Although development skills are important, and most helpful to own from the start, staff can learn them. Some believe that a person can also learn initiative. It seems to be a fact of life that by nature either people are driven toward success or are comfortable coasting through their responsibilities without ever breaking a sweat. You cannot afford the latter personality.

Then Look for a Plan

Assuming that your vice president and staff are acceptable or better, which issues should you address first? Look for a written plan. It should clearly articulate the mission of the development office, and specific measurable goals and objectives tied to deadlines and a budget. It should also encompass programs to address each of the major constituencies of the college. Such a plan is the necessary first step if the staff is to accomplish anything concrete.

The development program, regardless of the number of staff or the staff administrative structure, must be concerned with these types of donors: individual major, individual general, corporate, and foundation. Some church-affiliated colleges will also focus on a religious constituency.

Without exception, all development programs must concentrate on "the critical few," that small number of potential donors in each of those constituencies who, by their ability and inclination, will determine the program's success. With your vice president, examine this small list first. There should be a written plan for each of these 50 to 100 donors. Many will be familiar names: trustees, important alumni, local corporations. Determine your personal development priorities from this list.

Next, Look at the Programs

Review next the programs designed to provide to those constituencies information and opportunities for involvement and investment in your college. They should include annual-giving programs for operating purposes, major giving programs for endowment and capital needs, a program to encourage gifts through trusts and bequests, and a program to seek support from corporations and foundations. Here's more about each:

Annual Giving. Annual giving is the backbone of most development programs. It provides a mechanism for all alumni, parents, and friends to support your college. It builds a base of support for your college and begins the process of identifying potential major donors. Annual giving, discussed in depth in Chapter 11, also provides many opportunities for voluntarism through which interested individuals can become more personally involved in your college's future.

To reach the greatest number of alumni, parents, and friends, the annual fund will employ face-to-face solicitation, direct mail, volunteer phonathons, phonathons employing paid callers, or a combination of these techniques. You should look for detailed organization of this program, and a reporting mechanism that allows you to see on a weekly or biweekly basis the results of the program. See one such report in Table 15.1.

Like a major campaign in microcosm, the annual fund must have strong volunteer leadership. Like a major campaign, the annual fund should have a table of gifts so that staff, volunteers, and you will know

Table 15.1. SAMPLE REPORT FOR ANNUAL-GIVING PROGRAM

TO: President Smith
FROM: Jane Jones
 Director, Annual Fund
DATE: February 22, 1988
RE: ANNUAL FUND STATUS REPORT

Period Ending	02/17/88		02/18/87	
	$	# Donors	$	# Donors
Alumni	$1,780,362	10,395	1,853,223	10,053
Parent	24,295	213	17,929	131
Friends	84,430	118	71,695	152
Corporate Match	285,986	315	223,319	283
GRAND TOTAL	$2,175,073	11,041	2,166,166	10,619

Average Alumni Gift thru 02/17/88 $171
Average Alumni Gift thru 02/18/87 $184
Outstanding pledge balance as of 02/17/88 = $ 663,683
Number of pledges with balances = 5,371
Average pledge balance = $123
Outstanding pledge balance as of 02/18/87 = $ 362,798
Number of pledges with balances = 3,324
Average pledge balance = $109

what is needed to reach your goal and how you are progressing toward that goal (see Table 15.2). Your vice president must focus the program to obtain the maximum number of leadership gifts. Quite often, leadership donors become members in the "President's Club" or a similar organization by some other name. By whatever designation, these are the gifts of $1,000 or more that will determine whether you reach your goal.

The President's Club is both a marketing and a recognition tool. It enables your college to encourage those who are able to support your college's mission with significant annual gifts. In return, most colleges publish the names of these individuals prominently in the annual report of gifts and in a separate membership directory. Generally there is a social event, often black-tie, to recognize the members of this club. Most colleges now have giving clubs at levels higher than $1,000—some at the $5,000 and $10,000 levels.

Volunteers should personally solicit as often as possible major gifts to your annual fund, whether they are $500-plus or $1,000-plus. A strong base of committed volunteer leadership with specific tasks and responsibilities is critical to your development program. Most often, you establish that leadership in your annual-giving program.

Table 15.2. 1987–88 ANNUAL FUND, INDIVIDUAL GIVING, TABLE OF GIFTS

Total # of Donors Needed	At $	# Donors through 02/17/88	For Cumulative $	# Donors through 02/18/87	For Cumulative $
6	25,000	3	84,500	4	103,441
25	10,000	17	223,433	15	186,492
40	5,000	27	141,657	32	183,237
200	2,000	139	317,365	143	342,697
210	1,000	124	133,133	154	169,764
375	500	270	145,524	276	151,090
2,000	200	1,275	299,398	1,234	289,540
4,100	100	3,011	326,004	2,791	304,036
3,600	50	2,435	132,926	2,370	129,950
5,200	0	3,425	85,147	3,317	82,600
15,756		10,726	1,889,087	10,336	1,942,847

Corporate match received through 02/17/88 = $285,986
Total cash received = $2,175,073
% Dollar Goal attained = 60% (Including pledges = 78%)
% Donor Goal attained = 68% (Including pledges = 99%)

Another activity that relies on volunteer leadership is your phone solicitation program. Phonathons have, over the past dozen or so years, assumed an ever greater role in annual-giving programs. In the middle 1960s, volunteers began to gather on campus, or in an office provided by an alumnus or friend, to call others to ask for support. This method, from the start very effective, over the years has improved in several ways. Today, experience shows that it is possible to *predict* how many people out of every 100 will answer the phone, how many will give, and how many will increase their gift compared to last year's. A really strong annual-giving program will include a broad geographic solicitation using *both* direct mail *and* telephones.

A critical component of the annual fund is the discipline brought by the staff to the details of organizing lists of potential donors, volunteers, tasks to be achieved, and deadlines to be met. Staff must maintain these lists religiously, and refer to them regularly to ensure that each required task is completed on time. The annual fund works on a very short timeline. One year passes all too quickly. Watch for reports on results!

Major Giving. Major giving programs focus your resources to reach the "critical few," that group of people who are capable of making very substantial gifts. Each college develops its own programs to inform and involve potential donors; each decides its own levels of "major" gift. For purposes of discussion, let's assume we are talking about a gift of $10,000 or more given in one year.

While all your programs seek to identify and involve donors at every level, you will personally succeed or fail in your development program by your ability to persuade "the critical few" to support you and your institution. Some experienced development professionals subscribe to the 80–20 rule (80 percent of the gift support will come from 20 percent of the donors). Others say the ratio is 90 to 10 and some say 95 to 5. Many colleges and universities now find that two-thirds of the financial support in any year comes from thirty or fewer donors. During one major campaign, 66 percent of the support came from 1 percent of the donors, and 93 percent of the giving came from 6 percent of the donors.

The fact is that the small number of donors who may or may not provide relatively large gifts can determine the success or failure of your overall program. Understanding that it is *those* donors who are in the driver's seat, how should you operate your programs to ensure success?

The task assigned to major giving is to identify, cultivate, and solicit all major and potential major donors, and to provide them with stewardship (see Glossary). Your vice president should have a written list of major potential donors, with an estimate of potential giving and a proposed sequence of cultivation steps leading to a solicitation. Without such a list, the task will fail.

If there is no list when you ask for one, your vice president should "screen" lists of potential donors, to discover potential major donors. Assessing their past giving, their business titles, their addresses, and their other known indicators of wealth will provide an idea of their ability to give. Only personal visits and invitations to involvement in college activities will help assess inclination to give. This is called "rating." It is the combination of ability and inclination that determines what a reasonable request for support might be, and the timing of that request. While it is best to begin with a staff screening, it is also wise to seek corroboration of these ratings from alumni and friends.

Once you have the list, work begins. Visits by staff and volunteers will help determine inclination, and also raise the individual's awareness of the people, programs, and aspirations of your college. You should limit your visits to individuals who have been assessed. If you're starting from scratch, begin by visiting your board of trustees while your vice president prepares other recommendations for your time.

During your visits, your job is to demonstrate a vision of what you can achieve if others join you. You must articulate that vision—that plan—and the personal leadership to reach your objectives. Generally, a first visit is not the time to solicit a gift.

After a donor's first visit, you should issue an invitation to return to campus. Our students and faculty are really our best salespeople. They are the reason our donors are interested in our institutions. Find ways for potential donors to meet, know, and appreciate your faculty, students, and campus. During such a visit, listen to your visitors: Often they will tell you what they want to support, and what they think is a comfortable level of support.

When a potential donor develops a relationship with you and your institution, it will be time to solicit this person.

1. *Do it in person.* If you are seeking a major gift, you will more than likely be the right person to ask for it. At other times a volunteer or staff person will be more right. It is best when two people visit the potential donor. The presence of a volunteer will help you carry the conversation more easily and will support the request's importance.

2. *Do it with a written proposal.* A written proposal provides the formal request that deserves an answer. It will also help you, before the request, to review the specifics for your conversation. After you have left, the proposal will help the donor to recall the importance and specifics of your request.

3. *Do it with sensitivity to the donor's circumstances.* Rarely do you

know all of the elements of a donor's private life. Sensitivity to this fact in your request is important. For particularly large requests, remind the donor that a pledge payable over a number of years is acceptable. You'd be surprised how often a donor does not consider this as a way to make a large commitment.

4. *Do it.* More large gifts are lost because no one asked than for any other reason. There is no magic to seeking support. You are the best person to understand your vision for your college. Organize your thoughts to explain the big picture to the potential donor. Then express your reasons why one or more particular needs that deserve support will help accomplish those dreams. A potential donor wants first to know how you will use the gift, not the machine or activity it helps to pay for. Your ability to sell the dream is your first objective.

Then present the written proposal asking the potential donor to consider a specific gift. Explain it thoughtfully. Then stop talking. Wait for an answer. The second biggest reason for losing gifts is not allowing the donor to respond.

5. *Say thank you.* Thank the potential donor immediately. Follow up with a personal letter of thanks for considering or making the gift.

6. *Say thank you again.* Thank the donor often and sincerely. One of the ways to seek a major gift from a previous major donor is through providing stewardship: a report that both thanks the donor and outlines how you have used previous gifts to improve your institution. Such a report helps you to move easily into more current needs.

Corporate Giving. Corporate giving programs offer great opportunity to research and technology universities. For smaller liberal arts colleges, the ability to attract large corporate donations is more difficult. It is often said that corporate donors give from a position of enlightened self-interest: They provide most of their support to institutions that are sources for employees (check your placement statistics), for research (do any corporations support the research of your professors?), and to colleges that are part of the communities where they have plants.

Your development officers should seek the logical connections through which you can develop the correct strategy for each potential corporate donor. Keep in mind that *people* at corporations make the decisions about corporate gifts. You should invest as much time in providing information to the right people at the potential major corporate donors as you do to individual major donors.

Look for the list of top corporate employers of your graduates. Look for companies where your alumni are leaders. Look for the list of companies supporting research at your college. Look for the list of past corporate supporters. Look for written strategies and for written proposals to deliver to your most important corporate friends. For corporations, just as for individuals, the rules are to concentrate on the critical few, visit judiciously often, and invite them to your campus.

Foundation Giving. You stand the best chance for success when you know foundation programs (they are readily available from foundation officers). Find foundations with shared areas of interest. Then have your staff prepare well-written proposals that link a campus program to a foundation. Most proposals will have the greatest impact when *you* sign them.

Don't overlook the small, community-based foundations in your area. Often they are capable of contributing substantially to your program. Again, as with individuals and corporations, you won't receive gifts unless you ask. If your development office is not preparing, submitting, and discussing written proposals with foundation program officers, obviously foundations cannot respond.

Signs of Success

There are many signs of a strong development program. The most obvious, of course, is an ever-increasing total of gift support. However, there are things to look for from the start:

1. *Look for a staff seeking you out to meet with potential and current donors.* Leadership is critical when dealing with donors, and if the program is to function well you must be part of that leadership. During noncampaign periods you should devote at least 20 percent of your time to development activities. During a campaign, that portion of your effort may need to reach 40 or 50 percent.

2. *Monitor the volume of proposals and acknowledgments that you are signing.*

3. *Look for a regular report (at least monthly) of all gifts by source (alumni, friends, parents, corporations, foundations) and purpose (expendable, endowment, physical facilities).*

4. *Look for strong volunteer involvement.* Do you know our leadership volunteers? Do they know you and your aspirations for your

college? No matter how good your staff, the leverage of volunteers improves your program's quality and shows constituent involvement. Look for breadth of involvement by alumni, parents, and friends.

5. *No one can raise money while sitting behind a desk.* Look for a program that involves you, your staff, and faculty in visiting potential donors and hosting guests on campus. When potential donors see your campus first-hand and meet your faculty, staff, and students, your opportunities for seeking support increase.

6. *Look for feedback.* Does your development staff regularly provide you with feedback about your involvement? Remember, too, to ask volunteers and donors for feedback.

Putting It All Together

Meet with your development vice president regularly. Discuss what the development staff is accomplishing, the opportunities for new gifts, and future plans to seek those gifts. Involve yourself in the program. Discuss the annual fund, the major gifts program, and the corporate and foundation gifts programs. Discuss potential donors and volunteers.

This is your agenda. Tell your vice president that you expect a written agenda when you meet. Keep your copy, and look at the collection regularly to ensure that you focus on these.

Finally, *have fun* with your development program. The program can produce wonderfully enjoyable human relationships as you work with staff, volunteers, and donors. It can also produce tangible successes that will benefit your program, faculty, students—indeed, your entire institution.

Development Glossary

annual fund The program to seek expendable gifts from all alumni, parents, and friends (sometimes also faculty, staff, local business, and industry). The cornerstone of the development program. Generally, a mixture of personal solicitation, telephone solicitation, and direct mail.

capital campaign The program to seek major gifts for capital (endowment and facilities) support within a specified period (generally one to three years). More often, although the name doesn't change, such major efforts really are comprehensive campaigns that also seek expendable current support and include the proceeds of the annual fund.

case statement The written statement of need, urgency, and justification for a donor to consider as a campaign proceeds. Generally explains the proposed plan for raising the money required, and discusses how to make gifts. Also describes the people who lead and direct the campaign.

cultivation The planned combination of information and activity directed toward a potential donor to increase that party's inclination to commit the greatest amount of his or her resources to the needs of your college.

gift clubs One way to recognize donors. Dinners, plaques, and/or certificates often are features or benefits for those meeting club requirements. They usually recognize donors of $10,000, $5,000, $1,000, $500, and $100. You can choose the ones appropriate to your institution. Clubs also recognize donors whose lifetime giving reaches levels of $1,000,000, $100,000, $50,000, and $10,000.

LYBUNT A person who gave Last Year But Unfortunately Not This Year.

major gift A large gift, generally meant as one for capital purposes (probably a gift of $10,000 or greater).

nucleus fund The gifts and pledges of the leadership donors who, in anticipation of a major campaign, make their commitments to set the pace for others.

phonathon The organized program of telephone calling to solicit donors. Sometimes called a *telefund,* particularly when paid callers do the calling.

planned gift Part of the major gift strategy for an individual, generally through a bequest or trust. A gift like this always gives you the chance for an *in vivo* gift as well.

screening/rating Identifying potential donors of considerable wealth and determining their ability and inclination to give.

stewardship A program of annual reporting to major donors on the use of their gifts. This wonderful cultivation program often inspires repeat giving.

SYBUNT A person who gave Some Years But Unfortunately Not This Year.

telefund A more sophisticated phonathon program (sometimes called *phone/ mail*), incorporating a strong marketing letter followed by a phone call from a well-trained, generally paid caller. Aggressive negotiation is a trademark of this largely successful technique.

IV

REACHING THE
APEX IN
FUND RAISING

16

MAJOR GIFTS

David R. Dunlop

The gifts of a few individuals can make the difference between what your college is today and what it can become. One fund-raising consultant, in reviewing the last twenty-three campaigns his firm assisted, found that 2.5 percent of the givers provided 98 percent of the dollars given.

In the last decade we have seen a dramatic increase in the number and magnitude of very large gifts. A recent informal study of publicly announced gifts of $5 million or more to higher education confirms this trend:

	Number of Gifts	Total Amount Given
1977	8	$119 million
1979	6	139
1981	14	162
1983	16	235
1985	25	280
1987	36	380*

* This figure omits the gift to UCLA of the Norton Simon art collection, valued at $750 million.

The future strength of your institution may depend on how well you understand the steps that lead to a major gift, and what you and your college can do to encourage donors to advance along those steps.

Kinds of Gifts

To appreciate what leads a person to make a major gift, you must first understand the three kinds of gifts: *regular gifts, special gifts,* and *ultimate gifts.*

1. *Regular gifts* are made repeatedly and at regular intervals. The gift placed in the church collection plate every week, the check written

173

to support the public television station every quarter, and the gift made once every year to the United Way, the Cancer Crusade, or a college annual fund are examples of regular giving. The timing of these gifts relates largely to the calendar. Regular gifts usually are the smallest gifts the individual will make. For comparison with a person's other types of giving, we can ascribe a unit value of 1 to the regular gift.

$$\text{Regular Gift} = 1x$$

2. *Special gifts* are those that a person makes to help a charitable organization or institution meet a special need. They usually are made to an institution that the giver also supports with regular gifts. The three-year pledge to help pay for the new roof on the church, the two-year pledge in support of the YMCA building fund for a new pool, and the three-year pledge to support a college's campaign for a new library are typical special gifts. The needs of the institution receiving special gifts influences their timing. Special gifts are typically five to ten times larger than the regular gift the person makes to the same institution.

$$\text{Special Gift} = 5x \text{ to } 10x$$

3. *Ultimate gifts* are an exercise of the giver's full giving capacity. They are the largest philanthropic commitment the giver can make. Givers make most of these gifts by trust or bequest. Some wealthy individuals, however, have sufficient resources to make their ultimate gift during their lifetime. In contrast to the case with regular gifts and special gifts, factors in a giver's life most influence the timing of ultimate gifts. Typically 1,000 to 10,000 times larger than the giver's regular gift to the same institution, they may go to a single institution or be divided among several.

$$\text{Ultimate Gift} = 1,000x \text{ to } 10,000x$$

What a college calls a "major gift" is usually defined by two factors:

1. The size of the institution's need

2. The college's gift-receiving history

On the other hand, what a giver perceives as a "major gift" is usually determined by his or her financial circumstance and past giving.

Whether the college or the giver views the gift as "major" relates to the size of the gift—but that should not be the only factor in determining the type of fund raising you should use. It is whether the gift being sought will be a "regular gift," a "special gift," or an "ultimate gift" in the experience of the giver that will tell you what method of fund raising your institution should use to secure the major gifts it needs and hopes for.

Methods of Fund Raising

The fund-raising method your institution uses is vital to your success in securing major gifts. Your fund-raising philosophy and concepts need to fit the type of gifts you seek.

Speculative fund raising characterizes one end of the fund-raising spectrum. *Individualized* fund raising characterizes the center. And *nurturing* fund raising—the relationship between the giver and the institution—characterizes the other end of the spectrum.

1. *Speculative fund raising* focuses on asking for the gift. It is based on the speculation that if you ask enough people for gifts, a sufficient number will respond favorably to make the effort worthwhile. Direct-mail appeals, phonathons, telethons, and even some personal solicitations are typical of speculative fund raising. The time and resources invested in this kind of fund raising focus primarily on asking, with little time or resources invested in developing the individual giver's sense of commitment. In speculative fund raising the proportion of effort devoted to encouraging the giver to give before he or she is asked, versus the effort invested in asking, might look something like this:

asking

Fund raisers most often use speculative fund raising to solicit regular gifts and, occasionally, special gifts.

2. *Individualized fund raising* focuses on the process of asking. But before the actual solicitation, the fund raiser invests more time and resources in preparing the prospect for the request. For example, you invite a prospect to campus to meet the college's curator of rare books before a classmate calls on him or her to consider a special commitment to the college's library campaign. The initiatives undertaken before the solicitation, preparing the giver before he or she is asked, versus the effort invested in asking, might look something like this:

preparing	asking

You use individualized fund raising to solicit special gifts and to increase the size of regular gifts.

3. *Nurturing fund raising* focuses on building, over time, the prospective giver's sense of commitment to the institution so that the institution becomes the giver's priority for all types of giving, including the giver's ultimate gift. Fund raisers invest much more effort and resources in building that sense of commitment than in the processes of asking. The proportion of effort put into building the individual giver's sense of commitment before asking, versus the effort put into asking, might look something like this:

preparing

All three methods of fund raising affect major gift-giving. However, nurturing fund raising will have the greatest impact on ultimate gift-giving.

Prospect Versus Project Emphasis

To be successful, your college's fund raising must respond to both the priorities of the institution and the interests of prospective givers. Fund-raising programs tend to emphasize one or the other. A campaign for a new library or a reunion class project to endow a professorship are examples of project-oriented fund raising. Corporate, foundation, and major gifts fund raising tend to be prospect-oriented, although they too can pursue nurturing fund raising. Coordination between your prospect- and project-oriented fund raising allows complementary activities. A lack of coordination creates frustration and distraction.

Your major gifts program, with its emphasis on fund raising that nurtures prospect awareness, knowledge, interest, involvement, and commitment should focus on initiatives responsive to both the institution's priorities and the prospect's interests. This requires you to share the college's strategic plan with your major gifts officer and others responsible for designing and implementing those initiatives. And you must factor into your college's strategic plan estimates of how feasible it will be to obtain gift support for specific purposes.

The Role of Major Gifts Fund Raising

As you determine where the major gifts program fits into your institution's fund raising program, you must take many things into account. You must consider the different kinds of gifts you hope to secure, and their relative size and significance to the institution's future. You must also decide on the most appropriate fund raising methods to secure them, and the prospect-versus-project emphasis of the programs you organize to do this fund raising. Although oversimplified, Table 16.1 may help to put these choices in perspective.

What Leads a Person to Make an Ultimate Gift?

While the experiences that lead a person to direct an ultimate gift to an institution are unique, the types of experiences are almost always the same. They begin with experiences that develop their *awareness* of the institution and the purposes to which they eventually designate their ultimate gift. Other experiences develop their *knowledge and understanding*. Then there are experiences that enhance the giver's *interest and caring*. Still other experiences provide the opportunity for the giver's formal or informal *involvement* with the institution. Some of these experiences will happen by chance, but you must carefully plan most of them.

Based on experiences that have nurtured the giver's awareness, knowledge, interest, and involvement, a *sense of commitment* will develop.

Table 16.1. THE CONTEXT FOR MAJOR GIFT FUND RAISING

Kinds of Gifts	Regular	Special	Ultimate
Relative size	1x	5x to 10x	1000x to 10,000x

Methods of Fund Raising	Speculative	Individualized	Nurturing
Emphasis: ■ preparing prospect □ asking prospect	▮▭▭▭	▰▰▭▭	▰▰▰▯
Period for bottom line evaluation	annual	length of fund raising campaign or project	lifetime of prospect
Dominant emphasis in organizing	project oriented		prospect oriented
Programs typically involved	annual fund, capital campaign, and special project fund raising		major gift program

With that sense of commitment come *expressions of commitment*—not only financial but personal, political, moral, and even spiritual. It is through such experiences, and the resulting sense of commitment, that your institution can move to a position in the giver's priorities so that it may qualify for part or all of that person's ultimate gift.

Fund raising that encourages regular and special gifts rarely brings about ultimate gifts. However, nurturing fund raising, with its focus on building the giver's awareness, knowledge, interest, and involvement will almost guarantee a stream of regular and special gifts, as well as all or part of the giver's ultimate gift. Because of this, you should base your institution's major-gifts fund raising on the concept of nurturing fund raising.

Why not, then, concentrate all your fund-raising efforts on nurturing fund raising? There are two reasons why you can't. First, achieving success with this method demands so much of your institution's time and resources that you must limit it to those few individuals with the greatest potential and likelihood. Second, the habits of giving, and the sense of commitment encouraged by regular and special gift-giving help set the stage for securing ultimate gifts. This requires a balanced development program, one that includes speculative and individualized fund raising as well as nurturing fund raising.

The Need to Focus Efforts

Not only is nurturing fund raising time-consuming, it is costly. It is costly in budget and development staff required, but even more costly in its demands on your best volunteers, key administrators, trustees, faculty, and you. Developing institutional friendships requires the same kind of investment that your personal friendships require: frequent, thoughtful, and sustained personal attention. Consequently, the institution that seeks major gifts must limit the number of prospects who receive this kind of attention—perhaps only five or ten.

Selecting Prospects for Major Gift Fund Raising

You must balance several criteria against each other in selecting your prospects:

1. Financial capacity
2. Charitable nature
3. Existing and/or potential interest

Financial capacity is relatively easy to recognize. Residences, possessions, life style, business position, social standing, investments, and charitable commitments all provide evidence of financial capacity. In assessing financial capacity to give, you must take into account present and future financial demands and commitments. Family obligations, business requirements for capital, community expectations, and an expensive life style can make a person of substantial means a less promising major gift prospect than others with fewer resources.

It is harder to determine the second criterion for selecting major gift prospects: a charitable nature. The late Harold Seymour, in speaking to a group of fund raisers at Cornell in 1959, said that all fund raising constituencies include:

1. Those who see the need and respond without being asked

2. Those who respond when told of the need

3. Those who will respond when persuaded of the need

4. Those who may or may not respond, even when heavily persuaded

5. The inert fifth—nothing will get them to give

He concluded that the efficiency of major gift fund raising is greatly affected by how well you are able to discern people who are in one of the top three categories.

The very nature of an institution makes the third criterion for selecting major gift prospects—existing and/or potential interest in your college or university—one for which most individuals will qualify. Year after year, about half of the support given to campuses by individuals comes from nonalumni. Don't underestimate your college's *inherent* appeal.

Who Should Do the Work of Major Gift Fund Raising?

At most institutions the responsibility and most of the work of major gift fund raising falls on the shoulders of the president and the chief advancement officer, who often is the vice president for development. Recognizing that both have many other time-consuming and important responsibilities, some campuses began about fifteen years ago to appoint a senior development staff member to help ensure that frequent and continuous attention go to prospects for large gifts. In order to help, colleges enlisted major gift committees composed of trustees and other ranking friends and alumni.

Most prospective givers have several friends who play a key role in their relationship with the campus. Your institution will be much more effective in its major gift fund raising if, instead of asking for volunteers to take responsibility for a given prospect, you try to discover the natural partners in each prospect's relationship with the college. Some of the most effective natural partners will be members of your faculty, staff, or board of trustees. Well-developed major gift programs typically discover five to ten key natural partners who can play a key role in nurturing a major gift prospect's relationship with the college or university.

Often one natural partner will stand out as being in the best position to help plan and implement campus initiatives with a prospective giver. In 1974 one of our nation's leading advancement officers, G. T. "Buck" Smith, now president of Chapman College, called this key natural partner "prime." He called the other natural partners involved with the same prospect "secondaries." In focusing attention on the primes' and secondaries' initiatives with prospective major gift prospects, Smith created what we now refer to as the "moves concept" of major gift fund raising.

There is a problem with using the help of primes and secondaries in work so crucial to major gift support. When the primes and secondaries bound out of bed in the morning, they seldom have the institution or your prospective major gift givers on their minds. They may go for days, weeks, or even months without focusing their attention on these donors. Therefore, your campus needs to encourage primes and secondaries to take the initiatives required to build their prospective major gift givers' awareness, knowledge, interest, involvement, and commitment. The development staff member who encourages, supports, and manages these initiatives that Smith called moves is known as a "moves manager." What distinguishes moves managers from other fund raisers is their focus on identifying the primes and secondaries and working with them to carry out initiatives that create the meaningful experiences leading to a major gift.

You base selection of primes and secondaries on two criteria: (1) the person's relationship with the prospective giver; and (2) his or her willingness and ability to help build the institution's relationship with the giver. As president, you will be the prime or secondary for many of your major gift prospects. Others who may serve as primes and secondaries include deans, department heads, faculty, trustees, students, alumni, and other close friends. Like the president, the vice president for development and members of the development staff will probably become the primes or secondaries for a number of prospects.

Occasionally the advice that one person gives about what is appropriate to do or not do will conflict with another's advice. Because the group of prime and secondaries for each prospective giver will involve people of various positions and rank, it is important to sort out these differences in an environment that respects knowledge and familiarity rather than rank and position. As president, you will play a key role in creating such an environment.

Managing Moves

Your major gift prospects will undoubtedly be involved with a number of other institutions and organizations. Unless your campus enters their lives and consciousness every few weeks, it is likely that their ultimate gift, and larger special gifts, will go to the institutions and organizations that involve them more frequently and meaningfully. Therefore, each prospect must be assigned a moves manager to ensure the quality, frequency, and continuity of initiatives. The responsibilities of the moves manager are:

1. *Review* what has transpired in the relationship with the prospective giver.
2. *Plan* the next initiative required.
3. *Coordinate* the initiative with the appropriate prime and secondaries.
4. *Implement* the initiative.
5. *Assess* the results.
6. *Report* and *record* the results.

Although the work associated with this process is ongoing, the cycle begins again at least every month. Some of the moves will require only a few hours or days; others will require weeks or months. Consequently, more than one move may be going forward for a single prospect at the same time.

The initiative or move may be as simple as a phone call or as elaborate as a testimonial dinner. You must decide which move is appropriate, based on an informed assessment of what is most likely to bring the prospect closer to your institution. Should the next move simply be to gain more information? Or should it advance the prospect's awareness, interest, and involvement? Perhaps the time is right to ask for a commitment?

The types of moves or initiatives that accomplish these objectives fall into two categories: *background* initiatives and *foreground* initiatives.

You conceive, plan, and execute *foreground* initiatives with a specific person in mind. They include such things as:

1. A request to borrow art for display on campus
2. An invitation to dinner with the president
3. A request for advice in an area of special competence
4. An invitation to meet with the dean
5. Flowers to celebrate an anniversary
6. A testimonial dinner
7. A visit from a faculty member
8. A message of congratulations over a business promotion
9. A request to represent the institution at the inauguration of another campus president
10. A letter reporting on the impact of a previous gift

You conceive, plan, and execute *background* initiatives with a group of people in mind. They may involve one or more major gift prospects. Some common background initiatives are:

1. Class reunions
2. Newsletters and alumni magazines
3. Films and slide shows
4. Alumni club activities
5. College-sponsored travel
6. Annual reports of the college
7. Musical, theatrical, or athletic events
8. Campus tours
9. Campus advisory councils
10. Continuing education programs

The quality of initiatives will be influenced by how well the people helping you understand the interests and needs of the prospects. Institutional friendships, like personal friendships, take time to grow and develop naturally. The person who presumes friendship and familiarity, when these are not based on mutual feelings and experiences, diminishes the relationship. The best safeguard for ensuring the quality of major gift initiatives is the patience and sensitivity of the people who conceive, plan, coordinate, and execute those initiatives.

Frequency and continuity are as essential to success as is quality in managing initiatives. An alumnus of my alma mater has presented to it a remarkable series of gifts, including two buildings, four professorships, another professorship given by his wife in his honor, and an arboretum. When he agreed to help us create the arboretum, we realized that this was the gift closest to his heart. Its dedication in his honor provided us an opportunity to express our thanks, appreciation, regard, and affection.

If, however, six weeks or six months were to go by without fresh initiatives to bring his alma mater back into his consciousness, much of what we invested to create that dedication would be lost. We waste one initiative if we do not follow it with other initiatives designed to maintain and incrementally advance the friendship.

Staffing Considerations

Senior development officers whose background and experience qualify them to serve as your major gifts officer often are qualified to serve as director or vice president of development, or planned-giving officer. At the same time, increasing numbers of institutions are establishing fund-raising programs. As a result, the demand for experienced major gifts officers exceeds the supply. If you choose to fill this position from outside the college, beware of applicants whose career shows a record of frequent job changes. Your major gifts officer helps build some of your institution's most important friendships. You need continuity in this position.

With demand outstripping the supply of experienced and qualified major gift officers, and with the high compensation required to attract them, you should consider selecting a person already at your institution. The Council for Advancement and Support of Education (CASE) conducts training conferences that provide an excellent orientation for such officers. These conferences provide an introduction to other major gift officers, who in turn become a valuable resource and support network for newcomers. You and your chief advancement officer might consider hiring a consultant to coach your home-grown major gifts officer as he or she gets started. As with the selection of any consultant, be sure to check out the proposed consultant's credentials and performance record first.

Here are a few qualifications to keep in mind as you consider candidates:

1. *A kind and forgiving nature is essential.* Your major gifts officer should look for the good in people and, while recognizing their

faults, still like and appreciate them. People who are judgmental or insincere quickly fail in this role.

2. *Integrity is an absolute requirement.* Unless the institution's trustees, faculty, staff, alumni, and friends have total confidence in the honesty and discretion of your major gifts officer, he or she cannot succeed.

3. *Sensitivity is another essential.* Your major gifts officer must be able to deal as astutely with feelings as with facts. No amount of experience can make up for a lack of sensitivity.

4. *Conscientious hard work is another requirement.* Despite the advantages of maturity, financial knowledge, and so on, this is not a position for a person who views it as a last stop before retirement. There will always be more work for your major gifts officer than time or resources to do it.

5. *Commitment to higher education and your institution's unique role in it also are important.* The person you want as a major gifts officer probably is one of your donors already and more than likely supports a number of other charitable causes.

6. *Maturity is valuable.* Maturity will help your major gifts officer to relate to, and be accepted by major gifts prospects and volunteers.

7. *Knowledge of finances is desirable.* For example, a local bank trust officer with knowledge of personal investments and finances combined with human relations skills could be an excellent candidate.

8. *Knowledge of the means of giving is advantageous.* Some familiarity with planned/deferred giving is essential, but your officer can acquire this. He or she need not be an expert on tax law. Although the knowledge and skill of such a person should be available to your institution to prepare legally qualified trust agreements and other gift instruments and to offer advice, your major gifts officer needn't be the primary source. The demands of keeping that knowledge current, and of exercising it on behalf of the campus, would keep that party from his or her primary function of stimulating, managing, and supporting initiatives.

Tools Required

To function efficiently in its major gift fund raising, your campus should keep track of at least *two* types of information: Facts about prospective major gift givers, and records of the interactions between the campus and the prospective major gift givers. (Most institutions already have a system for researching prospective givers and storing the information.) There are *three* sources from which your campus should draw for prospect data: public information researched by your development staff, peer information provided by volunteers, and information from the prospects themselves. The lattermost is by far the most helpful and reliable.

Prospect tracking systems to monitor the institution's interaction with key prospects have developed in recent times. Prospect tracking systems record, store, and allow ready access to information about initiatives. If well conceived, the prospect tracking system will provide a basic tool for managing, communicating, coordinating, and stimulating initiatives. Your prospect tracking system should not duplicate the contents of your institution's prospect information system, but may be integrated with it.

Measuring Progress

The bottom line for evaluating fund raising is the number and amount of gifts received. While this is as true of major gift fund raising as it is in other areas of your institution's fund raising, your time frame for evaluating your major gift program is much longer.

You can evaluate regular or annual gift fund raising by dollars and donors on a year-to-year basis. For special gifts, an appropriate time frame is typically the length of the campaign for those special gifts. For ultimate gifts, the time frame for measuring the bottom line is the lifetime of your prospects.

The dollars and donors that your campus records from major gifts prospects in a single year can be misleading. One or two ultimate gifts that are based on the cumulative effect of initiatives taken over ten or twenty years may make a currently poor program look great. Conversely, a program that is doing an outstanding job of building a sense of commitment among the right prospective givers may not produce measurable results for several years.

Because the number and value of gifts received in a given year may not accurately reflect the current strength or weakness of your institution's gifts program, you must also look to other measures of its performance. The best indication of your program's performance will come from examining the quality, quantity, frequency, continuity, and effectiveness of its initiatives with each prospective giver.

Your Role as President

In *The Power of Ethical Management* (William Morrow and Co., 1988), coauthors Kenneth Blanchard and Norman Vincent Peale quote the chairman of the board of Matsushita Electric. When asked what his primary job was as chairman of the great international company, he responded, "To model love. I am the soul of this company. It is through me that our organization's values pass." Your first and foremost role as president in major gift fund raising is to be the soul of your institution through which its values pass. Through you, those values are recognized and given voice.

17

PLANNED GIVING
Winton C. Smith, Jr.

One aspect of an effective development program is planned giving by contributors who believe in an institution and desire to make substantial gifts to it. The purpose of planned giving is to encourage your contributors to select the most appropriate among a wide range of gift opportunities. Frequently, contributors discover that they can give more than they thought possible. Often the result is an increased gift for your institution.

Planned giving includes major current gifts, gifts that provide a life income, and estate gifts. Successful planned giving programs include the following elements.

Training for Development Staff

You, the president, and your development team must have a thorough knowledge of planned-giving opportunities. You must know the various types of gifts and who makes them, and why and how. Moreover, you must know how to promote the various types of gifts, and how to talk to people about them.

CASE provides a comprehensive training program to inform development professionals about all aspects of planned giving. These national, yearly conferences include "Introduction to Planned Giving" workshops, "Advanced Planned-Giving" conferences, and annual refresher courses. Too, each year, colleges and universities employ an experienced consultant to train the development team on campus. This provides a cost-effective way for an institution to train the team, and an opportunity for all parties involved to concentrate on those planned gifts that are most important for the institution.

A Successful Planned-Giving Committee

You and your development team should establish a successful Planned-Giving Committee that will endorse your planned-giving program. It will also encourage bequests and other planned gifts for your institution: bequests, the foundation of a successful planned-giving program, provide the greatest financial results of any planned gift.

The chairman of your Planned-Giving Committee should be committed to making a leadership bequest and to enlisting a committee of people who will make similar bequests. Ideally, that chairman should be a member of your board.

(You should also set up a Planned-Giving Advisory Committee that includes lawyers, certified public accountants, trust officers, certified financial planners, and other financial planners. But I'll discuss that committee later.)

You should recruit the committee chairman and convey the importance of this program and of estate gifts for all institutions. You and the committee chairman should summarily establish a date to finish recruiting the committee. Then the two of you should identify the fifteen people in a position to make a leadership bequest or other planned gift for your institution. Consider board members, emeritus board members, major gift contributors, annual contributors, and (especially) those who have made repeat gifts. You should also consider contributors who have chosen not to have children but demonstrate a strong interest in your institution.

You and your chair should then visit each prospect, to ask him or her to join. You should explain that the program's purpose is to encourage contributors to consider the many types of planned gifts that may benefit them as well as the institution. The chairman should explain, however, that the committee will emphasize the simplest planned gift: the bequest. Committee members must understand not only the importance of estate gifts for your institution, but also the importance of their bequest or other planned gift to the success of your program. Committee members must agree to include your institution in their own estate plan. If any prospective committee member cannot (or will not), thank that person graciously and indicate that you understand that some cannot make estate gifts. Mention that you would appreciate support in other areas, but don't include that prospect on your committee.

A Bequest Recognition Society

Your board of trustees should approve a Bequest Recognition Society to honor and recognize those individuals who make an estate gift to your institution. Honor as charter members the members of the Planned-Giving Committee and the trustees who approve this society. Also include as charter members all contributors who have notified the institution over the years that they have put your college in their will. The Planned-Giving Committee should also recommend an annual dinner, or some other annual special event, to honor and recognize those who make this important type of gift. This celebration will help you to remember to thank the group annually, and also to measure the success of your program from year to year.

Guidelines

Your board of trustees should also adopt guidelines clarifying the nature of your planned-giving program. The guidelines should incorporate the various types of planned gifts and administrative procedures necessary to implement a successful program. Guidelines both convey information and provide an effective marketing approach. Some board members will learn about the various planned-giving opportunities for the first time, and may consider a gift themselves. Or perhaps they will suggest names of other potential contributors. Figure 17.1 illustrates a sample set of guidelines, while Figure 17.2 offers a sample description of planned-giving opportunities that your institution can adapt and use. (Figures will be found at the end of this chapter.)

Charitable Gift Planning Seminars

To explain planned-giving opportunities to the board and other contributors, many institutions offer annual seminars on charitable gift planning or charitable tax strategies. These seminars generate substantial gifts *and* provide an opportunity for an outside consultant and the staff to work together, thus offering additional staff training. You can adapt the sample invitation letter (Figure 17.3) and program description (Figure 17.4) for use on your campus.

A consultant can conduct an effective seminar for the board and other major contributors in about two to three hours and adequately cover the most important planned-giving opportunities. For the board alone, a consultant can run through an effective planned-giving program in from say forty-five to ninety minutes. A member of the development team can supervise brief presentations that last only five to ten minutes yet produce significant gifts. (The lattermost presentations frequently focus on a single planned-giving idea.)

A Presidential Wills Emphasis Letter

Again, bequests are the most important type of planned gift for your institution. Many colleges and universities find that most of their endowment comes through estate gifts. An annual letter from you discussing the importance of estate gifts for the institution and requesting consideration of an estate gift, is a cost-effective way to encourage bequests. Spring, when many contributors review their wills, is an excellent time for this letter to go out.

A Reunion Class Bequest Program

A reunion class bequest program—similar to an annual-fund agent program—can also be extremely effective. Reunion classes take special pride in announcing the number of class members who have provided a bequest to the institution. Typically, a class agent writes to class members encouraging a will provision for the college. You can recognize the class at reunion and emphasize the importance of these provisions for the college. The college can also list in an annual development report the number of bequests from each class, in order to recognize further the importance of these provisions.

A Planned-Giving Advisory Committee

You should invite trust officers, life insurance underwriters, certified financial planners, and other financial planning professionals to serve on a Planned-Giving Advisory Committee. This committee enlists an elite group of professional advisors who can help you implement your program. The committee also provides an opportunity for you to involve an important group of professional advisors in plans for your institution. You come to know the very group of advisors with whom you may later work on a major gift. The committee also encourages this group to consider the importance of charitable gift planning for their clients.

Seminars on Making Wills

Wills seminars encourage your contributors to recognize the importance of a proper will, and provide an excellent opportunity to suggest a possible estate gift for the institution. The chairman of the Planned-Giving Committee might ask a select group of lawyers specializing in the wills area to speak at the wills seminars. The program should include attorneys who are members of your Planned-Giving Advisory Committee, as well as others thoroughly knowledgeable about wills and who speak clearly before a group. Lawyers who specialize in wills often appreciate the chance to participate in such a program.

Charitable Gift Planning Seminars for Professionals

Many institutions conduct annual charitable gift planning or charitable tax strategies seminars for attorneys, accountants, trust officers, life insurance professionals, investment advisors, and other financial planning specialists interested in the campus and who advise potential donors. Lawyers and other financial planning specialists are trained to help people acquire and conserve assets, and they provide an excellent service. The simple fact is that many financial planning specialists are not trained in planned charitable gifts, so the seminars provide helpful information to the professionals helping clients to make taxwise gifts. (Professionals attending the program should receive continuing-education credit.) You and your development team will find that the seminar offers you the chance to become acquainted with planners you may work with later, on a major gift for the institution.

Printed Communications

A planned-giving program should use many techniques to stimulate interest among potential donors.

A quarterly planned-giving newsletter emphasizing feature articles can call attention to recent donors and to the importance of planned gifts. Articles written in nonlegal language can explain how various types of planned gifts can help the donors and their families as well as the institution. Newsletters should include a response card to allow donors to request additional information about various planned gifts, as shown in the sample newsletter in Figure 17.5.

A series of brochures, each covering in simple language a single planned-giving idea, helps the development staff respond to donor inquiries about various planned gifts.

Articles on planned giving in the campus newspaper or in other campus publications also are helpful because they reach an important target audience: alumni and friends of the institution. A series of articles, each focusing on a single planned-giving idea, often produces major gifts for institutions. You should also consider placing in campus publications a string of advertisements, or brief reminders, about the advantages of planned gifts.

Legal Advice

The development staff should retain an attorney specializing in the tax consequences of all types of planned gifts. Federal tax laws change rapidly. Counsel should send to the development staff each month a summary of the major changes in federal tax laws, and their potential effects on planned-giving opportunities. Of course, counsel should be available at all times to help your development staff present the most effective taxwise giving opportunities to donors.

Figure 17.1. SAMPLE GUIDELINES FOR PLANNED-GIVING PROGRAM.

The Planned-Giving Program of ABC College provides donors many opportunities to present a tangible expression of care and interest in ABC College by sharing their resources in a meaningful way and by helping donors meet their needs. This program exists both to provide support for the institution's mission, and to assist donors through a comprehensive portfolio of taxwise giving alternatives. The following general policies shall govern the program.

1. *Protection of Donor's Interest*
   ABC College and its representatives shall always consider the donor's financial situation, and shall encourage no donor to make an inappropriate gift.

2. *Use of Legal Counsel*
   ABC College shall seek the advice of legal counsel in all matters pertaining to its planned-giving program. Legal counsel will review all planned-giving agreements. All prospective donors will be urged to seek their own counsel in matters of estate planning, taxes, and planned gifts. It is not the province of ABC College staff to give legal advice. The donor's counsel must bear responsibility for all legal conclusions and advice.

3. *Authority for Negotiation*
   The following persons are authorized to negotiate planned-gift agreements with prospective donors: [designate college officials]—all of whom have been trained in this area. All agreements must be approved by the [designate college official] upon the advice of counsel. The [designate college official] is authorized to sign planned-gift agreements.

4. *Confidential Information*
   Donors shall be encouraged to notify ABC College, in writing, concerning all will provisions and other planned gifts. ABC College shall keep all information concerning wills and other planned gifts confidential, unless donors or their counsel permit this information to be released.

5. *Investments*
   The Investment Committee will make all investment decisions. All funds shall be invested under procedures established by the Investment Committee.

6. *Payment Schedule*
   ABC College life-income plans will make monthly, quarterly, or semi-annual payments, according to the donor's and income recipient's desires.

7. *Funding*
   Cash, securities, real property, personal property, or a combination of these, may fund planned gifts. Listed assets traded on a recognized exchange are accepted at their value on the date of the gift, which ordinarily is the mean between the high and low selling price on that date.

Figure 17.2. PLANNED-GIVING OPPORTUNITIES.

ABC College's Planned-Giving Program includes the following comprehensive taxwise giving alternatives.

I. Current Gifts

1. *Gifts of Cash, Securities, Real and Personal Property*
   Federal tax laws encourage gifts of cash, securities, and real and personal property to ABC College by permitting the donor to take a charitable contribution deduction for a gift to support ABC College's mission. The donor therefore gives ABC College the full dollar value of the gift to support its mission, and simultaneously removes the amount of the gift from being taxed at the donor's top income-tax bracket.

2. *Gifts of Undivided Interest*
   Donors may make gifts of a percentage interest of their entire interest in real and personal property. Federal tax laws encourage gifts of undivided interests by granting the donor a current income-tax deduction for the gift. Therefore, the donor makes a gift to support

Figure 17.2. *continued*

ABC College's mission and simultaneously removes the amount of the gift from being taxed at the donor's top tax bracket.

3. *Gifts of Closely-Held Stock*
Donors may make gifts of closely-held stock to ABC College and receive a charitable contribution deduction for the value of the stock.

4. *Gifts of Insurance Policies*
Donors may make gifts of insurance policies to ABC College and receive a charitable contribution deduction for the value thereof. Donors also may purchase life insurance policies, name ABC College as the owner, and take a charitable contribution deduction for each premium payment.

II. Deferred Gift Annuities

1. *Charitable Gift Annuities*
Donors may make gifts to ABC College and receive a guaranteed income for life. The donor receives a current income-tax deduction that produces current tax savings and also receives a large portion of guaranteed, tax-free income.

2. *Joint and Survivor Gift Annuities*
Donors may make gifts to ABC College, receive a guaranteed income for life, and also provide a guaranteed income for a spouse, parent, brother, sister, or other person for life. The gift produces current income-tax savings, and a large portion of the guaranteed income is tax-free. These gifts often save estate taxes, too, thus providing an increased income for a spouse or other survivor.

3. *Deferred Payment Gift Annuities*
Donors may make gifts to ABC College and receive a current income-tax deduction, and a guaranteed lifetime income to begin at some future date. Donors therefore may make a current gift, save income taxes, and also provide a guaranteed income for retirement.

4. *Charitable Remainder Unitrusts*
Donors may make gifts to ABC College in trust and provide for the trustee to pay them a fixed percentage each year of the value of the trust assets for life. These gifts often provide current income-tax savings, capital gains tax savings, and (frequently) estate taxes. Charitable remainder unitrusts enable donors who own highly appreciated low-yield assets to make a gift and also increase their return for life.

5. *Charitable Remainder Annuity Trusts*
Donors may make gifts to ABC College in trust and provide for the trustee to pay them a fixed amount each year, either for their lifetime or for a period of years. Charitable remainder annuity trusts enable donors who own appreciated low-yield assets to make a gift and increase their return for life.

6. *Life Estate Contracts*
Donors may make a gift of a personal residence or farm to ABC College, receive a current income-tax deduction, and retain use of the property for life.

7. *Charitable Lead Trusts*
Donors may make a gift to ABC College in trust and provide that the trustee shall pay an income to ABC College for a fixed period of years. They further provide that at the end of the period of years the trustee will transfer the property to children, grandchildren, or other specified persons. These gifts produce dramatic gift- and estate-tax savings, and thus provide a way both to make a gift and to preserve assets for the donor's family and other heirs.

III. Estate Gifts

1. *Will Provisions for ABC College*
Wills provide many donors an excellent opportunity to support ABC College's mission. Donors may bequeath either a fixed percentage of their estate, or a specific amount, to ABC College to support its mission. Donors also may provide in their wills for specific heirs to disclaim in favor of ABC College if they later decide to do so. State laws often provide for assets to go to the state if other heirs are unavailable. Donors may avoid this possibility by including ABC College in their wills as a final contingent beneficiary if other heirs are unavailable.

2. *Testamentary Charitable Gift Annuities*
Donors may include charitable gift annuities in their wills and thus provide for an eventual gift to ABC College. They may also provide a guaranteed income for a spouse, parent, brother, sister, or other survivor. These gifts often provide estate-tax savings, and thus frequently provide an increased income for a survivor for life.

3. *Testamentary Charitable Remainder Trusts*
Donors may include charitable remainder trusts in their wills and thus provide for an eventual gift to ABC College, and an income for a spouse, parent, brother, sister, or other survivor for life. These gifts often save estate taxes, and can provide an increased income for a spouse or other survivor.

Figure 17.2. *continued*

---

4. *Testamentary Charitable Lead Trusts*
   Donors may save estate taxes, and also provide for ABC College, by including a charitable lead trust in their will. This provides for an income payment to ABC College for a period of years, with the property going to children, grandchildren, or other private heirs at the end of the trust term. These gifts produce dramatic estate-tax savings and preserve their estate for heirs.

Figure 17.3. SAMPLE INVITATION LETTER.

Dear _____ :

You are cordially invited to be our guest at a Special Seminar on Charitable Tax Strategies, sponsored by _____ .

This seminar explains the latest income-, gift-, and estate-tax rules affecting the tax consequences of charitable gifts. The program explains a variety of ways in which you can increase your tax savings as you make charitable gifts. You learn how to plan your charitable gifts to your maximum advantage, as well as to the advantage of charitable institutions.

Winton Smith, Esq. conducts the program. Mr. Smith specializes in Estate-Tax Planning and Charitable-Tax Strategies. He lectures extensively for bar associations, estate-planning councils, colleges, and national philanthropic, religious, and other organizations. There will be an opportunity for questions after the presentation.

I hope you will join us for this special program. The Seminar will be held at [location] on [date] at [time].

I look forward to seeing you.

Sincerely,

Figure 17.4. PROGRAM TOPICS, CHARITABLE GIFT STRATEGIES
               SEMINAR.

- Latest income-, gift-, and estate-tax rules. How to make taxwise charitable gifts, including outright gifts, life income gifts, and estate gifts.
- Taxwise gifts of appreciated property, including stock or real estate, closely held stock, insurance policies, and other special gifts.

- How to make charitable gifts, save income- and capital-gains taxes, and increase your spendable income.
- How to make taxwise estate gifts through your will or through a revocable trust.
- How to make gifts through your will that increase the spendable income of surviving family members as well as provide a magnificent gift for our institution.
- How to make gifts through your will and protect your estate from estate taxation, thus preserving your estate for family members while providing an important gift to our institution for a specific period of time.
- Latest tax law changes and proposals.

Figure 17.5. SAMPLE NEWSLETTER.

A FINANCIAL
AND TAX PLANNING GUIDE
FOR FRIENDS OF
ABC COLLEGE

QUARTERLY NEWSLETTER   SPRING

WHY WRITE A WILL

Your Plan or the State's Plan

Whether single, married, or widowed, you need a will to distribute your assets and express your plan for family, friends, and other interests. State laws, called the laws of intestacy, dictate the disposition of your estate if you have no will. These laws vary from state to state, but they rarely dispose of your estate in the manner and proportions that you would desire.

THE STATE'S PLAN FOR YOUR SPOUSE

The State Provides One-Third for Your Spouse

You may wish your spouse to receive your entire estate or you may prefer to arrange for the management of assets for your spouse for his or her lifetime. If you have no will, state intestate laws frequently dictate that your spouse shall receive only one-third of your estate or share equally with your children, whichever is greater. This may leave your spouse with insufficient assets, and it often produces unnecessary estate taxation that further reduces your spouse's share of your estate.

Figure 17.5. continued

PLANNING FOR YOUR SPOUSE

*You can
Provide
Your Entire
Estate
Tax-Free
for Your
Spouse*

You can plan your will to leave your entire estate to your spouse free of federal estate taxes. You then insure that your spouse will receive the full value of your estate. Federal estate-tax laws change, and these changes influence the way wills are written to provide for spouses and other heirs. Your current will, if based on pre-1981 laws, may leave only $250,000 or one-half of the estate to the surviving spouse, and therefore the remaining one-half of the estate remains subject to the federal estate tax.

*Old Wills
Often
Provide
One-Half
for Your
Spouse*

Many wills written before the Tax Reform Act of 1981 leave the maximum amount allowable to the surviving spouse in order to qualify for the federal marital deduction. These wills, if written before September 13, 1981, are often interpreted to give only $250,000 or one-half of the estate to the surviving spouse, and therefore the remaining one-half of the estate remains subject to the federal estate tax.

*Consult
Your
Lawyer*

To make certain that your estate passes tax-free to your spouse, you should consult your lawyer, who can advise you whether or not to revise your will and make certain that you are leaving your entire estate to your spouse free of estate taxes.

PLANNING FOR MINOR CHILDREN

*Providing
for Minor
Children*

Parents of minor children have two special reasons for obtaining a properly written will. Through your will you have an opportunity to select the person or persons who will care for your children if you are not available. Your will also provides a way for you to specify your financial plans for their future. You can arrange for the management of property and thus assure an income for your children until they reach specified ages.

THE STATE'S PLAN FOR YOUR CHILDREN

*Court-
Appointed
Guardians*

If you have no will, the state steps in and selects a guardian for your children, often turning to the nearest surviving relative, rather than to the most suitable. The guardian must obtain the court's permission for the expenditure of funds. The guardian is also required to pay an annual bond premium to insure proper handling of the estate. In the absence of a will, even your spouse is subject to these requirements. The state also apportions your estate, often distributing your assets equally to your children, after the minimum legal age. When you consider the children's ages, educational and medical needs, or other factors, you may conclude that such a distribution would be inappropriate.

PROVIDING FOR MINOR CHILDREN

Financial Planning for Minor Children

Through a will you can name a guardian and an alternate guardian after considering the specific needs of your children and the willingness of the guardian to serve. You should talk to the guardian about your hopes and dreams for your children and the financial arrangements you have made to help them. You can eliminate the costly bond requirements and the annual accounting, and instead use the money saved for the children's support.

How Trusts Help

Although you need a guardian to provide for the actual care of your children, guardianships often do not provide the best financial plan for your children because they terminate and distribute the assets when a child becomes an adult—18 in most states. A more flexible option is the use of a trust in your will. This simply means that you leave your estate to a trustee who manages your assets as you direct in the terms of the trust. Because your trustee is under legal obligation to manage your property as you specify instead of as the Probate Court decides, you have greater control over the way the money will be spent. For example, assets can be distributed to your children at any age or at several different ages. You may direct that a portion of your estate be released when your child is 25 and the rest at age 30, thus ensuring a "second chance" for a child who might use his first inheritance unwisely. You may even direct that the assets be held until the last child completes his education. The value of a trust is that you can establish a financial plan for your children in the manner you wish and for the length of time you wish.

How to Provide a Second Chance for Your Children

Figure 17.5. *continued*

THE STATE'S PLAN FOR ITSELF

Your State Could Receive Your Property

Your final beneficiary under many state intestate laws is the state where you live. If your state-appointed heirs are unavailable, your property passes directly to your state. You can avoid an unintended gift to your state by naming our college, or some other charitable institution, to receive your estate if your other heirs are unavailable.

PLANNING FOR ABC COLLEGE

Your Plan for ABC College

Just as you have provided for our college throughout your lifetime, you can include a provision for our college in your will and continue your support of our mission. Wills offer many donors a way to make gifts that might not have been possible during their lifetime. Your will can reaffirm your commitment to our college.

PERCENTAGE OF ESTATE

How to Provide a Percentage Bequest

Because estates are frequently divided by percentages, it may be simplest to designate that our college receive a percentage of your estate. This is especially convenient if you are uncertain of the exact value of your assets and therefore wish to avoid naming a specific sum. Many donors, however, choose to designate a percentage so that they may contribute their estates as they have contributed their income over the years.

SPECIFIC SUM OF SPECIFIC PROPERTY

How to Provide a Specific Bequest

If you wish to know the exact amount of your gift, so as to direct the use to which it will be put, you can also select an amount which, when invested, will continue your present annual contribution to our college on a permanent basis.

TWOFOLD BEQUEST

How to Provide for a Survivor

You can include a trust in your will that assures life income for your survivors but that ultimately provides for our college. The trustee manages the assets, your heirs receive a lifetime income, the estate is saved federal estate taxes, and our college ultimately receives the assets.

AN ANNUAL GIFT FOR A PERIOD OF YEARS

*How to
Preserve
Your
Estate*

Charitable Lead Trusts make an annual contribution to our college for a specified period of years, after which time the property goes to your heirs. Thus, you provide for our college, save estate taxes, and preserve your property for your heirs.

RESIDUE OF ESTATE

After providing for your other heirs, you leave the remainder of your estate to our college, thus removing the possibility that your property might go to the state if your other heirs do not survive you.

*A Gift to
ABC College
Through
Your Will*

All gifts to our college through wills are important. If you have our college in your will now, please advise us of your current provision. As you consider your desire to support our mission through your will, we will be pleased to send sample provisions for your consideration, and additional information concerning the tax advantages of charitable provisions for our college.

For Further information, write or call:

Director of Planned Giving
ABC College
College Town, USA
(202) 328–5900

© Winton C. Smith, Jr., 1988

18

The Capital Campaign:
Benefits and Hazards

Rita Bornstein

A capital campaign is more than a special fund-raising endeavor. It celebrates an institution's history and creates a vision of its future. This type of campaign calls for the reassessment and reaffirmation of an institution's mission, goals, and priority needs. It fires the imagination of all those connected with the institution, and inspires to action those with the resources necessary to convert the vision into reality. It raises fund raising to a new conceptual and technical level, akin to the difference between making a home movie and a major film classic. Indeed, an ambitious and successful campaign is one of the greatest legacies a president can leave a university or college.

But beware: Such a campaign should not be launched until both the president and vice president are as ready as the institution for the rigors and hazards of the undertaking. The president's role, being central, will demand an extraordinary commitment—well beyond the already heavy demands of the office. And supporting the president, and directing the campaign backstage, must be a strong and able vice president.

The President's Role

As I have said, both the institution and the president must be ready for a capital campaign. To undertake it too early or too late in a president's tenure is to doom it: A campaign led by either a brand-new or a lame-duck president will lack both credibility and power.

You, the president, are the pivot of a campaign, the institution's chief fund-raiser. Thirty to 40 percent of your time should be spent on this enterprise, much of it in building close relationships with those individuals who can make it a success. You will soon discover that such activity greatly increases the normal round of dinner parties, meetings, receptions, and special events. This means that you will need to have regular assistance from the development vice president (just one of whose tasks is to help you to manage your time judiciously).

The success of a campaign will depend in large measure on the extent to which you develop an appetite for fund raising. You should conduct many, if not most, of the major gift solicitations. A trustee or dean may be present, but *you* carry the banner of the institution and are its chief spokesperson and advocate. You are the commander-in-chief who articulates the vision that inspires the troops. It is you who must kindle and keep aflame staff and volunteer confidence and enthusiasm.

A great advantage to a president in a campaign is a strong provost to whom you can delegate much of the internal institutional activity. You must be free to focus on the campaign and to meet frequently with volunteers, alumni, and donors.

The president sets the moral tone of a campaign. You ensure that the institution is always presented honestly to its publics, that volunteers and staff do not pressure prospects to make gifts not in their best interests, that gifts with unacceptable restrictions are renegotiated or rejected, and that gifts from inappropriate sources are not accepted. In these and other situations the most ethical course of action may not always be apparent to others. You should set a high standard and insist on being involved in decision-making as problems arise.

The Development Vice President's Role

A campaign is a team effort and should not be launched until you have a vice president in place whom you trust.

You and your vice president should meet weekly to plan the campaign, chart strategy for key prospects, and discuss issues to be brought before volunteer leaders. The vice president is responsible for keeping you informed about fund-raising activities and is involved in campaign-related policy decisions. It is also imperative that the vice president be fully aware of what you know and do in relation to the campaign.

The vice president should participate in the academic goal-setting process and in the opening academic discussions at the institution. He or she should be present at board meetings in order to (1) understand the issues surrounding the institution, (2) be available to answer development-related questions, (3) develop good relationships with board members, and (4) keep the campaign high on everyone's agenda. Participation in planning and policy arenas ensures that the vice president has the institution's direction firmly in mind when managing the campaign.

The development vice president is the linchpin of the campaign, orchestrating and driving the entire effort and coordinating the fund-raising activities of staff, deans, faculty, and volunteers. The vice president singlemindedly focuses on the campaign while the president and key volunteers attend to their many other responsibilities.

Elements of Success

Timing. A feasibility study determines the institution's state of readiness. Staff can conduct such a study, but an outside consultant produces a more objective result. The study investigates the strength of the institution's case for support, tests a financial target among potential donors and volunteers, assesses the prospect pool and volunteer leadership, and appraises the ability of the development staff to execute the campaign.

Board Involvement. The board must be involved from the moment a campaign is contemplated, in order to ensure the commitment of its members as the process unfolds. Every important policy decision should be taken to the board. The most crucial campaign issues the board will face are: approval of a strategic plan for the institution; when to launch the campaign; the amount of the financial target; and gift-counting and reporting standards.

Board members should accept primary responsibility for providing and soliciting financial support for the campaign according to their capabilities and resources. A capital campaign at a private college or university provides a rationale for asking inactive members to step aside, and for recruiting powerful new members.

Volunteer Leadership. Volunteers are the *sine qua non* of major campaigns. Although staff involvement in campaign fund raising is important, there is no substitute for peer solicitation. Assessment of an institution's campaign readiness must include an honest appraisal of the experience and commitment of its volunteers.

One of the most important steps in a campaign is to identify and enlist a campaign chairperson. This individual, perhaps a member of the governing board, certainly should be someone knowledgeable about, and committed to, the institution's goals. The campaign leader should also be a well-respected individual of high status, able to devote considerable time to cultivating and soliciting prospects, and willing to make a significant personal gift. This appointment will send a clear message about the importance of the campaign to the institution's constituencies, both internal and external.

The campaign chairperson, president, and development vice president constitute the "first team" of the campaign. The chemistry among these three must be especially good, laced with a great deal of mutual respect.

Academic Planning and Identification of Needs. Before a campaign is undertaken, you should initiate or update institution-wide strategic planning. Through a comprehensive planning process vice presidents, deans, faculty, and staff review academic and nonacademic strengths and weaknesses, endorse or redefine the institutional mission, project goals, and identify needs. The plan serves as the stage for the drama of the campaign, for from this process you can develop the case statement and gift opportunities for the campaign.

A campaign offers an opportunity to institute academic change in a system that is notoriously slow to change. The academic planning that must undergird a campaign provides a mechanism for identifying both long- and short-term institutional priorities, fortifying or building selected departments and research areas, and reallocating resources to support those decisions.

Aggressive fund raising calls for entrepreneurship among scholars. Often of interest to foundations and corporations are projects at the margins of the disciplines. To secure such support, new academic configurations may be developed in conformance with identified institutional priorities.

Although the president usually has little direct control over the curriculum, change can be influenced through the academic priorities emphasized in fund raising. As programs and projects stand to benefit from the president's special interest during the campaign, so also will this emphasis be implicitly communicated to faculty as they make decisions about the curriculum.

Setting the Campaign Goal. In determining the financial target of a campaign, you will weigh your institution's needs against its fund-raising potential. The president has the challenge of determining whether the development vice president, board members, and consultants are too cautious in their recommendations. Vice presidents are professionally committed to meeting their goals. Board members are determined to be successful. Consultants want to add a win to their scorecard.

The campaign goal must be attainable, but should represent a stretch for everyone involved. A bold campaign attracts attention from the media and the community. It also stimulates prospects, alumni, faculty, and staff to give more and work harder to achieve the future envisaged through the campaign. Of course, the more ambitious the goal, the harder the president's work. But once the president sets the challenge, board members and development officers will accept it as their own.

Donors. Part of the preparation for determining the campaign goal is analyzing the range and levels of support possible from prospects. Campaign success depends on having enough good prospects to meet the goal, and the organization to cultivate and solicit those prospects.

A gift range table will provide a rough approximation of the number of gifts needed at various gift levels to make the goal. For every donor at the top levels, you need two or three good prospects. As part of the intensive preparation for a major campaign, the development office will identify those individuals and organizations to consider as prospects for the necessary levels of giving. If a strong prospect base does not exist, the development office should raise a caution flag about proceeding with campaign plans. Focus special attention throughout the campaign on that relatively small number of prospects who are the key to success.

Before you can solicit individuals of wealth for support, they must develop an interest in the institution. Building those relationships is of critical importance to managing a campaign. A wide variety of opportunities for prospect involvement with the institution probably already exist, and you can create many more. Prospects can serve as members on advisory, visiting, campaign, and other committees. They can also participate in a variety of meetings, lectures, seminars, colloquia, receptions, parties, lunches, and so on.

Gift-Counting and Reporting Policies. The time to reach agreement on gift policies is before you launch the campaign. Policies and procedures should conform with those at comparable institutions, and you should adhere to them rigorously. Most institutions are already scrupulously following the CASE–NACUBO (National Association of College and University Business Officers) guidelines in their annual reporting to the Council for Financial Aid to Education. (Comprehensive campaigns often go beyond these annual reporting guidelines and include pledges and deferred gifts in their count.)

The credibility of a campaign depends on the integrity of the reporting process. As a successful campaign evolves, many, including board members who approved the policies, will call into question campaign procedures for accepting and counting contributions. Refer these doubters to the board policy.

Budget. Launch no campaign without an adequate investment of resources in the development operation. Requirements vary, based on the size of the institution and the campaign, but you should spend between 5 and 15 percent of the campaign target on the development operation. Consider setting up a separate campaign budget, which can be amortized for accounting purposes and funded in a variety of ways. Also consider budget enhancements, including additional staff, entertainment, travel, counsel, and computer hardware and software.

Staffing. A successful campaign depends in large measure on the adequacy and range of staff positions, and the competency of the development staff. Before entering a campaign, centralize operations under the development vice president to the extent possible. This ensures coordination, the recruitment of top fund-raising talent, appropriate training, team building, and the planning necessary to ensure a high level of productivity.

There is no substitute for a fully coordinated, organized, institution-wide effort. In large universities with professional schools, unless development is carefully orchestrated, school-based fund raisers may be directing proposals and solicitations to individuals and organizations without regard to approaches conducted by others in the institution. The embarrassment and inefficiency resulting from such a lack of coordination can be costly.

Development operations should become highly organized and sophisticated in the course of planning and managing a large campaign. You should see that key areas such as major giving, planned giving, donor research, and proposal writing are adequately staffed, and the staff well trained. (Computerize financial and biographical records.)

A major opportunity exists through a campaign to bridge the historic schism between the development and academic sectors of the institution. The effective collaboration that must emerge during a campaign depends on mutual respect and confidence.

Consultants. Seek help from consultants when you contemplate a major campaign. Consultants bring a national perspective, broad campaign experience, and an unbiased view of the institution. They can conduct the feasibility study and remain with the campaign full-time by placing a manager on site, or part-time through regular visits. Consultants can be especially helpful in setting forth to board members and volunteers their responsibilities for financial and leadership support in the campaign.

Public Relations and Publications. The public relations and publications staff and operations must be ready to support a campaign. You may need to call on consultants, but in-house expertise will be vital to oversee the preparation of campaign materials and the timing and preparation of news releases. You must see that relations with the media are managed effectively during a campaign. Fund-raising success depends on donors who hold positive attitudes toward the institution, and the institution's portrayal in print and nonprint media strongly influence such attitudes.

Alumni Relations. A comprehensive campaign will seek special gifts from alumni, upgrade general alumni giving, and increase the number of alumni who contribute. Key to these efforts is the effectiveness of an institution's alumni relations program. Graduates are more likely to provide financial support if they had a good experience while at the institution and if they maintain close ties to it. A good, current relationship can even overcome any negative residual from a less-than-happy college experience.

You should see that the alumni and public-affairs operations, as well as the development office, are carefully assessed before the campaign. If the campaign is to be a success, you will require much of the alumni professionals.

Hazards of a Campaign

Campaigns, like other human endeavors, generally produce a number of unintended negative consequences. In the early campaign euphoria, no clouds appear on the sunny, dollar-laden horizon. Because you as president will be responsible for campaign failures as well as victories, you should know the pitfalls you may encounter.

Long-Term Problems. No matter how successful a campaign, chances are it will not solve long-term accumulated problems such as low faculty salaries, deferred maintenance, and budget deficits. When this becomes apparent, some deans and faculty become disenchanted. To forestall such expectations, explain early that a fund-raising campaign is most successful when it focuses on programs and projects that excite prospects.

Future and Restricted Commitments. Most commitments to the campaign are likely to be restricted to special projects, and not all of the cash does come in at once. In fact, in many campaigns, a significant percentage of the commitments secured are in the form of deferred gifts that will not mature for many years. Other commitments will be paid out over a period of time, generally three to five years.

Because most of the money comes in for restricted purposes, the president may not have significantly more flexible dollars to spend, even though the campaign results are very good. Faculty members, alumni, and others will want to know why the president is not funding their favorite projects. You will have to explain this over and over again.

Rich Nations vs. Poor Nations. Units of the institution that are less successful at fund raising will begin to resent greatly the more successful. This is particularly acute if the campaign includes fund raising for a school of medicine or a big-time athletics program. But it can be just as thorny a problem among disciplines in the liberal arts. The problem of "rich nations vs. poor nations" erupts during a campaign because those units with the greatest resources and reputation are disproportionately successful at fund raising.

The Edifice Complex. Another hazard of campaigning is limited donor interest in erecting the many facilities generally included among the institution's priorities. This problem is especially acute at private institutions, which receive little or no support from the state for facilities. A campaign provides a powerful stimulus for the "edifice complex" that seems to exist in virtually all deans and presidents. The huge sums necessary to build facilities are hard to raise, although there are a few individuals and families for whom naming an important college or university building is attractive and possible. You must see that those few are identified, involved, and solicited during the course of the campaign.

Unmet Needs. Not only will some faculty needs go unmet, but so will many other programmatic and endowment needs identified early in the planning process. At the same time, the institution will have opportunities to establish programs, endowments, and even facilities not high on the priority list. Some of these will be hard to refuse, but those whose priorities have found no sponsor through the campaign may view these actions negatively. It falls to you, together with the board, to determine when to refuse a gift and to redirect the donor's interest. As the campaign evolves, you can refocus attention of staff and volunteers to units and projects that are severely underfunded.

Incremental Costs. Successful fund raising often incurs unanticipated incremental financial costs. For example, the income distribution from an endowed chair probably will not be enough to support the salary of a nationally known professor, and certainly not his or her requirements for graduate and clerical assistance, library resources, laboratory equipment, space, and so on. Then there is the generous gift to build a facility that does not establish a maintenance endowment, creating a financial albatross for the future.

State Support. News of an institution's fund-raising success travels quickly to the state legislature. Even key alumni and friends in the capitol may be tempted to eliminate or reduce some state support and to ignore arguments for new or special projects. As the campaign moves toward its successful conclusion, state representatives must regularly be briefed on the separate objectives for state and private support.

Secrets. The uncontrolled flow of confidential information can be hazardous to a campaign. "Don't tell anyone" is a phrase that begs for clarification. How anonymous does a donor intend an anonymous gift to be? Does the request simply mean no news release, so that the donor will not be besieged by requests from other charitable organizations? Can you tell the dean and faculty affected by the gift? Development officers? Can you use the information as leverage in other solicitations?

To protect the donor and the integrity of the institution, you should define the degree of confidentiality at the time of the gift and record it in development files for future reference. Memories fade rapidly and, without a record, what was confidential in April may be common knowledge by December.

The casual handling of confidential information may have serious consequences. A president or other institutional representative can inadvertently damage relations with a donor by making a chance remark before the conclusion of a final agreement. Also, avoid releasing information about a donor that can risk embarrassment—or even the possibility of a lawsuit.

Opportunities Created by a Campaign

A bold, successful campaign brings prominence to an institution and its president. Alumni, corporate leaders, foundation executives, and others see the institution as a winner, a place that others find worthy of support. They will want to participate.

A campaign forges a sense of common purpose among all segments of the academic community, and extends these bonds outward to the larger institutional family. A campaign affords the opportunity to tell the institution's story to many audiences.

Through a campaign you can establish a powerful fund-raising apparatus. At its conclusion, the tendency will be to dismantle this machinery, slash the budget, and focus on other priorities. For the long-term health of the institution, you should be wary of, and counter, such actions.

Planning for the next campaign must begin, quietly, before you end the current campaign. Within a few years you will announce another campaign, but in the interim the big challenge is to keep annual-giving totals at the new levels. The institution will have begun to depend on this new level of funding. Backsliding in staffing and organization can be extraordinarily costly when gearing up for the next effort. Some tightening will be in order, but the institution is now permanently in a campaign mode.

Historians writing about American universities and colleges and their presidents in the late twentieth century will pay great attention to the strategies they pursued to secure the financial support necessary for continued growth. The campaigns that made a difference will figure prominently in this record.

19

THE HISTORICAL IMPORTANCE OF MAJOR GIFTS

James L. Fisher

"We must find a wise man of means who wants to make a difference." These reportedly were the words of James Pierpont about the struggling Collegiate School of Connecticut in 1711. And, with the help of Jeremiah Dummer and Cotton Mather, he found that man in Elihu Yale. Although Yale had never seen the Collegiate School, he was persuaded not to bestow his gifts on Oxford. Instead, he became convinced that his benefaction could make a more formidable impact on the new college in the colonies. The following letter from Mather may also have helped persuade him.

> Sir, though you have your felicities in your family, which I pray God continue and multiply, yet certainly, if what is forming at New Haven might wear the name of YALE COLLEGE it would be better than a name of sons and daughters. And your munificence might easily obtain for you a commemoration and perpetuation of your valuable name, which would indeed be much better than an Egyptian pyramid.

Thus was born Yale College from a gift of Elihu Yale.

So it was later with the Brown family, as their 760 pounds sterling gave vitality to the College of Rhode Island (Brown University); with the Penn family and the college of Philadelphia (University of Pennsylvania); and with the Earl of Dartmouth and Moor's Charity School of Lebanon (Dartmouth College—although the donor thought he was giving money to teach Christianity and educational skills to the Indians). And so it has been with almost every great college and university in America. Each has received life and potential greatness from a single major gift.

Here we distinguish major gifts from big gifts. While both are important to an institution, the major gift is at once more speculative and more life-giving, and makes a fundamental difference in the institution's condition and potential. The major gift makes the big gift possible. It is axiomatic that without a major gift, the enterprise will fail.

Certain characteristics seem to distinguish major givers from others. In general, they appear more inclined to take risks, are visionaries, and tend to be idealists. They are entrepreneurial in nature, are more likely to be self-made and strong-willed, have a realistic view of the world, and are highly disciplined. They are bottom-line oriented and tend to invest their resources in the president rather than in the institution itself.

In the Beginning

In America it all started with John Harvard some 350 years ago, when he bequeathed his gift of books and money to the new college north of Boston. It was only then that an uncertain Harvard College gained sufficient momentum to send three clergymen—Thomas Weld, Hugh Peters, and William Hibbens—to England to raise support for "a school of learning, acceptable to God and man." Parenthetically, to help them present the case for the college, they used a publication, *New England's First Fruits,* which was the prototype of thousands of fund-raising publications to be used by colleges and universities.

Indeed, philanthropy (also discussed in Chapter 2), which in its most successful practice is uniquely American, began in America with the founding of Harvard. Historian Henry Steele Commager wrote:

> Americans managed so long without energetic government that they came to prefer volunteer public enterprise. If they wanted a college, they built one; if they wanted a hospital, they raised the money for it; whatever was called for, they did it . . . and they kept right on doing it into the twentieth century.

It was as if, in order to ensure that their government not become too powerful, Americans chose to do many of the important things themselves, never arrogating to the government the full responsibility for the public welfare. If there was a need to educate, heal, or defend, Americans would do it themselves. And through the centuries, if the country started slipping one way or another, some dynamic American seemed always to step forth to restore the balance—usually backed by those most rational American institutions, our colleges and universities. Although the multitudes would eventually become involved, initially it was, much more often than not, those who benefited from major gifts to institutions of higher learning who made the balancing possible.

It is important to point out that a number of America's first colleges received some *public* support (Dartmouth, King's College). But the primary source of support for all early American colleges was *private*, and the moral force therefrom was to effect a better society, usually through religion.

From the founding of Harvard until the Civil War, over a thousand colleges opened in America. Fewer than two hundred survived, the rest having died for want of a major gift. The survivors that exist today are among the most prestigious colleges and universities in the world. And they are here because of the wisdom of a handful of our forebears who had the foresight, goodness, and resources to invest in our future.

Carnegie, Rockefeller, and Big Giving

Andrew Carnegie and John D. Rockefeller were major givers. As I have noted in Chapter 2, Carnegie's "Wealth" (1889) first proposed benevolent foundations created by the rich. In that same year, Rockefeller gave the first of the millions of dollars he was to donate to the University of Chicago. And Commodore Cornelius Vanderbilt led his family over the next seventy-five years to contribute millions to Central College, now Vanderbilt University.

Out of this largesse came bad as well as good—the inevitable result of colleges, and universities, unaccustomedly administering great amounts of cash. For instance, the infamous "tainted money" controversy grew out of accusations that rich robber barons were trying to buy public acceptance. Through the years, however, the wisdom of Carnegie and Rockefeller prevailed as major gifts from individuals proved to be a primary source of educational (and therefore societal) direction in America.

There is an amusing story about Andrew Carnegie, suggesting that one cannot take ethical behavior for granted:

> While touring rural Ireland in his declining years, Mr. Carnegie developed an intestinal problem and went to a local hospital administered by nuns. He quickly recovered, and on the evening before his discharge the Mother Superior paid him a visit. She acknowledged his international reputation as a philanthropist and asked if he would give the hospital $5,000. Grateful for the excellent care he had received, Mr. Carnegie quickly said yes.
>
> The next day, as he prepared to leave the hospital, he saw a copy of a local newspaper with the headline, "Andrew Carnegie Gives Hospital $50,000." Immediately the Mother Superior rushed into his room and

apologized for the error. It seems a young nun had added a zero when she reported the amount to the local editor.

His reputation at stake, Mr. Carnegie analyzed the situation and told Mother Superior that a correction wasn't necessary. He would increase the original amount to $50,000, but in return the hospital would have to mount a plaque in its lobby. He said the check and plaque would be mailed to her soon. When the plaque arrived, it was inscribed: "And When I Was Sick, You Took Me.—Andrew Carnegie."

Major Gifts Create Great Institutions

In 1864, President William C. Cattel of Lafayette College had a dream goal that depended on major support. He wanted to build his small, struggling Presbyterian college into a dynamic model based on the finest American traditions. Out of a combination of commitment, brass, and desperation, he went to a man who had never even heard of Lafayette College: Azio Pardee. Pardee, a prosperous "man of business," helped refine Cattel's dream goal, and gave it life through his generosity. By the time Cattel died (1892) he had contributed $522,800 to Lafayette—more than Ezra Cornell gave in major gifts to found Cornell University at about the same time. Since that time Lafayette has received more than a dozen multimillion-dollar gifts, has attained a net worth of $400 million and an endowment of $150 million, and recently completed a $54 million campaign. But no gift has been so telling as that of the man who gave to support an idea without having seen the college.

A $3.5 million gift by Johns Hopkins to the university that bears his name literally revolutionized research and medicine in the United States (and indeed the world). Yet Johns Hopkins University, like all of its colonial predecessors, has retained its fundamental commitment to the liberal arts. In fact, today the undergraduate liberal arts college at Johns Hopkins enrolls only about 2,200 students, a telling reminder of its origins and continuing purpose.

Then there is the classic story of Stanford University, a lesson to all college presidents:

> In the year 1884, a young man from America died while on a visit to Europe. His middle-aged, grieving parents returned with the body. They were heartbroken; they had loved their son very much. After the funeral, they began to discuss some kind of memorial. . . .not a tombstone or ornate grave, but a living memorial, something that would help other young men like their son. After considering many alternatives, they decided that something in the field of education would be most appropriate. It would be the kind of memorial that would go on year-after-year helping educate

young people. That would be the best kind of tribute to their son's memory.

They arranged an appointment with Charles Eliot, then president of Harvard University. He received the quite ordinary, unpretentious couple in his offices, asking what he could do for them. They told him about the death of their son, and apologized for taking up his valuable time. They explained that they wanted to establish a memorial. . . .Eliot looked at the unprepossessing couple with some impatience and a certain suggestion of aristocratic disdain. "Perhaps you have in mind a scholarship," he said crisply. "No," said the woman, her mild manner belying the quickness and sharpness of her mind. "We were thinking of something more substantial than that—perhaps a new building or so. . . . " "I must explain to you," said Eliot with what seemed a patronizing air, "that what you suggest costs a great deal of money. Buildings are very expensive." Obviously, Eliot did not think from their appearance that they were capable of that kind of donation.

There was a pause. Then the lady rose slowly and said, "Mr. Eliot, what has this entire university cost?" Eliot shrugged, and muttering, stated a figure that amounted to several million dollars. "Oh, we can do better than that, " said the lady, who had now seemed to make up her mind about the entire thing. "Come, dear," she motioned to her husband, "I have an idea." And they left.

The following year, President Eliot of Harvard learned that the plain, unpretentious couple had contributed $26 million for a memorial to their son. The memorial was to be named Leland Stanford, Jr. University.

Although Lee A. Iacocca leads Lehigh University's impressive fund-raising efforts today, those began with Asa Packer. Packer was a farm hand, carpenter, canal boat builder and captain, railroad builder, judge, congressman, and philanthropist. In 1869, Bishop Stevens, president of the university's Board of Trustees, described as follows a conversation he had with Packer:

> I asked him how much money he proposed to set aside for this institution, when he quietly answered that he desired to give $500,000. At the time of this interview no one in this country, it is believed, had offered in a single sum such an endowment. It was the noblest offering which an American had ever laid on the altar of learning.

At the time of Asa Packer's death, his contributions had reached the "enormous" sum of $3.25 million, while his aggregate charities within fourteen years exceeded $4 million. He did it because of his faith and a conviction that, with the coming of the industrial revolution, a new kind of education would be needed.

In a rare memorial tribute, the nineteenth-century humorous magazine *Puck* said:

No need to wait for the opening of his will to know what sort of a man he is. . . .Oh, ye millionaires, scatter your dollars while you live, and while you live receive the love and admiration of your fellow man. . . .You will all imitate Asa Packer in his business shrewdness: Imitate him also in his charities.

Paul J. Franz, Jr., tells another Lehigh story:

Henry Kemmerling, a bachelor and school teacher from Scranton, PA, visited Lehigh in 1936 to give $50,000 to establish tuition scholarships. When I started my work in development for Lehigh in the late '40's, one of my first trips was to Scranton to meet Mr. Kemmerling. I was quite surprised to find him living in a small, bleak, single room in the Scranton YMCA. This was his home. It was also evident that he had given to Lehigh just about everything he owned except his school teacher's pension. I was shocked and even a little bit embarrassed, but it was soon evident that Mr. Kemmerling thoroughly enjoyed his situation. In glowing terms he told me how he would often walk by the high school and watch the young men and women leaving. He was delighted to think that a few among the crowd would receive an education at Lehigh as a result of his gift. I estimate today that the Kemmerling Memorial Fund has provided an education for 114 students, and this is just the beginning of its work.

The Role of Families and Major Gifts

As we have seen to some extent, families—the Browns, Penns, Rockefellers, and Vanderbilts, for example—have played a crucial role in developing many great institutions.One of the best recent examples is the Robins family of Richmond, Virginia. The family commitment to the University of Richmond was born in the late 1960s when President William Modlin expressed the fear that the university might have to "become a public institution without a major infusion of private resources." Clairborne Robins, a man committed to private initiative and enterprise, accepted the challenge with a $40 million gift. At that time this was the largest single gift in the history of American higher education.

Robins gave because, in his words, "I feel that the problems of society today can only be solved by education." Since his initial gift, the Robins family has given over $110 million to the university. The institution has become a first-rate institution with a $225 million endowment, eight applicants for each opening in the freshman class, and entering students with combined SAT scores of over 1200.

As is invariably the case, the Robins major gifts attracted other big gifts: The Gottwalds gave $4 million, the Hanes $3 million, the Gumenicks over $1 million; and the Oldhams $2 million. But it was the Robins gift that got the university over the hump.

All of this is topped by two impressive gifts: the $100 million single gift to Emory University by Robert W. Woodruff, following the more than $110 million he and his family had given earlier. In 1979 the family gave the entire assets of the Emily and Ernest Woodruff Fund, Inc., which consisted of three million shares of Coca-Cola stock valued at over $105 million. They gave because of Robert Woodruff's "confidence that the funds would be used by Emory to enhance his vision of the future." He would not tell them how to spend the money, but he knew that his gifts would be "tended carefully" by the university and used to advance the best in American life.

Then there is the $18 million gift to Buena Vista College, initially donated anonymously but later acknowledged by Harold Siebens. Siebens' gift was the largest per-student gift in the history of higher education. Since that time the credentials of the student body and faculty have improved dramatically, the enrollment has more than doubled, the endowment has grown to over $50 million, and the college is listed in *U.S. News & World Report* as one of the "best colleges in America."

What Motivates the Major Giver

As with Woodruff and Siebens, all major gifts (gifts that have made a difference) seem to be motivated by confidence and vision—that is, confidence in the institution, particularly its current president. Every major giver and every involved president has had this rare and precious combination. When the two come together, sparks fly and the future becomes as it were today. Father Theodore M. Hesburgh, president emeritus of the University of Notre Dame, said about the more than $300 million in gifts and pledges during his administration, "It was the vision."

The same is true at Texas Wesleyan College today, where Eunice and James L. West of Fort Worth donated $12 million to give the ninety-year-old college "an opportunity to improve the order of things in society." They said, "A college without a vision is a college without a mission." Without directly seeking recognition, major givers seem to believe that there is great satisfaction in knowing that they have done something for generations to come. While such giving provides a kind of immortality as well as a sense of obligation, it also demonstrates a profound belief that the donor can help to make things better.

And the story goes on: Buck Duke, the tobacco tycoon, gave over $110 million to the little Methodist College (which became Duke University) that forbade smoking on campus. At Bates College, Elmer W. Campbell used the product of his lifetime to establish endowed professorships that might inspire high-quality teaching at Bates. His effort fired another alumnus, Kazushige Hirasawa, to do the same thing. Apparently both men were convinced of the fundamental importance of the self-made man and woman, and of the significant role that colleges and universities play in the process of creating them.

At Massachusetts Institute of Technology, the faith and support of two early major givers, T. Coleman du Pont and George Eastman (of Kodak), prompted later big gifts from Mrs. Katherine Dexter McCormick ($32,700,000 in 1967), and Alfred P. Sloan ($64,620,358 over fifty-six years)—the largest amount received by MIT from a private source), as well as others. In 1964, it was the vision of Samuel Newhouse and his $13 million gift that reshaped Syracuse University. At about the same time, James S. McDonald contributed $13 million to Washington University in St. Louis, moving it onto the national stage. McDonald's contribution was certainly the inspirational precursor for Washington University's recent record-setting $500 million campaign. Indeed, major gifts seem to be the turning point for all the colleges and universities listed among the best endowed.

Major Givers and Big Givers

Although big gifts represent from 80 to 95 percent of an institution's fund drive, they would not be possible without the major gift. Big gifts make the difference between success and failure in a capital campaign. But the major gift makes a fundamental difference in the life of the institution itself.

Author's Note

Most of the material in this chapter was compiled from letters and conversations with a number of people. I am particularly indebted to: Brad Barber, University of California at Berkeley; Keith Brisco, Buena Vista College; David Dunlop, Cornell University; Marilyn Dunn, University of Washington; Leslie Fox, Harvard University; Arthur Frantzreb, consultant; Paul Franz, Lehigh University; Pat Harrison, MIT; Father Theodore Hesbergh, Notre Dame University; Perk Robbins, University of Georgia; Jerry Smith,

Vanderbilt University; John Stone, University of Vermont; Jan Strahler, Lafayette College; Gina Tangney, Bates College; and Chris Withers, University of Richmond. I hope that in time their contributions can be developed into a worthwhile book.

20

THE HEART OF
THE MATTER
Joan M. Fisher

And so we close where we began. The ultimate gift to you and your institution, and the philanthropic motive that brings gifts to your college, can make real the dreams and hopes for the educational enterprise that you work to shape.

Remembering that "no one must give anything to anybody (or place) for any reason" makes accepting and adopting what you have read here easier. What these writings do not do is give you the vision and/or the reasons for external (or internal) support. As the presidential leader, *you* must shape the compelling reasons for philanthropic support. And you must do this relying on your conscience and capacity for leadership and contribution, and in consonance with the institution and environment you serve. Virtually all of this book's contributors, who know best the means and methods, imply that your vision and behavior both are at the heart of this process.

Armed with your vision and these considerations written by tested and respected educator practitioners of institutional advancement, you can ensure that the necessary programs of activities and patterns of relationships mature for your institution. For, above all, this is a book about relationships: between a president and his or her public, between a president and donors, between a president and the advancement staff, and between a president and the institution's promise.

Chapter 2 begins with a description of the historical context and the ethics of philanthropy. From the earliest of civilized history, the act of giving in support of another's welfare—with no expectation of return—is recorded. From the earliest days, there has been a distinction between charity and philanthropy, with charity the precursor to the higher mode of gifts given "uncounted" and only to aid a higher good.

While American generosity is well documented and unique in history, it is the practiced and historic love of mankind that is indefinable. Philanthropy informs much of the morality of voluntary service and association with others. In your quietest moments as president you will wonder at the unexplained motivation leading some (not all) among your constituents to give you unfailing and generous support. You will marvel at the beneficence that you and your institution enjoy because of belief in the importance of what you try to accomplish. And your efforts and the gifts of others have in common a greater good than either would have achieved alone.

Remembering this will help you and your colleagues maintain a level of respect and ethics in acquiring private resources. The higher calling of philanthropy can inform presidential participation in the process of development in the same way that it informs the work of the best and most effective development officers. Just as the president must embody the institution and its programs to bring collaboration within the institution, so must the development programs, processes, and techniques aid the president in securing the resources to improve the institution.

How you legitimize, support, and lead the development function in the institution can and will have a profound effect on how others understand and participate in the search for philanthropic support. Whether you are genuinely convinced of the importance of the development endeavor and the promise that philanthropy holds for your institution, or are a begrudging contender for charitable handouts, will sooner or later communicate itself to your public, donors, faculty, and staff. The program will reflect not only your institution's style but also your consciousness, conscience, as well as your commitment. Sincerity and beliefs eventually will prevail. Better for all concerned with the institution that its leaders' link with philanthropy be one of ease and wise counsel.

Laying the Foundation or Positioning the Institution

To lay the necessary foundation for a successful philanthropic response from the public you must know your institution's history, the resources it brings to the public it serves, the resources and expertise it brings to the development function, and your institution's potential for short-term and long-term success. It certainly can help immeasurably if planning, clarity of vision, consistent assessment, and evaluation and goals are part of the institution's culture.

To take first steps is the most challenging part. The processes that can help establish the successful fund-raising program are well defined in chapters by Fisher, Snelling, Stuhr, and Frantzreb. These focus on departmental set-up, the use of consultants, feasibility studies, case statements, and the selection of staff.

"The Value of Fund-Raising Counsel" by Snelling, and "The Feasibility Study" by Pendel and Thompson, will give you the essence of the consultant's value to the organization. Here you will find the best ways to both select and use outside evaluation. The objective guidance that comes from complete and unbiased review of your institution's staff, public, and programs can help with the first critical steps you take in establishing or monitoring a strong program.

The chapters about the case statement (Stuhr), the use of consultants for a feasibility study (Pendel and Thompson), and the alternative ways of using feasibility studies (Frantzreb) encourage you to explore and clarify your institution's values fully. How you can bring together the elements of a strong case for your institution, first through consensus-building with faculty, trustees, and others and through your own personal alchemy, will create the document that sells the grand plan for the institution. The authors describe how to use consultants, draw responses from test markets, and get help with action plans to help you launch or sustain the best integrative effort to advance your institution.

But, you've still never raised funds. And all of this discussion about conveying your compelling case, planning and communicating your vision, and testing the opinions of your public can seem like academic strategic planning made poetic. It may seem like academic consensus-building made competitive. It may also seem a long way from receiving the votes of confidence that gifts can mean.

Running the Program: The Means to the Vision

What brings gifts to an institution is unceasing attention to the development process. That process identifies, communicates, cultivates, and achieves an investment by others in the purposes and goals of the institution. Around the relentless tasks of identifying, interesting, informing, involving, and acquiring investment from others has grown a series of skills and practices that when coordinated and combined become the institutional advancement function.

Section III, "Conducting the Fund-Raising Program," details key elements in a comprehensive development program. After you learn about the most fundamental needs through the public relations program, and your relationships with and expectations of trustees, and alumni, you progress to the interim stages of running annual funds and developing corporate and foundation giving programs. You also learn how to determine the necessary costs and tools for the program. In these eight chapters you learn a basic understanding of the ways in which fundamental programs in a successful development operation best function.

Without a clear understanding of your institution's value, your public relations people will be hard put to engender understanding and support for your institution. With a compelling vision and a program that hears responses from its public, a sound public relations program can help create a positive and supportive climate for providing extra resources for the institution. Richard W. Conklin, in "The Role of Public Relations," makes us understand that a prudent president, by using the public relations staff and tools effectively, can help strengthen both institutional self-identity and pride of association.

Whether private or public, presidents who garner the understanding and willingness to work of trustee members of clout and resources will have an easier time in acquiring private resources for their institutions. According to Gale ("The Role of the Governing Board"), the special constituency of trustee members who "give generously themselves," talk up the institution, and "identify and cultivate prospects" will serve the president, extend the staff's effectiveness, and help promote the compelling vision. If identified, chosen, oriented and cultivated well, trustees can help ensure the well-being of your institution.

So, too, do the alumni of your institution require attention. Because the alumni have such a vested interest in the quality and strength of their alma mater, you can see why they can also be your single greatest resource. Forman's chapter, "The Role of Alumni Relations," helps you know what kind of staff, "peopling" of programs and activities, and structure you can expect to produce results. His convincing argument is that the president who "understands, cultivates, nourishes, and utilizes" alumni wisely will build connections for the institution that can have an admirable effect in both services and future support.

That most basic yardstick of support will come from the annual fund, the "teething ring" of development professionals, and the initial "kitty" for your vision. The obvious elements—the marketing segmentation, the records, the appeals, the volunteer training and involvement—are the basics for any speculative or maturing program. What Lowery ("The Annual Fund") urges you to do is to think and approach your supporters with the creativity and imagination that will allow them to give because they believe that they and their gifts are integral to the college's success. Operate this first-level program in your resource outreach by funding a marriage between the donor's perspective and the vision.

Because people rather than corporations and foundations give the largest amounts of supportive charitable and philanthropic endeavors, you and your development staff should recognize that diversifying a development program to include corporation and foundation support will require an acceptance of the *quid pro quo* as a catalyst to external support from corporations and foundations.

In deciding whether your institution should pursue corporate or foundation fund raising, consider whether the academic and research pursuits of your institution interest corporations and foundations, and whether you can afford twelve- to eighteen-month proposal preparation time. Also consider whether you can afford the one- to three-years investment in prospect research and cultivation, withstand the vagaries of economic conditions, and have the personal or lay/trustee clout to influence corporations or foundations. Most of all, you need to know whether you want to create the climate in your institution for projects that interest corporations and foundations. Are you willing to use the time necessary to build relationships that will result in support? Once you decide this, you can just follow the guidelines laid out by Murphy ("Corporations and Foundations") for the program, its setup, and how to deploy yourself and your staff.

The plans and programs you establish in your development program will depend in large measure on how you choose to use your people and resources. In early stages, your public relations effort may take more time and investment simply to interest, inform, and communicate. Obviously, starting a program will cost more in relative terms than ongoing funding of an established program.

Evans, Wisdom, and McGoldrick who are concerned (in Chapters 13, 14, and 15 respectively) with helping you know which tools are necessary, and how to assess the costs and benefits required to engender external support, caution you to understand that development programs, like all the other relationships you are building, are built over time. A centralized program will have less staff and services, and consequently will cost less. You must allocate your resources to consultants, cultivation activities, computerized records, donor recognition, and travel. The goals and objectives you set for each of your major constituencies, and the kinds of annual or major support that you want to garner, can help you decide how to allocate your resources.

You'll know that you have a viable and dynamic program when you can readily see the identification, communication–cultivation, and investment processes flowing smoothly in all of the advancement offices. Once established the process repeats itself, refining and maturing with more sensitivity and care for each successful measure of support.

The Potential and the Philanthropic Promise

This is a book about seeing clearly relationships you must achieve in order to realize dreams in a public arena, and about how to best organize the ways to nurture those relationships.

Because you will always measure the effectiveness of fund-raising people (staff and volunteers), plans, and programs by whether there are increasing donors and dollars, you should be prepared for your development professionals to consistently and actively press you to meet and engage with donor prospects. As your programs become established, a test of your effectiveness as a leader and a builder of relationships will be whether you can sustain interest, credibility, and integrity with your donors—not as a means to an end but, as Payton ("The Ethics and Values of Fund Raising") suggests, as an end in itself.

If, after reading the early chapters (1, 2, and 3) by Fisher and Payton, you still need convincing about the efficacy of embarking on an advancement program, or as a skeptic you question the charitable gift, turn to Fisher's "The Historical Importance of Major Gifts." Here you will come to know how institutions both previously unknown and unsung have been marked (indeed, blessed) by beneficence beyond their quietest wishes and most imaginative dreams.

Is there a way to guide the development process toward the philanthropic promise? Dunlop, Smith, Bornstein, and Fisher (Part IV) believe it can happen with organization, technical skills, careful cultivation, and care of the vision. To move from speculative giving to nurturing the ultimate gift requires, according to Dunlop, balanced initiatives and efficient running of the development function. More importantly, acquisition of the gifts that make the difference between a vision realized and slow-step improvements requires an informed understanding. To acquire major gifts requires caring and commitment between your institution, its public, and you. The frequent, thoughtful, and sustained effort from the president and chief development officer requires collaboration and consensus.

These authors also describe how the efforts for larger gifts can be institutionalized. Both the well-shaped capital campaign and the well serviced planned-giving program can bring a vitality and inspiration not only to the development areas and the entire institution, but also to donors and friends.

In the capital campaign an entire institution and its publics gear up and are motivated to pursue a challenging goal for resources that will enable the institution to thrive and prosper. In a planned-giving program, you make a range of gift opportunities available to your donors to enable them to help your institution thrive and prosper. While each program can occur without the other, they both must have at their base a willingness to build relationships that develop in your constituents a deepening belief and commitment to what you and your institution represent. The assertive, sometimes aggressive, but always nurturing efforts that mark capital and planned-giving efforts require that your development professionals and you have experienced the process that generates philanthropic support.

The dream you envision and the hopes you have for a strong and contributing future for your institution will require that your development function evolve and mature. Together you need to have worked your values and objectives into effective messages; to have researched, identified, cultivated, captivated, and recognized supporters. Together you need to have established the working functions and plans, and the discipline within them, that will enable your staffs to support you in building relationships. You need to have built enough close relationships with those who can make an impact, and you need to have sustained their enthusiasm.

If your way is one of confidence and vision, then you may be able to inspire the confidence and vision of those ready and able to take risks and to build with you through an ultimate and life-giving gift.

Although many major gifts may come to your institution through your leadership and your staff's administration and enthusiastic participation, the real measure of your skill will be whether you can convert voluntary charitable gifts into gifts inspired by a philanthropic motive. If the idealistic, strong-willed, risk-taking, and/or wealthy among you are caught up by the dream of what you want to build, a philanthropic gift may yet emerge from the pages of these chapters.

May you be successful in getting one and all to build with you!

CONTRIBUTORS

James L. Fisher is president emeritus of both the Council for the Advancement and Support of Education (CASE) and Towson State University. He is the author or editor of *Power of the Presidency, The Effective College President, The Role of the President in Institutional Advancement, The Handbook of Academic Administration,* and *Leaders on Leadership.* Currently he serves as a consultant and resides in McLean, Virginia.

Gary H. Quehl came to the presidency of the Council for the Advancement and Support of Education (CASE) from serving as the president of the Council of Independent Colleges (CIC). Previously he served as executive director of the College Center, Finger Lakes, N.Y., and vice president and dean at Lindenwood College.

Robert L. Payton is a former president of the EXXON Education Foundation and immediate past scholar in residence in philanthropic studies at the University of Virginia. He is currently director of the Center on Philanthropy and professor of philanthropic studies at Indiana University. His latest book, *Philanthropy,* was published in the fall of 1988.

Barbara W. Snelling is president of Snelling, Kolb & Kuhnle Incorporated, following eight years as vice president for development and external affairs at the University of Vermont.

Robert L. Stuhr is a partner in the financial development consulting firm of Gonser, Gerber, Tinker, Stuhr, and is the editor of four bimonthly bulletins on development. He holds a Ph.D. degree in mass communications from Northwestern University and is accredited by the Public Relations Association of America.

Mary Helene Pendel is currently a partner in Thompson and Pendel Associates, working to join communications effectively with fund

229

raising on behalf of colleges and universities. Earlier, she had been a vice president at the firm of Frantzreb, Pray, Ferner and Thompson, Inc.

David M. Thompson, like his wife, Mary Pendel, was active in the firm of Frantzreb, Pray, Ferner and Thompson prior to establishing their own organization. Earlier, Mr. Thompson served a key role in the National Urban Coalition and the establishment of Common Cause.

Arthur C. Frantzreb has enjoyed personal and professional relationships as student and alumnus of a public and private university; board member, chairman, and honorary degree holder of a private college; and philanthropic management counselor, lecturer, and author helping countless non-profit organizations and institutions.

Richard W. Conklin is currently vice president for university relations and oversees the department of Public Relations and Information at the University of Notre Dame. He has been on the staff of Minneapolis and St. Louis metropolitan dailies, taught for twelve years in CASE's Institute in Communications, and received numerous awards within the communications field.

Robert L. Gale is currently president of the Association of Governing Boards of Universities and Colleges. His past activities have included serving as vice president of Carleton College, director of recruiting and director of public affairs for the Peace Corps, and director of public affairs for the Equal Employment Opportunity Commission.

Robert G. Forman has been executive director of the Alumni Association of The University of Michigan for the past 22 years. He was the first recipient of the Theodore Hesburgh Award for CASE trusteeship, and has written a number of articles on the role of the alumni administration profession in the field of institutional advancement. Mr. Forman is the past chairman of the board of directors of CASE and a former board member of the American Council of Education.

William R. Lowery is vice president for development and public affairs at Lake Forest College, Illinois. Previously he served as director of corporate and foundation relations and director of development at Pomona College, and dean of admissions at Pitzer College.

Mary Kay Murphy is director for development at the Georgia Institute of Technology. She directed the Institute's foundation relations program during the recent five-year $202 million capital campaign. She is chair-elect of CASE III and editor of a new CASE publication, *Cultivating Foundation Support for Education.*

Gary A. Evans is the vice chancellor for development and university relations at the University of North Carolina at Chapel Hill. Earlier he served as vice president for resource development at Rensselaer Polytechnic Institute, and vice president for development and alumni affairs at Lafayette College. He is a faculty member at the Williamsburg Development Institute and a lecturer at the Harvard Institute for Educational Management.

Paul E. Wisdom is vice president for public affairs at Colorado State University, where annual voluntary giving tripled to $13.5 million during his first three years. Programs Wisdom has headed have three times won the CASE (ACPRA) Grand Gold Award for most improved overall advancement program in the nation.

William P. McGoldrick is vice president for institute relations at Rensselaer Polytechnic Institute. He has served four colleges and universities in public relations and development positions for 17 years.

David R. Dunlop is the director of capital projects at Cornell University. He was the first recipient of the James L. Fisher award given by CASE for exceptional leadership and innovative management. He advocates the maximum use of volunteers in all levels of fund raising, whether speaking as a guest lecturer to groups from CASE, NSFRE, PDE, ATS or the National Planned Giving Assn., or as a contributing author to professional publications.

Winton C. Smith, Jr., a practicing attorney, specializes in estate tax strategies and charitable tax planning. His background includes twelve years of practical experience in the marketing of planned gifts. He represents charitable institutions, keeping them informed on the latest marketing strategies and tax law changes affecting charitable gifts.

Rita Bornstein is vice president for development at the University of Miami. She is responsible for a five-year, $400 million comprehensive campaign. She has published and spoken widely on philanthropy, administration, and educational equity.

Joan M. Fisher has been vice president for development at George Mason University in Northern Virginia, and at Mount Vernon College in the District of Columbia. She currently serves as director of development for B'nai Brith Women.

INDEX